The
1000s

HEADLINES IN HISTORY

Books in the Headlines in History series:

The 1000s

HEADLINES IN HISTORY

Brenda Stalcup, *Book Editor*

Bonnie Szumski, *Editorial Director*
Scott Barbour, *Managing Editor*

Greenhaven Press, Inc., San Diego, California

Library of Congress Cataloging-in-Publication Data

The 1000s / Brenda Stalcup, book editor.
   p. cm. — (Headlines in history)
   Includes bibliographical references and index.
   ISBN 0-7377-0527-2 (pbk. : alk. paper)—
   ISBN 0-7377-0528-0 (lib. bdg. : alk. paper)
   1. Eleventh century. 2. Civilization, Medieval. 3. Middle Ages
—History. 4. Crusades—First, 1096–1099. 5. Indians—History.
6. Asia—History. I. Title: One thousands. II. Stalcup, Brenda.
III. Series.

CB354.3 .A16 2001
940.1'46—dc21

00-052831

Cover photos: (top, left to right) Siege of Jerusalem, Giraudon/Art Resource, NY: Leif Ericsson off the coast of Vinland, © North Wind Picture Archives; (bottom, left to right) The Bayeux Tapestry: Bishop Odo encouraging the young men, Giraudon/ Art Resource; Sung dynasty portrait of an emperor. A painting from the Sung dynasty depicts the first Sung emperor, © Charles & Josette Lenars/CORBIS
Dover Publications, 43, 160
Library of Congress, 128
North Wind Picture Archives, 84

CONTENTS

Chapter 1: Western Europe: Emergence from the Dark Ages

1. Awaiting the Apocalypse
Western Europe greeted the year 1000 with apprehension, fearing that the turn of the millennium would signal the beginning of the apocalypse.

2. The Rise of Feudalism
After the virtual anarchy of the Dark Ages, the rise of the feudal system in eleventh-century Europe allowed for the growth of strong governments.

3. The Peace of God Movement
During the late 900s and the 1000s, the Catholic Church supported the Peace of God movement in an attempt to eliminate the internal warfare that plagued western Europe.

4. The Truce of God for the Diocese of Cologne
Decreed in 1083, this version of the Truce of God greatly restricts the times during which warfare will be permitted. It also delineates severe punishments for those who break the peace.

5. Papal Reform
The popes of the eleventh century strove to reform the Catholic Church by strengthening the position of the papacy and raising the moral standards of the clergy.

control of the Muslim kingdoms in the Near East and made inroads into Christian and Hindu lands, spreading Islam as they went.

Chapter 5: Asia's Cultural Renaissance

woman, is widely regarded as the world's first novelist. Her book, *The Tale of Genji,* represents a significant literary milestone by any standards.

Chapter 6: The Rise of New Civilizations in America

5. The Mound Builders of Cahokia

Located in the Midwest region of the present-day United
States, the city of Cahokia grew rapidly during the 1000s
to become an important center of culture and trade.

FOREWORD

Chronological time lines of history are mysteriously fascinating. To learn that within a single century Christopher Columbus sailed to the New World, the Aztec, Maya, and Inca cultures were flourishing, Joan of Arc was burned to death, and the invention of the printing press was radically changing access to written materials allows a reader a different type of view of history: a bird's-eye view of the entire globe and its events. Such a global picture allows for cross-cultural comparisons as well as a valuable overview of chronological history that studying one particular area simply cannot provide.

Taking an expansive look at world history in each century, therefore, can be surprisingly informative. In Headlines in History, Greenhaven Press attempts to imitate this time-line approach using primary and secondary sources that span each century. Each volume gives readers the opportunity to view history as though they were reading the headlines of a global newspaper: Editors of each volume have attempted to glean and include the most important and influential events of the century, as well as quirky trends and cultural oddities. Headlines in History, then, attempts to give readers a glimpse of both the mundane and the earth-shattering. Articles on the French Revolution, for example, are juxtaposed with the then-current fashion concerns of the French nobility. This creates a higher interest level by allowing students a glimpse of people's everyday lives throughout history.

By using both primary and secondary sources, students also have the opportunity to view the historical events both as eyewitnesses have experienced them and as historians have interpreted them. Thus, students can place such historical events in a larger context as well as receive background information on important world events.

Headlines in History allows readers the unique opportunity to learn more about events that may only be mentioned in their history textbooks, or may be ignored entirely. The series presents students with a variety of interesting topics that span cultural, historical, and political arenas. Such a broad span of material will allow students to wander wherever their curiosity will take them.

An Age of Fearful Anticipation

T he approach of the year 1000 held great import for the Christian world. According to the European calendar, it marked the thousandth year since the birth of Christ, and many people believed that it would also herald the onset of the apocalypse, the final battle between the forces of good and evil that was to occur at the end of the world. They took to heart the prophesy in the Book of Revelation, which stated that "when the thousand years are expired, Satan shall be loosed out of his prison, and shall go out to deceive the nations which are in the four quarters of the earth . . . to gather them together to battle: the number of whom is as the sand of the sea."[1] With much trepidation, they awaited the arrival of Satan's minion, the Antichrist, who was to rule the world in terror and bloodshed for several years until Christ's eventual triumph.

All around them, the Europeans saw heavenly signs described in the Bible as presaging the advent of the apocalypse. In 989, a strange new star streaked across the sky, blazing brightly for almost three months, then vanishing as mysteriously as it had appeared. Historians now know that this "star" was in fact Halley's comet, which passes by the earth in regular cycles of approximately seventy-five years. To the medieval Europeans, however, the comet was an inexplicable phenomenon, understandable only as a warning from God. Indeed, shortly after the comet's appearance, a fire devastated the church of a prominent Benedictine monastery in Mont-Saint-Michel, France. The Germans received their own celestial message in 998, when two balls of fire were hurled from the clouds; one of these meteorites smashed directly into the imperial cathedral at Magdeburg. The accounts increased as the new millennium drew nigh: A group of French nuns reported seeing fiery armies warring in the heavens, and residents of Aquitaine claimed that blood had rained from the skies. Perhaps most frightening of all, in the year 1000 an enormous bolt of lightning created the apparition of a dragon that grew until it stretched across the horizon. The terrified witnesses knew, as did all good Christians, that the dragon was the symbol of Satan and the Antichrist.

Omens of Doomsday

Besides the signs in the heavens, the Book of Revelation listed more omens that would signal the pending apocalypse, including war, famine, plague, and natural disasters. There was no shortage of such troubles in western Europe during the years leading up to the turn of the millennium, and many of the medieval chroniclers who recorded their occurrence described them as portents of the End Times. Warfare—both external and internal—was rampant, as author Richard Erdoes explains in his book A.D. *1000: Living on the Brink of Apocalypse*:

> Western Europe was beset on all sides by fanatic Saracens, Spanish Moors, Thor-worshiping Vikings, pagan Bulgars, and fierce Magyar horsemen—the proverbial Scourges of God. Christian barons slaughtered each other with a vengeance over a piece of land, killing their enemies' serfs . . . to weaken them economically, burning villages and crops, and cutting down fruit trees for good measure.[2]

The destruction wrought by barbarian invasions and feudal battles often led to crop failures. The European agriculture techniques of the tenth century were not highly effective, and a good harvest typically provided just enough food to maintain the population through the winter. With such a small margin for error, even a mild decrease in the annual crop production could mean months of tight rations and gnawing hunger. A significant crop failure due to war or unusual weather conditions such as drought could easily spark widespread famine. Beginning in 970, food shortages and famines became increasingly frequent and severe. According to the eleventh-century account written by the Burgundian monk Ralph Glaber, near the turn of the millennium "a most mighty famine raged for five years" throughout Europe,

> so that no region could be heard of which was not hungerstricken for lack of bread, and many of the people were starved to death. In those days also, in many regions, the horrible famine compelled men to make their food not only of unclean beasts and creeping things, but even of men's, women's, and children's flesh, without regard even of kindred; for so fierce waxed this hunger that grown-up sons devoured their mothers, and mothers, forgetting their maternal love, ate their babes.[3]

Lean times were not unusual during the Dark Ages, but people had rarely become so desperate in the past as to resort to cannibalism. The growing frequency of dire food shortages prompted many Europeans to wonder whether Famine, one of the Four Horsemen of the

Apocalypse described in the Book of Revelation, had not already arrived to scourge the earth.

According to this prophesy, War, Pestilence, and Death were the other three horsemen who would be unleashed against humanity in the final days before Christ's return. Pestilence referred particularly to plagues—epidemic diseases that were extremely virulent and deadly. In his chronicle, Glaber noted the outbreak in the 990s of a mysterious and devastating illness. "A horrible plague raged among men," he wrote, "namely a hidden fire which, upon whatsoever limb it fastened, consumed it and severed it from the body. Many were consumed even in the space of a single night by these devouring flames."[4] Most historians believe that Glaber's description refers to St. Anthony's fire, an infection caused by a fungus called ergot that typically grows on rye plants. Almost invisible to the naked eye, ergot was nearly impossible for medieval farmers to detect. They unwittingly harvested the infected rye and used it to make flour. Erdoes relates the horrific results: "People eating bread made from diseased rye first experienced a tingling sensation, as if thousands of ants were crawling over their bare skin. In severe cases, affected fingers and toes gangrened, turned black, and fell off. This was sometimes accompanied by respiratory failure, hallucination, madness, and death."[5] In his book *The Last Apocalypse: Europe at the Year 1000 A.D.*, author James Reston Jr. explains that St. Anthony's fire "seemed aptly named for the impending apocalypse, for in Christian legend the devil had taken the shape of a monk and had offered corrupted bread to St. Anthony as the communion host."[6]

In addition to a drastic increase in plague, war, and famine, the Book of Revelation also predicted that the world would be wracked by earthquakes, volcanic eruptions, and other natural disasters. As the tenth century drew to a close, the inhabitants of Europe experienced several frightening events that many considered to be auguries of the apocalypse. The Italian volcano Mount Vesuvius grew active around 993, triggering several earthquakes before it finally erupted. The mountain "vomited forth numberless vast stones mingled with sulphurous flames which fell to a distance of three miles around," Glaber remarked, "and thus by the stench of its breath, like the stench of hell, made all the surrounding province uninhabitable."[7] Subsequent earthquakes rocked Saxony in 998 and France in 1000. During the same time period, an unprecedented number of fires broke out in almost all the major cities of France and Italy—including Rome, the seat of the papacy. The conflagration in Rome even threatened St. Peter's Cathedral, the papal church; according to Glaber, "the flames caught the beams . . . and began to creep up to the bronze tiles" of the roof, until the watching crowd cried out in despair to Christ that "if he watched not over his own, nor defended his own church, many throughout the world would abandon the faith and fall back into paganism. Whereupon the devouring flames at once left the wooden roofbeams and died away."[8] Disaster was narrowly averted that day, but numerous Christians still considered the near-burning of the pope's cathedral to be an augury of the apocalypse. In fact, Erdoes points out, "many people believed that the dissolution of the world would begin at Rome and spread out from there until all of the earth should be consumed."[9]

"No Man Knows the Hour"

The year 1000 came and went, and still the world continued on its usual course. Not everyone was reassured, however: The new millennium might merely signal the beginning of the time of tribulation rather than the final doomsday. After all, the Bible specifically stated that no one could foresee the exact day and hour of the Second Coming. For decades, the people of Europe continued to anxiously mark the signs of impending doom. In 1009, for example, the Muslim ruler of Jerusalem demolished the Church of the Holy Sepulchre; this church was especially sacred to Christians because it was built over the site where Christ was believed to have been buried, and many Europeans took its destruction to be a significant omen. During the following year, a French chronicler named Ademar of Chabannes observed the occurrence of unusually violent storms and record floods, a rash of plagues and famines, and ominous signs in the sky.

In England, the early years of the new millennium were filled with warfare and bloodshed as Danish invaders scoured the land. England had survived Viking raids before, but this new conflict was far more dire: Instead of a few boats of marauders, they faced a mighty host of battle-hardened warriors intent on conquest, headed by the king of Denmark himself. The English forces were unable to resist the onslaught. As their towns and cities capitulated one by one to the Danes, the English began to view their desperate situation in terms of the apocalypse. Even the English king "retreated into apocalyptic thinking," writes Reston. "He issued a royal edict identifying the 'Great Army' of heathens with the forces of the Antichrist"[10] and ordered his people to fast and pray for deliverance from the enemy. Their pleas did not prevent the Vikings from capturing London in 1013. The Danish army put the English king to flight and installed their own ruler on the throne.

To Wulfstan, the archbishop of York, this tragic defeat was a clear indication that the end of the world was at hand. In a famous sermon that was distributed throughout England during 1014, Wulfstan declared that the people had brought their misfortune on themselves through their sinful wickedness. "For long now the English have

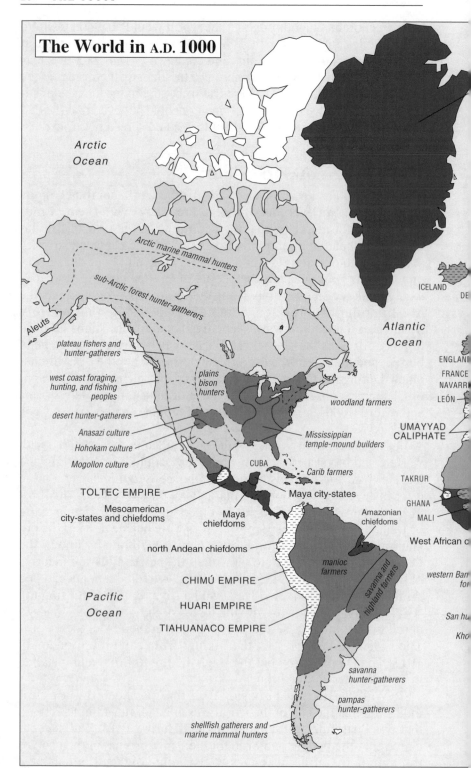

The World in A.D. 1000

Arctic
Ocean

Arctic marine mammal hunters

sub-Arctic forest hunter-gatherers

Aleuts

plateau fishers and
hunter-gatherers

west coast foraging,
hunting, and fishing
peoples

desert hunter-gatherers

Anasazi culture

Hohokam culture

Mogollon culture

plains
bison
hunters

woodland farmers

Mississippian
temple-mound builders

CUBA

TOLTEC EMPIRE

Mesoamerican
city-states and chiefdoms

Maya
chiefdoms

Carib farmers

Maya city-states

north Andean chiefdoms

CHIMÚ EMPIRE

HUARI EMPIRE

TIAHUANACO EMPIRE

Amazonian
chiefdoms

manioc
farmers

savanna and
highland farmers

Pacific
Ocean

savanna
hunter-gatherers

pampas
hunter-gatherers

shellfish gatherers and
marine mammal hunters

Atlantic
Ocean

ICELAND   DE

ENGLAND
FRANCE
NAVARR
LEÓN

UMAYYAD
CALIPHATE

TAKRUR

GHANA

MALI

West African c

western Ban
for

San hu

Kho

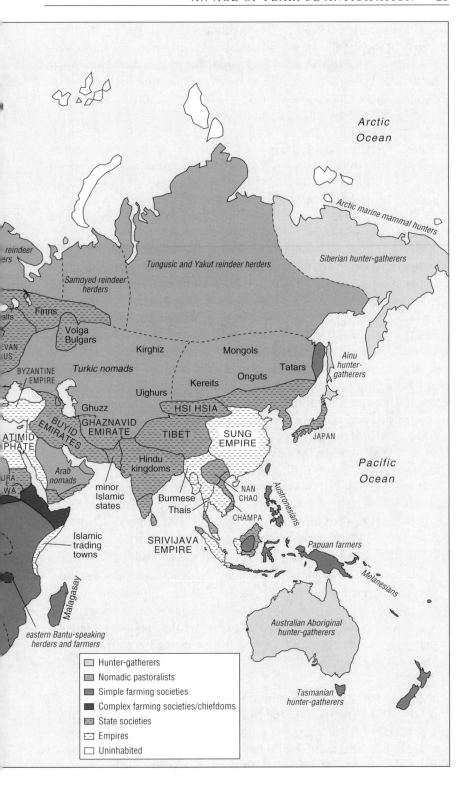

Arctic
Ocean

Arctic marine mammal hunters

reindeer
ers

Tungusic and Yakut reindeer herders

Siberian hunter-gatherers

Samoyed reindeer
herders

alts

Finns

Volga
Bulgars

Kirghiz

Mongols

Ainu
hunter-
gatherers

VAN
US

BYZANTINE
EMPIRE

Turkic nomads

Tatars

Onguts

Kereits

Uighurs

Ghuzz

HSI HSIA

BUYID
EMIRATES

GHAZNAVID
EMIRATE

ATIMID
PHATE

URA
WA

Arab
nomads

minor
Islamic
states

TIBET

SUNG
EMPIRE

JAPAN

Pacific
Ocean

Hindu
kingdoms

Burmese

Thais

NAN
CHAO

CHAMPA

Austronesians

Islamic
trading
towns

SRIVIJAVA
EMPIRE

Papuan farmers

Melanesians

Malagasay

eastern Bantu-speaking
herders and farmers

Australian Aboriginal
hunter-gatherers

Tasmanian
hunter-gatherers

- ▫ Hunter-gatherers
- ▫ Nomadic pastoralists
- ▪ Simple farming societies
- ■ Complex farming societies/chiefdoms
- ▨ State societies
- ▫ Empires
- ▫ Uninhabited

been entirely without victory," he maintained, "and too much cowed because of the wrath of God, and the pirates are so strong with God's consent, that in battle one will often put flight to ten." [11] He warned his flock to repent and mend their ways while time yet remained. "Beloved men, realize what is true," Wulfstan exhorted them. "This world is in haste and the end approaches." [12]

At approximately the same time that England fell to the pagan Vikings, the Christians of Spain mounted a new resistance against their Muslim enemies, who had dominated much of the Iberian peninsula since the 700s. Unlike the beleaguered English, the Spaniards enjoyed several decisive victories against their foes, but they too considered these events as fulfilling biblical prophesies concerning the apocalypse.

During the first decade of the 1000s, the Muslim caliphate that governed Islamic Spain from its seat in Cordoba weakened, primarily due to internal conflicts among the leading families. The Christian princes in the north of Spain gradually started to take advantage of the caliphate's impotence, regaining important fortresses that they had previously lost to the Muslims. They formed an alliance of sorts with the Berbers, Muslims from North Africa who had originally come to Islamic Spain as mercenaries for the caliph and who were often discriminated against by the Arab majority. In May 1013, after a prolonged siege, the Berbers overran Cordoba. They sacked and pillaged the once-glorious city in an unrestrained frenzy. "Most of the houses were demolished, the palaces burned or stripped of all worldly beauty, as if such sensuous delights were in themselves sins," [13] writes historian Elmer Bendiner.

"When the news of this conflagration reached the north of Spain," according to Reston, "there was rejoicing in the cities and in the farthest reaches of the Christian provinces." [14] The Spanish Christians associated Cordoba with the decadent city of Babylon described in the Book of Revelation, whose downfall was foretold as follows:

> I saw the angel come down from heaven, having great authority, and the earth was lighted up by his glory. And he cried out with a mighty voice, saying "She is fallen, Babylon the Great" . . . and the kings of the earth . . . will weep and mourn over her when they see the smoke of her burning. They will stand far off for fear of her torments, saying "Woe, woe, the great city, Babylon, the strong city, for in one hour, your judgment came!" [15]

The Cordoban caliphate continued to disintegrate until its final collapse in 1031. Meanwhile, the Spanish Christians steadily chipped away at the Muslim territory, with the ultimate goal of reconquering the entire peninsula. Although they would not achieve this goal during the eleventh century, with each new triumph they became more determined to reclaim all of Spain from the Muslims. "In millennialist terms," Reston asserts, "Babylon was burning, and the kingdom of a Christian God was [being] restored."[16]

Going to Jerusalem

As the century progressed, many Europeans began to look anxiously forward to the year 1033, the thousandth anniversary of the death and resurrection of Christ. In the medieval world, where the Catholic Church placed far more emphasis on Easter than on Christmas, it seemed reasonable to assume that the thousand years specified in the Book of Revelation should be counted not from Christ's birth but from his triumphant ascension into heaven. Again the believers pointed to the appearance of fearsome auguries, including more famines, plagues, and celestial wonders. Most spectacularly, they witnessed "a saffron sun and a solar eclipse which bathed the earth in a sapphire mist, turning the faces of men pale as death,"[17] in the words of Hillel Schwartz, the author of *Century's End: A Cultural History of the Fin de Siecle from the 990s Through the 1990s.*

Throngs of western Europeans set out on pilgrimages to the Holy Land, hoping to witness with their own eyes the Second Coming of Christ. Glaber described the unprecedented size of this pilgrimage movement at its height:

> So innumerable a multitude began to flock from all parts of the world to the sepulchre of our Saviour at Jerusalem, as no man could before have expected; for the lower orders of people led the way, after whom came those of middle rank, and then all the greatest kings and counts and bishops; lastly (a thing which had never come to pass before), many noble ladies and poorer women journeyed thither.[18]

This surge of pilgrimages was distinctly linked to the onset of the apocalypse:

> When some of the more truthful of that time were asked by many what might be the meaning of such a great flocking together of people to Jerusalem, unheard of in previous centuries, they cautiously responded that it presaged nothing else but the coming of the Lost One, the Antichrist, who according to divine authority stands ready to come at the End of the age. Then the road to the eastern region from which he was to come was opened to all nations, so that all might go forth to meet him without delay.[19]

According to Glaber, most of these pilgrims wholeheartedly believed that the end was near, and they wished to die in the Holy Land. They departed from Europe fully expecting never to see their homes again. During the fateful year of 1033, a timely earthquake shook Jerusalem and the surrounding area; when the ground began to tremble, the European pilgrims may well have thought—at least briefly—that the apocalypse had finally arrived.

They were mistaken, of course; yet millennialist thinking continued to have an indelible influence on the Europeans throughout the remainder of the eleventh century. Even as late as the 1090s, the apocalyptic concept was evident in the spirit that drove the First Crusade. Once again the Europeans cast their sights on the Holy Land, this time with the intent of liberating Jerusalem from its Muslim rulers. This act, many believed, would set the stage for the beginning of the apocalypse. In Guibert of Nogent's account of Pope Urban II's 1095 sermon proclaiming the First Crusade, the conquest of the Holy Land by the Christians was depicted as a necessary precursor to the final battle between good and evil:

> You should also consider with the utmost care whether God is working through your efforts to restore the church that is the mother of churches; he might wish to restore the faith in some of the eastern lands, in spite of the nearness of the time of the Antichrist. For it is clear that the Antichrist makes war neither against Jews, nor against pagans, but, according to the etymology of his name, he will move against Christians. And if the Antichrist comes upon no Christian there, as today there is scarcely any, there will be no one to resist him. . . . According to the prophet, [the Antichrist] will undoubtedly kill three kings pre-eminent for their faith in Christ, that is, the kings of Egypt, of Africa, and of Ethiopia. This cannot happen at all, unless Christianity is established where paganism now rules. . . . It is necessary, before the coming of the Antichrist in those parts . . . that the empire of Christianity be renewed, so that the leader of all evil, who will have his throne there, may find some nourishment of faith against which he may fight.[20]

Until the western Europeans regained control of the Holy Land and reestablished Christian kingdoms there, this reasoning goes, the apocalypse would necessarily be delayed.

In this text can be seen the radical difference between the millennialism of the 990s and that of the 1090s: the absence of fear. Rather than cowering in dread as comets crossed the sky, the knights of the First Crusade took bold action calculated to *trigger* the apocalypse, which they were prepared to meet head on. This new attitude reflects the overall gain in confidence and strength that western Europe experienced during the course of the eleventh century.

Ragnarok

The focus on the significance of the turn of the millennium was uniquely Christian. Only those who believed in Christ and anticipated the apocalypse predicted in the Bible would place any special meaning on the year 1000. In fact, during this time period the different civilizations of the world did not follow a single system of dating years. Each culture adhered to its own calendar, none of which counted the years or centuries in the same manner as did the Christians of western Europe. For most of the world, the year 1000 was expressed in completely different numbers.

Yet the eleventh century was still a time of tension for many of these civilizations as well. They had their own conceptions of the final days, their own predictions of how the earth would end—and they felt a sense of unease, a vague fear of impending doom. In the ancient pagan religion of the Vikings of northern Europe, doomsday was known as Ragnarok (literally, "the fate of the gods"). Like the Christian apocalypse, Ragnarok involved a final battle between the good gods and the forces of evil, but in this version the battle would end only when both sides were utterly destroyed.

As discussed above, the English equated the pagan Vikings with the armies of the Antichrist, and certainly these ferocious warriors had struck terror into the hearts of many Christians as they rampaged throughout western Europe during the Dark Ages. But by the beginning of the eleventh century, the world of the Vikings was changing rapidly and irrevocably. Particularly unsettling was the trend toward conversion to Christianity, which often occurred under duress or threat of violence. The first Christian king of Norway, for instance, persecuted those of his subjects who would not accept baptism and did not hesitate to kill his religious opponents in the most gruesome and torturous fashion he could devise.

Some Vikings saw these developments as a sure sign that Ragnarok was imminent. Historian Gwyn Jones explains that the Vikings believed the onset of Ragnarok "would be preceded by an age of faithlessness and depravity; all ties and restraints would vanish between kinsfolk."[21] As families and friends divided over acceptance of the new religion, as the old faith was increasingly abandoned, those who still held to the pagan gods braced themselves for the coming of the end. Around the year 1000, an anonymous poet composed the *Voluspa*, a prophesy depicting the terrible times to come:

Brothers will fight, will kill each other.

Kin will break the bonds of kin.

A harsh world it will be, whoredom rampant,

An axe-age, a sword-age, shields shattered,

A wind-age, a wolf-age before man's age tumbles down.

No man will spare his neighbour. . . .

All mankind must depart this world. . . .

The sun blackens. The earth sinks into the sea.

The brilliant stars dash down from the skies.[22]

While this prophesy concerning the death of the gods was not literally fulfilled, in one respect it did come true: By the close of the eleventh century, most of the Scandinavians had renounced their traditional beliefs and converted to Christianity. They abandoned the Viking lifestyle, no longer roaming to far lands to pillage and plunder, no longer glorying in the clash of sword and shield. As Erdoes states, "For the idol-worshiping people of the North, their world, the world of Thor and Odin, did indeed come to an end." [23]

Anxiety in the East

Apocalyptic tensions ran high not only in Europe but in the Middle East as well. Because the religion of Islam springs from Judeo-Christian roots, the apocalyptic vision of the Muslims of the eleventh century shared many similarities with that of the Christians. The Muslims believed that the End Times would be heralded by the arrival of the Antichrist in the Holy Land. There he would rule for forty days, performing false miracles in mockery of Christ. At the end of the forty days, Christ would return to earth and triumph over his foe. Following this final battle, the souls of all the men and women who had ever lived would be summoned to Jerusalem for the Day of Judgment. Many of these same elements can be found in the Christian view of the apocalypse. One concept unique to Islam, however, was the belief in the Mahdi (literally, "the rightly guided one"). A messianic figure destined to appear shortly before the Antichrist, the Mahdi would reveal the complete truth of Islam, establish perfect justice and equality, restore virtue, and bring victory to the followers of Muhammad.

While the Muslims' conception of the end of the world can accurately be labeled as apocalyptic, it would be mistaken to refer to their belief as millennialist. The medieval Muslims followed their own dating system; according to the Islamic calendar, the time period known to the Christians as the year 1000 fell between the years 390 and 391 after the Hegira (Muhammad's flight from Mecca, which occurred in A.D. 622). For the Muslims, the turn of the millennium was many centuries yet to come, and they placed no special significance on the year 390 A.H. On the other hand, as Schwartz notes, "By the end of the 4th century A.H., Islamic lore . . . had it that the beginning of each century A.H. would be graced with the emergence of a Mahdi to reform the faith and lead Muslims into a new age." [24] At the turn of the Christian millennium, therefore, numerous Muslims were looking ten years ahead in anticipation of the coming of the Mahdi.

Some felt that the Mahdi had indeed arrived in the person of al-Hakim, the caliph of Egypt, who in 400 A.H. implemented a policy of extreme adherence to the strictest interpretation of Islamic law. Previously his Islamic subjects had been accustomed to a rather lax enforcement of such religious restrictions as the ban on alcohol and the social segregation of the sexes, but al-Hakim worked vigorously to compel the Muslims to obey the dictates of Islamic law—and he severely punished them when they did not. He also reversed his predecessors' policy of toleration toward the Jews and Christians who lived in the lands ruled by the Egyptian caliphate. According to Schwartz,

> The revival of intolerance for Jews and Christians, both subject to humiliation and persecution under al-Hakim, was meant as manifesto that the Islamic world was about to be purified by the Mahdi. . . . Al-Hakim had gone much further than the appropriation of the role of Mahdi; he had declared that he was not only inaugurating a new age but was himself an aspect of the godhead. It was as deity incarnate that al-Hakim in 400 A.H. (1009 A.D.) could without qualm demolish the Church of the Holy Sepulchre in Jerusalem.[25]

Initially, al-Hakim's campaign to advance fundamentalist Islam struck a chord with many Muslims, but his increasingly cruel and erratic behavior—including his insistence on his divinity—alienated even the most conservative of his subjects. Only a few years after his ascendancy to power, al-Hakim mysteriously disappeared; presumably he was assassinated, although no body was ever found.

Despite al-Hakim's ignominious end, anticipation of the imminent coming of the Mahdi grew steadily throughout the eleventh century. The expectations of many Muslims were specifically centered on the approach of the year 500 A.H. (A.D. 1106–1107). As historian Robert Irwin explains, "For Muslims, . . . the late eleventh-century Near East was a time of acute insecurity. While some expected the revival of the Islamic faith at the end of the fifth Islamic century, others fearfully awaited the appearance of the Mahdi and the End of the World."[26] To some extent, the arrival of the armies of the First Crusade in the final years of the eleventh century simply served to heighten these expectations. As described above, the crusaders viewed their conquest of Jerusalem as essential to bringing about their version of the apocalypse, in which Christian victory was assured. But the Muslims had a slightly different opinion of these events: While the loss of Jerusalem was upsetting, it was not inconsistent with their scenario for the final days. In Irwin's words,

> Speculations about the Last Days and the role of the Mahdi in them were frequently intertwined with prophecies about Islam's triumph over Christianity and about the future fates of Jerusalem, Constantinople, and Rome. . . . The prophecies tended to stress that the Muslims would face many hardships and setbacks—they might even lose Jerusalem to the Christians for a while—before ultimately triumphing.[27]

Thus, the Christian occupation of Jerusalem could be seen as a sign that the long-awaited Mahdi would soon arrive to lead the forces of Islam to victory.

Troubled Times

Overall, the eleventh century was a turbulent era in human history. Relentless wars, famines, epidemics, fires, earthquakes, floods, and storms plagued the men and women of the 1000s. Whether or not these devastating events were considered omens of the imminent destruction of the earth, their combined impact contributed to a continual awareness of human frailty and the transitory nature of life. Even in civilizations that were not actively anticipating some sort of apocalyptic event, there was a marked sense of insecurity about the future.

And the future was indeed insecure: Over the course of the century, mighty empires crumbled, religions vanished, ways of life altered irrevocably. The once proud and powerful Mayan civilization fell to brutal invaders, who imposed their own traditions and culture on the Maya. At the start of the 1000s, the sub-Saharan kingdom of Ghana was an economic powerhouse, controlling the profitable African gold trade; by the close of the century, Ghana had been overrun by Muslim warriors and was in the process of losing its competitive edge. India also lost considerable territory to the armies of Islam, as did the Byzantine Empire of the Greeks. Even China— arguably the most secure and prosperous nation in the entire world during the eleventh century—felt the tension of the times. Many Chinese of the Sung period compared their age unfavorably to the more vigorous dynasties of the past, calling it decadent and soft. The government's policy of placating hostile border tribes with gifts of money and silk did little to reassure those who worried that China's military had become too weak to protect the country.

Yet the tenor of the times was not one of complete despair. Instead, there was a mingling of anxiety and expectancy, of fear and hope. People cast their thoughts nervously toward the future, worrying about what it might bring, trembling at apparent omens of doomsday. But they also continued to plan for the future as if it were certain. Even at the very peak of millennial fever, they continued to marry, to have children, to build homes, to conduct business deals, to go on with the everyday concerns of life. And despite the many troubles of the age, there was much to be hopeful about during the eleventh century. During the 1000s, the scholars of the Islamic world synthesized knowledge from Greece and India, advancing mathematics and science exponentially. The Chinese initiated a cultural renaissance that encouraged intellectual achievement throughout all strata of society. In the Americas, though the Maya declined, other civilizations—the Toltecs, the Anasazi, and the Cahokians—emerged and flourished. Western Europe awoke from the long nightmare of the Dark Ages and made the first few tentative steps toward recovery and resurgence.

The individuals who lived during the eleventh century could only glimpse the future through a misty haze, and more often than not the visions they saw troubled and disturbed them. But they continued to work and plan ceaselessly for the future, whatever it might bring. In this respect, they are little different from their descendants a thousand years later, who stand at the threshold of a new millennium, peering uncertainly but hopefully into the future.

Notes

1. Rev. 20:7–8 King James Version.
2. Richard Erdoes, *A.D. 1000: Living on the Brink of Apocalypse.* New York: Harper & Row, 1988, p. 5.
3. Quoted in G.G. Coulton, *Life in the Middle Ages.* New York: Macmillan, 1931, p. 3.
4. Quoted in Coulton, *Life in the Middle Ages,* p. 2–3.
5. Erdoes, *A.D. 1000,* p. 7.
6. James Reston Jr., *The Last Apocalypse: Europe at the Year 1000 A.D.* New York: Doubleday, 1998, p. 206.
7. Quoted in Erdoes, *A.D. 1000,* p. 3.
8. Quoted in Erdoes, *A.D. 1000,* p. 4.
9. Erdoes, *A.D. 1000,* p. 3.
10. Reston, *The Last Apocalypse,* p. 93.
11. Quoted in Robert Lacey and Danny Danziger, *The Year 1000: What Life Was Like at the Turn of the First Millennium: An Englishman's World.* New York: Little, Brown, 1999, p. 77.
12. Quoted in Reston, *The Last Apocalypse,* p. 96.
13. Elmer Bendiner, *The Rise and Fall of Paradise.* New York: Putnam, 1983, p. 239.
14. Reston, *The Last Apocalypse,* p. 155.
15. Rev. 18: 1–2, 9–10. Quoted in Reston, *The Last Apocalypse,* p. 155.
16. Reston, *The Last Apocalypse,* p. 156.
17. Hillel Schwartz, *Century's End: A Cultural History of the Fin de Siecle from the 990s Through the 1990s.* New York: Doubleday, 1990, p. 37.
18. Quoted in Coulton, *Life in the Middle Ages,* p. 7.
19. Quoted in Bernard McGinn, *Visions of the End: Apocalyptic Traditions in the Middle Ages.* New York: Columbia University Press, 1979, p. 90.
20. Guibert de Nogent, *The Deeds of God Through the Franks,* trans. Robert Levine. Woodbridge, UK: The Boydell Press, 1997, pp. 43–44.
21. Gwyn Jones, *A History of the Vikings.* Oxford, UK: Oxford University Press, 1984, p. 318.
22. Quoted in R.I. Page, *Chronicles of the Vikings: Records, Memo-*

rials, and Myths. London: British Museum Press, 1995, pp. 209–10.
23. Erdoes, *A.D. 1000*, p. 138.
24. Schwartz, *Century's End*, p. 45.
25. Schwartz, *Century's End,* p. 45.
26. Robert Irwin, "Islam and the Crusades, 1096–1699," in *The Oxford Illustrated History of the Crusades*, ed. Jonathan Riley-Smith. Oxford, UK: Oxford University Press, 1995, p. 218.
27. Irwin, "Islam and the Crusades," pp. 217–18.

Western Europe: Emergence from the Dark Ages

Compared to many other regions of the world, western Europe was an insignificant backwater at the turn of the millennium. The disintegration of the Roman Empire during the fifth century had sent western Europe spiraling into the Dark Ages, a turbulent period characterized by the breakdown of political, religious, economic, and educational institutions. By the year 1000, the Europeans had endured almost five centuries of frequent warfare, hostile invasions, political instability, and widespread corruption in the Catholic Church. In both economic vitality and innovative scholarship, Europe lagged far behind such countries as Egypt and China.

Despite these handicaps, however, at the beginning of the eleventh century Europe was posed on the brink of a monumental recovery. The near-constant invasions by the Vikings, Arabs, and Magyars that had so wracked the continent in the preceding centuries were finally starting to taper off. Internal hostilities were also decreasing in frequency, partly through the efforts of the clergy who promoted the new Peace of God movement, urging war-minded nobles to set aside their quarrels and maintain truces. This respite from the overwhelming violence of previous centuries afforded Europe the opportunity to begin to rebuild the societal structures that had been in disarray since the fall of the Roman Empire.

Europe's revival had three main components: political, economic, and religious. Politically, the nations of western Europe abandoned the last archaic remnants of Roman imperial government, which lacked effectiveness in the medieval age. Instead, they embraced the feudal system, which—by clearly establishing the hierarchy of allegiance among the noble class—allowed monarchs to consolidate control and build strong central governments. This change gave the Europeans more political stability and security than they had experienced during the Dark Ages, which fostered an environment conducive to further improvements.

The economic revival stemmed from an increase in agricultural productivity and urban commerce. In the troubled times after the dissolution of the Roman Empire, the cities of western Europe had declined as trade and manufacturing came to a standstill. "As trade and industry dried up," explains historian Bryce D. Lyon, "so did the middle class of merchants, artisans, and professional people. And as the middle class disappeared, so too did the towns in which it had lived." During the Dark Ages, the majority of Europe's population lived as impoverished peasants in the countryside, where they struggled to grow enough food to survive another year. But around the beginning of the eleventh century, several agricultural innovations enabled farmers to produce surpluses of food. These surpluses in turn freed more people to engage in nonagricultural activities, such as manufacturing and commerce. Europe's cities quickly increased in population, and new towns sprang up throughout the region. The resurgence of the merchant class, combined with the growth in political stability, greatly stimulated trade.

The revitalization of the religious world centered around the rise of a reform movement intended to reduce the amount of corruption in the Catholic Church. This movement had its main roots in the monasteries, although it also became popular among some members of the secular clergy (i.e., priests, bishops, and others who ministered to the public rather than living a cloistered life). The reforming monks addressed problems within their own monasteries and orders, attempting to restore monastic life to high standards of piety and poverty. However, they focused their strongest protests against the abuses of the secular clergy. For example, many members of the secular clergy came from powerful families among the nobility, and they strove to appoint their relatives to lucrative posts within the church. Kings and other secular lords often had control over important church positions and tended to grant these offices to the highest bidder. The reformers attacked these and other corrupt practices, and by the end of the eleventh century they had succeeded in abolishing many of the worst types of offenses, which contributed to a renewal of trust in religious institutions among the common people.

For western Europe, the eleventh century was largely devoted to recovery and rebuilding. And though other civilizations surpassed the Europeans during this period, the medieval renaissance of the 1000s planted the seeds for Europe's future greatness in centuries to come. The developments of this century, in the words of historian C. Warren Hollister, "would define and vitalize Europe across the next millennium."

Awaiting the Apocalypse

Robert Lacey and Danny Danziger

In the following selection from their book *The Year 1000: What Life Was Like at the Turn of the First Millennium: An Englishman's World,* Robert Lacey and Danny Danziger describe the anxiety that gripped western Europe as the year 1000 approached. According to the authors, many Europeans feared that the turn of the millennium would usher in the apocalypse—the terrible events presaging the end of the world. In the years leading up to and immediately after the new millennium, they write, Europe experienced comets, fires, outbreaks of heresy, and other disasters that were widely believed to be harbingers of doom. These portentous signs added to the overall climate of fear and apprehension, Lacey and Danziger explain.

Lacey is a historian and biographer whose works include *The Life and Times of Henry VIII* and *The Queens of the North Atlantic.* Danziger is a journalist and the author of several books on modern issues. Together, they are the founders and editors of *Cover* magazine, a British news digest.

Then I saw an angel coming down from heaven with the key of the abyss and a great chain in his hands. He seized the dragon, that serpent of old, the Devil or Satan, and chained him up for a thousand years; he threw him into the abyss, shutting and sealing it over him, so that he might seduce the nations no more till the thousand years were over. After that he must be let loose for a short while.

—Revelation 20:1–3

There were no such things as gossip columnists in the year 1000, but if *Vanity Fair* had existed, it would certainly have found room for the writings of Ralph Glaber. Glaber was a Burgundian monk who wrote a five-volume history of his times which constitutes our principal surviving source as to how people might have felt in the year 1000 about the shift in the calendar from one millennium to the next. Computer anxieties aside, most people today are looking forward to 2000 and the years beyond with reasonable optimism. But a thousand years ago people had never lived through such a major milestone, and biblical passages like the Revelation of St. John proposed unpleasant possibilities. Would the world come to an end? Would there be another millennium? Would life continue, but in some less pleasant form, reflecting the unchaining of Satan that St. John had described?

Ralph Glaber wrote his history with these questions in mind. He entered his first monastery in 997 A.D. Scarcely a dozen years old, he seems to have been possessed of a troublemaking character which set him apart from his fellows. As historian Henri Focillon has put it, Glaber had an "instinct for dissent," for in the course of his fifty years, the troublesome monk was shown the door of monasteries in Auxerre, Champeaux, Dijon, Beze, Suze, and finally the great abbey of Cluny. But Glaber's wanderings provided him with a patchwork of perspectives that was rare for his time. He was in touch with the bush telegraph [grapevine] of the year 1000. No cell-bound hermit, he wrote in a chatty, over-the-garden-fence style, and if it is impossible to confirm everything that he wrote, he still provides a vivid and believable glimpse of how some people, at least, experienced the first millennium.

Strange Phenomena

In the lead-up to 1000, Glaber gathered reports of a terrifying comet that had crossed the sky:

> It appeared in the month of September, not long after nightfall, and remained visible for nearly three months. It shone so brightly that its light seemed to fill the greater part of the sky, then it vanished at cock's crow. But whether it is a new star which God launches into space, or whether He merely increases the normal brightness of another star, only He can decide. . . . What appears established with the greatest degree of certainty is that this phenomenon in the sky never appears to men without being the sure sign of some mysterious and terrible event. And indeed, a fire soon consumed the church of St. Michael the Archangel, built on a promontory in the ocean [Mont-Saint-Michel off the coast of Brittany] which had always been the object of special veneration throughout the whole world.

In conjunction with his description of the portentous comet of 989—known today as Halley's comet—Glaber described other auguries:

In the seventh year from the millennium . . . almost all the cities of Italy and Gaul were devastated by violent conflagrations, and Rome itself largely razed by fire. . . . As one, [the people] gave out a terrible scream and turned to rush to confess to the Prince of the Apostles.

Many eminent men died around this time, recorded Glaber—though this could be said of almost any era—and there was an outbreak of heresy in Sardinia. "All this accords," wrote the monk, "with the prophecy of St. John, who said that the devil would be freed after a thousand years."

Glaber had met the Devil, who appeared at the end of his bed several times. As the monk recalled from his visions, the Prince of Darkness was a shaggy, black, hunched-up figure with pinched nostrils, a goat's beard, and blubbery lips with which he whispered seditious thoughts in an attempt to subvert the holy man: "Why do you monks bother with vigils, fasts, and mortifications?" cooed Lucifer on one visit. "One day, one hour of repentance, is all you need to earn eternal bliss. . . . So why bother to rise at the sound of the bell when you could go on sleeping?"

Some historians have cited this Dr. Faustus–like episode as discrediting the reliability of Glaber's testimony. But the monk's account of his vision neatly voiced the paradox which the doctrine of repentance poses to any Christian: if repentance guarantees salvation, why not enjoy a few good juicy sins before you repent? If anything, Glaber's dream indicated the reasoning of a sceptical mind—and his history did not dwell excessively on St. John's gloomy prophecies of millennial misery. After the monk's account of the natural disasters of the 990s, he moved smartly on to the year 1003:

Just before the third year after the millennium, throughout the whole world, but especially in Italy and Gaul, men began to reconstruct churches, although for the most part the existing ones were properly built and not in the least unworthy. But it seemed as though each Christian community were aiming to surpass all others in the splendour of construction. It was as if the whole world were shaking itself free, shrugging off the burden of the past, and cladding itself everywhere in a white mantle of churches.

Glaber described a world that had been holding its breath, expecting the worst. The worst had not happened, and as the monk travelled the countryside between Burgundy's great monastic houses, he had the chance to observe at firsthand the explosion of ecclesiastical stone building that marked the start of the eleventh century. It was echoed all over northern Christendom. To judge from the evidence of Anglo-Saxon England, there were teams of masons who travelled from community to community, offering package deals by which they erected parish churches to virtually Identikit plans. Their buildings must have shimmered, light and beautiful in the green medieval countryside just as Glaber described them—and so they still do.

The Second Wave of Millennialism

Glaber linked his "white mantle" of new churches to a world that was making a fresh start, but thirty years later another set of anxieties loomed. Strictly speaking, the reign of Christ on earth did not begin until the death and resurrection of the Saviour, which occurred, according to the New Testament, when Jesus was thirty-three years old. So might 1033 prove to be the year when the dire predictions of the book of Revelation would be fulfilled?

> After the many prodigies which had broken upon the world before, after, and around the millennium of the Lord Christ [wrote Glaber], there were plenty of able men of penetrating intellect who foretold others, just as great, at the approach of the millennium of the Lord's Passion, and such wonders were soon manifest.

Heresy broke out again around 1030 A.D., this time among the Lombards. There were horrendous famines which forced men into cannibalism, more beloved and distinguished church figures passed away, while pilgrims set off for Jerusalem in vast and unprecedented numbers. "It was believed," wrote Glaber,

> that the order of the seasons and the elements . . . had fallen into perpetual chaos, and with it had come the end of mankind. . . . It could portend nothing other than the advent of the accursed Anti-Christ who, according to divine testimony, is expected to appear at the end of the world.

Book IV of Glaber's *History* then described the manifestations that followed the happy passing of the 1033 "apocalypse":

> At the millennial anniversary of the Passion of the Lord, the clouds cleared in obedience to Divine mercy and goodness and the smiling sky began to shine and flow gentle breezes. . . . At that point, in the region of Aquitaine, bishops, abbots, and other men devoted to holy religion first began to gather councils of the whole people. . . . When the news of these assemblies was heard, the entire populace joyfully came, unanimously prepared to follow whatever should be commanded them by the pastors of the church. A voice descending from Heaven could not have done more, for everyone was still under the effect of the previous calamity and feared the future loss of abundance.

Glaber's reporting is confirmed by other sources. For several decades in the middle of the eleventh century huge crowds gathered in open fields in France to venerate relics and to swear oaths of peace. The movement was known as the "Peace of God," and economic historians have explained the phenomenon in terms of the church's wish to protect its estates in an era of petty warfare. Populist preaching whipped up feeling against lawless noblemen, and it is highly likely that some preachers may have called on millennial frettings for their purposes.

The theologian Abbo of Fleury recalled a premillennial sermon in his youth which did precisely this. A Parisian preacher had announced that "as soon as the number of a thousand years was completed, the Anti-Christ would come and the last judgement would soon follow." Abbo pooh-poohed the preacher's anxieties by quoting some alternative passages of scripture, but in England the eloquent Archbishop Wulfstan of York had no reservations about invoking millennial fears. It was in 1014, when the war between King Ethelred and the Danish invaders was at its bitterest, that England's greatest preacher composed his famous *Sermon of the Wolf to the English*:

> Dear Friends. . . . This world is in haste and is drawing ever closer to its end, and it always happens that the longer it lasts, the worse it becomes. And so it must ever be, for the coming of the Anti-Christ grows ever more evil because of the sins of the people, and then truly it will be grim and terrible widely in the world.

Wulfstan's corruscating sermon has come down to us in written form. It was intended to be read by monks and delivered by priests from parish pulpits, but in its mesmeric passion one can almost hear the tones of the archbishop as he himself declaimed it. Even in translation, his prose rings with the compelling rhythm of a Jesse Jackson or Martin Luther King:

> The devil has deceived this people too much, and there has been little faith among men, though they speak fair words, and too many crimes have gone unchecked in the land. . . . The laws of the people have deteriorated altogether too often since [King] Edgar died; and holy places are everywhere open to attack, and the houses of God are completely deprived of ancient rites, and stripped of all that is fitting; and religious orders have now for a long time been greatly despised; and widows are forced to marry unrighteously; and too many are reduced to poverty; and poor men are wretchedly deceived, most cruelly cheated and wholly innocent, sold out of this land far and wide into the possession of foreigners; and through cruel injustice, children in the cradle are enslaved for petty theft widely within this nation; and the rights of freemen suppressed and the rights of slaves curtailed, and the rights of charity neglected; and, to speak most briefly, God's laws are hated and His commands despised.

Preaching in 1014, Wulfstan made no reference to the anniversaries of 1000 and 1033 on which Glaber dwelt, but his words carried the same sense of crossing some awesome threshold in time. People were holding their breath in England, as Glaber described in France. Dates were not Wulfstan's concern, but the miseries of England were, and the archbishop had no doubt that the Vikings in their dragonships were acting as instruments of the Anti-Christ: "We pay them continually, and they humiliate us daily. They ravage and they burn, plunder and steal and carry off to their fleet. And lo! What other thing is clear and evident in all these events, if not the anger of God?"

The Historical Debate

Modern historians have debated whether the concerns expressed by Glaber and Wulfstan constitute evidence that Christendom marked the first millennium as a specially significant point in time. Those who doubt the reliability of Glaber's testimony, and who explain Wulfstan's sermon solely in terms of England's sufferings at the hands of the Vikings, point to the many English wills that were composed in the 990s. These were all written with the clear and calm assumption that the world was going to continue exactly as it always had. Not a single Anglo-Saxon will or charter makes any reference to a forthcoming apocalypse, and it would certainly be wrong to imagine crowds gathering together to count down in modern style to the end of an old era and the beginning of a new. . . .

Only the literate were in a position to concern themselves greatly with what would happen when the year DCCCCLXXXXVIIIJ [999—the Anglo-Saxons followed the older Roman style of numbering] became a simple M, and they would have had little agreement as to the specific day and hour at which the moment should be marked: December 25th? January 1st? Lady Day?

The profusion of possible starting points for a "new year" showed how imprecisely time was divided for most people in the year 1000—and they had heavyweight authority for their vagueness. It was ludicrous and impertinent, argued the philosopher St. Augustine of Hippo, for man to impose his own mortal calculations on the workings of God. According to the "business as usual" school of modern historians, the millennial preoccupations of Glaber and Wulfstan hold no more significance than the jeremiads of the gullible and doom-laden who agonise in every society—the medieval equivalents of believers in UFOs, the Bermuda Triangle, and the X files.

And yet. And yet . . . The appeal of Wulfstan's remarkable sermon derives from the power with which it captures and gives expression to the spirit of its times. Its pervading feeling of doom has a resonance that is deeper than the imagining of a single clergyman, while Ralph Glaber's history rings with the same echo. Glaber's narrative may have been colourful, but it was not concocted out of thin air. Sin, punishment, and Anti-Christ were clearly linked in these vivid contemporary visions to a common concern with a crossroad in time. The world was turning, and though it is in the nature of the world to turn, the ending of the first millennium clearly provided some people with the stimulus to contemplate that fact with extra seriousness, and to ponder the wonder and despair contained within the eternal platitude.

The Rise of Feudalism

Sidney Painter

In the following article, Sidney Painter examines the rise of feudalism in France and its spread throughout western Europe during the eleventh century. The feudal system—in which each knight pledged loyalty to a lord, and each lord swore allegiance to the king—provided the states of western Europe with the type of political structure that had largely been absent during the turbulent Dark Ages. While feudalism was not perfect, as the author notes, it did allow the growth of strong governments in the kingdoms of Europe. Painter was a professor of history at Johns Hopkins University in Baltimore, Maryland. His books include *Mediaeval Society*, *The Rise of the Feudal Monarchies*, *Feudalism and Liberty*, and *A History of the Middle Ages: 284–1500*.

One of the most important features of the eleventh century was the crystallization and extension of the feudal system. Feudal institutions had been developing since the eighth century. Charles Martel had given benefices [landed estates] to men who swore loyalty to him and were ready to serve him as soldiers. By the time of Charles the Bald benefices were becoming hereditary in practice if not in theory and the same tendency was affecting the countships and other royal offices. In eleventh-century France the benefice had become the hereditary fief. Although the office of count was not absolutely hereditary, a competent heir was practically certain of the inheritance. When an office changed hands, this was less likely to

Excerpted from Sidney Painter, "Western Europe on the Eve of the Crusades," in *A History of the Crusades*, edited by Kenneth M. Setton. Copyright © 1969 The Regents of the University of Wisconsin. Reprinted with permission from The University of Wisconsin Press.

be the result of royal action than of the successful aggression of a powerful rival. Moreover, during the ninth and tenth centuries when civil war combined with Viking raids to keep France in a state of anarchy, the landholders had but two practical alternatives. One could obtain military support and protection by becoming the vassal of a powerful neighbor or one could sink into the category of an unfree villager. Almost every landholder whose resources permitted him to equip himself as a soldier chose the former course. Only the most powerful and most stubborn could stay outside the feudal system. Although eleventh-century France contained *allods*, that is, lands held from no lord, they were quite rare and most of them disappeared in the twelfth century. In short, eleventh-century France, especially in the north, was almost completely feudalized and the principle so dear to feudal lawyers of "no land without a lord" was nearly true of it.

As the feudal system spread over France its members became arranged in a hierarchy. At the head stood the Capetian king, who was suzerain of the great lords of the land. Below him came a group of feudal potentates who may best be described as feudal princes. . . . Each of these great lords who held directly of the king had his own vassals many of whom were counts or had usurped that title. It was by no means uncommon for a vigorous lord to wake up some bright morning and decide he was a count, and usually no one bothered to dispute the claim. These secondary vassals in turn had their own vassals and rear-vassals, and the hierarchy continued down to the simple knight who had just enough land and peasant labor to support him. This minimum unit of the feudal system, the resources that would enable a man to be a knight, was called the knight's fief or fee. . . .

Feudal Obligations

Each member of the feudal hierarchy had obligations to his lord and his vassals. These obligations were defined by feudal custom. Whenever a dispute arose between lord and vassal, it was settled in the lord's *curia* or court. There the lord acted as presiding officer and the vassals rendered the decision. In every fief the feudal custom for that fief was created by these decisions in the lord's court. Thus feudal custom varied from fief to fief. Moreover, in the eleventh century the formation of this custom was far from complete, for questions were decided only when they arose and many came up but rarely. Take for instance the customs governing inheritance. It was generally accepted that if a man had sons, one of them was his heir, but in the eleventh century the idea of primogeniture was by no means absolutely accepted. If the eldest son looked unpromising as a warrior, the vassals felt free to choose one of his younger brothers. If the two eldest sons were twins, the fief might be evenly divided between them. When a man died leaving a son under age, who cared for the fief and performed the service due from it? Sometimes it was the nearest male relative on the mother's side, sometimes on the father's side. In other fiefs the custody of minors belonged to the lord. But despite the variations from fief to fief it is possible to make certain general statements about feudal obligations that are reasonably valid.

The fundamental purpose of the feudal system was coöperation in war. Every lord was bound to protect his vassal from enemies outside the fief and every vassal owed military service to his lord. In some cases the vassal owed only his own personal service; in others he was bound to lead a certain number of knights to his lord's army. By the thirteenth century the military service owed by vassals was carefully defined and limited, but this process was not complete in the eleventh century. In most fiefs a distinction was made between offensive and defensive campaigns and the length of time a vassal had to serve in the former was limited. . . . When the fief was in danger, obviously the vassals were bound to stay in service as long as they were needed. Then the feudal system was political as well as military. When there was a question of feudal custom to be decided, the vassals were bound to obey the lord's summons to his court. Moreover, as the vassals had a strong interest in the welfare of their lord and his fief, they expected him to consult them before making an important decision. When their lord was about to marry, he was expected to summon his vassals to aid him in deciding what lady had the most useful marriage portion and the most potent relatives. If a lord wanted his vassals to serve him with enthusiasm in a war against

A knight takes a solemn oath during a dubbing ceremony. Each knight was given just enough land and peasant labor to support himself.

a neighbor, he sought their counsel before embarking on it. In short, the important business of the lord's fief was conducted in his court. Finally a man's prestige in the feudal world depended very largely on the number and importance of his vassals. When he wanted to display his power and dignity, he summoned his vassals to "do him honor". Thus attendance at the lord's court was second in importance only to military service as a feudal obligation.

In addition to service in his lord's court and army the vassal had certain obligations that were essentially economic. One of these was known as relief. By the twelfth century, relief was a money payment due to the lord when an heir succeeded to a fief, but there is evidence to indicate that in some fiefs at least in the eleventh century it was also demanded when a new lord came into his inheritance. Moreover, in the eleventh century it was often, perhaps usually, paid in horses and armor rather than in money. When a lord had a need for additional resources for some purpose that he considered important for his fief as a whole, he asked his vassals for an aid. By the twelfth century feudal custom defined very strictly the occasions on which a lord could demand an aid—for other purposes he could simply request one. The accepted occasions were the knighting of the lord's eldest son, the wedding of his eldest daughter for the first time, and the paying of ransom for the lord if he were captured. In all probability this clear definition had not been achieved by the eleventh century. When a lord wanted an aid, he asked his vassals for it and unless the request seemed too unreasonable, he received it. . . . Finally, in some fiefs in the twelfth and thirteenth centuries, the vassals were obliged to entertain the lord and his household when he visited them, and there is reason for believing that this obligation had been more general and more important in the eleventh century.

The Lord's Rights

Beyond the actual services owed by the vassal the lord had certain rights over the vassal and his fief. As the marriage of a vassal's daughter gave a male from outside the family an interest in her father's fief, the bridegroom had to be approved by the lord. If a vassal died leaving an unmarried daughter as an heir, it was the lord's right and duty to choose a husband for her. This was a valuable prerogative as it allowed the lord to reward a faithful knight at no cost to himself. When a vassal died leaving children under age, the lord could insist that someone be found to perform the service due from the fief unless custom gave him the custody of the heirs and their lands. If a vassal died without heirs that were recognized by the custom of the fief—second cousins were rarely accepted and more distant relatives practically never—the fief escheated, that is, returned to the lord. In case a vassal violated the feudal bond by some offense against his lord and was condemned by his fellow vassals in the lord's court, he could forfeit his fief. Forfeiture was rather rare. The assembled vassals hesitated to declare a fief forfeited because each of them felt that he might be in the same position some day.

When a man became a vassal, he did homage and swore fidelity to his lord. There has been a great deal of essentially fruitless discussion about the distinction between homage and fidelity. The fact that prelates often were willing to swear fidelity but refused to do homage would seem to indicate that fidelity was personal loyalty while homage represented a promise to perform the services due from a fief. But household knights who held no fief often swore fidelity and did homage. Actually it seems doubtful that there was any clear, generally accepted distinction. Ordinarily the two were part of a single ceremony. The vassal knelt before his lord, put his hands between his lord's hands, and swore to be faithful to him "against all men living or dead". Often the lord then gave the vassal a clod of earth to symbolize the granting of the fief. The personal relationship between lord and vassal was an important element in feudalism — each was expected to be loyal to the other. It was a horrible crime for a vassal to slay or wound his lord or seduce his wife or daughter, but a lord was also bound not to injure his vassal in person or honor. The vassal was expected to aid his lord in every way possible.

A System Based on Warfare

As a form of government feudalism had both advantages and disadvantages. It supplied a military force of heavy cavalry at every stage in the hierarchy. Thus each barony, each county, and each kingdom had its army. It also furnished vigorous and interested local government. The extensive reclamation of land and the founding of towns [that began in the eleventh century] were largely the result of the desire of feudal lords to increase their resources. It is highly doubtful that mere agents working for the benefit of a central government could have accomplished so much. But as a means of keeping peace and order the feudal system was no great success, for it was based on the assumption that there would be continual warfare. In theory, quarrels between lords and vassals and between vassals of the same lord were settled in the feudal courts. Actually when two vassals of a lord quarreled, they went to war and the lord did not intervene unless he thought one might be so seriously weakened that he could not perform his service. And no spirited vassal accepted an unfavorable decision by his lord's court until he was coerced with armed force. Between vassals of different lords there was no hindrance to war. In short, in eleventh-century France, feudal warfare was endemic and it was a fortunate region that saw peace throughout an entire summer. The church tried to limit this warfare by declaring the Peace and

Truce of God. The Peace of God forbade attacks on noncombatants, merchants, women, and peasants while the Truce prohibited fighting on weekends and on religious days. Unfortunately, neither Peace nor Truce was taken very seriously by the feudal lords.

Fighting was the chief function of the feudal male. From early youth he was conditioned to bear the weight of knightly armor and drilled rigorously in the use of arms. He had to learn the extremely difficult feat of hitting a target with his spear while riding at full gallop with his shield on his left arm. When he was considered adequately mature and trained he was made a knight. This was a simple ceremony in the eleventh century. An experienced knight gave him his arms and then struck him a terrific blow with his hand or the flat of his sword. Throughout his life the knight spent most of his time in practising with his arms or actually fighting. . . .

The castle was an extremely vital factor in feudal politics. If adequately supplied and garrisoned a castle could hold out almost indefinitely against the siege methods of the day. Rarely could a feudal army be held together long enough to take a resolutely defended castle. Hence its lord was practically independent. If a baron was so unfortunate as to be condemned by his lord's court, he could simply retire to his castle until his discouraged suzerain was ready to make peace. Not until the advent of mercenary troops who would stay in service as long as they were paid and the invention of improved siege engines was it possible for a lord to exert any effective authority over a vassal who possessed a strong castle. And the castle was an integral part of feudalism. When feudal institutions spread to a new land, castles soon appeared. Within a century of the Norman conquest there were some twelve hundred castles in England.

At the beginning of the eleventh century France was the only feudal state in Europe. The Capetian king was essentially a feudal suzerain supporting his court on the produce of his demesne manors and raising his army from his vassals in the duchy of France and the tiny contingents that the great lords were willing to send him. The peers of France readily acknowledged that they were the king's vassals, but rarely bothered to render him any services. Actually France was not a single state but an alliance of feudal principalities bound together by the feeble suzerainty of the king. In real power the king was weaker than most of his great vassals. His demesne was small and he could not control the barons of the Île de France. The monarchy survived largely because of the support of the church, which was inclined to prefer one master to many, and the resources that could be drawn from church fiefs. While some of the great lords such as the count of Flanders and the dukes of Normandy and Aquitaine had obtained control of the bishops within their lands, the prelates of Burgundy and Champagne depended on the king. The bishops had large, rich fiefs with many knightly vassals. Hence the man who appointed the bishops had the use of extensive resources. Nevertheless, the Capetian monarchy of the early eleventh century could do little more than survive. In the Île de France it had little authority and outside none whatever.

Along the borders of France feudal institutions had spread into other regions. The county of Barcelona, once Charlemagne's Spanish March, was a thoroughly feudal state and there were strong feudal elements in the kingdoms of Aragon and Navarre. In Germany, Lorraine and Franconia were essentially feudal. The kingdom of Germany and the Holy Roman Empire ruled by the emperors of the Saxon dynasty did not constitute a feudal state. The base of the royal power lay in the duchy of Saxony, which was almost untouched by feudalism. It was a land of free farmers, noble and non-noble, who were always ready to follow their duke to war. Outside Saxony the imperial authority depended almost entirely on the prelates. The bishops and abbots of Germany, Lombardy, and Tuscany were imperial appointees with wide, delegated authority. Their great fiefs and their resources were at the emperor's disposal. Although the counts of Germany were non-hereditary royal agents, they were essentially judicial officers, and the military control rested in the hands of the dukes. The emperors, dukes, counts, and other landholders occasionally granted fiefs, but the offices of duke and count were not fiefs. The power of a duke depended on the extent of his estates and his ability to inspire the loyalty of the people of his duchy. Thus the dukes of Franconia, Swabia, and Bavaria were usually powerful figures while the duke of Lorraine was likely to be a mere figurehead. In this same period England was still a Teutonic monarchy. Small men commended themselves to great men, swore oaths of fidelity to them, and occasionally held land in return for military service, but there were neither vassals nor fiefs in the continental sense.

Spreading Feudalism: The Norman Invasions

During the course of the eleventh century feudalism expanded rapidly. The conquest of England by duke William of Normandy created a new feudal state. King William retained the powers that had been enjoyed by his Anglo-Saxon predecessors. In every shire there was a sheriff appointed by the king and removable at his pleasure who presided over the popular courts, supervised the king's demesne manors, and collected his dues. William also collected the land tax called Danegeld and was the only monarch of western Europe to have a source of revenue of this type. Moreover, when King William established a complete and formal feudal hierarchy in England, he made certain innovations in feudal custom. In France a vassal's primary obligation was to his lord, and if the lord waged war against the king, it was the vassal's duty to follow him. William insisted that every freeman owed basic allegiance to the crown. In the famous Salisbury Oath the freemen of England swore fidelity to him as against all others. If an English baron rose in revolt, his vassals were expected to desert him. Then William absolutely forbade private warfare. The vassals of an English baron owed him military service only when the baron himself was engaged in the king's service. Finally the Conqueror was extremely niggardly in granting rights of jurisdiction. All lords of any importance were given "sac and soc" or police court authority over their own tenants. A few great lords had the right to have their agents preside over local popular courts. But the higher ranges of justice were kept firmly in the hands of the crown. In short, William created a feudal state, but it was one in which the monarch had extensive non-feudal powers and resources and in which feudal custom was modified to favor royal authority.

At about the same time that William of Normandy established a feudal state in England a group of Norman adventurers were doing the same thing in southern Italy and Sicily. In the third decade of the eleventh century William, Drogo, and Humphrey, sons of a petty Norman lord named Tancred of Hauteville, entered the continuous quarrels between rival factions in southern Italy. First they served as mercenary captains, but soon they established themselves in lands and fortresses. They then sent for their younger brothers, Robert Guiscard and Roger. When Humphrey, the last of the elder brothers, died in 1057 the Hautevilles were masters of Apulia. Robert Guiscard took the title duke of Apulia and set his brother Roger to work conquering Calabria. In 1061 both brothers joined forces to attack Sicily, which was held by the Moslems. After some thirty years of continuous war the conquest was completed and Roger became count of Sicily as his brother's vassal. Robert, duke of Apulia and overlord of Sicily, did homage to the pope for his lands and was a firm ally of the papacy against the German emperors. But the possession of southern Italy failed to satisfy his ambition. He and his turbulent son Bohemond viewed with greedy eyes the Byzantine lands across the Adriatic and contemplated the conquest of Greece if not that of the whole Byzantine empire. Robert and Bohemond invaded Greece and might well have conquered it if their communications had not been cut by the Venetian fleet, which aided the emperor in return for extensive commercial rights in the empire. Robert Guiscard and Roger of Sicily built a strong feudal state on much the same lines followed by William of Normandy. There was a feudal hierarchy strictly controlled by a strong and effective central government.

In Germany the two great emperors of the Salian house, Henry III and Henry IV, attempted to build a strong, centralized monarchy on the foundations laid by the Saxon emperors. Already master of Franconia and with extensive estates in Swabia, Henry III planned to add

Thuringia and south Saxony to the family domains and thus gain a firm basis of power in the heart of Germany. He built a strong castle at Goslar, the chief town of south Saxony and the site of valuable silver mines, and strewed the neighborhood with fortresses garrisoned by troops from his Swabian lands. His son Henry IV continued his policy. But the nobles and freemen of Saxony fiercely resented the king's intrusion into the duchy and, led by the Billung family, which claimed the ducal dignity, they rose in revolt against Henry IV. At the same time the great pope Gregory VII chose to attack the very cornerstone of the imperial government—the emperor's control over the prelates. The German lords, who had no desire to see a strong monarchy, combined with the pope and the Saxon rebels against Henry. The emperor held his own and died victor over his foes in the year 1106. But the long struggle had ruined the hopes of the Salian kings for establishing a strong monarchy. The first half of the twelfth century was to be a period of anarchy in Germany in which feudal institutions were to spread rapidly until the Hohenstaufen emperors created a feudal state.

The Peace of God Movement

Thomas Head and Richard Landes

Thomas Head is a professor of history at Hunter College of the City University of New York. Richard Landes is a history professor and the director of the Center for Millennial Studies at Boston University. They are the editors of *The Peace of God: Social Violence and Religious Response in France Around the Year 1000*, from which the following passage is excerpted. The Peace of God movement, the authors explain, was a response to the frequent violence that plagued western Europe at the turn of the millennium. Bishops and other leading clergymen held public councils in which they required knights, nobles, and princes to take a holy oath to maintain the peace, the authors write. They also explore the related Truce of God, which strictly limited the times of year when warfare could be waged.

In the summer of 987, the West Frankish nobility passed over the claims of the last Carolingian and elected a new king. Although few at the time may have realized it, they had inaugurated a new royal dynasty, the Capetians. Whether this dynastic change triggered the changes that followed or merely provided added vigor to them, the next two generations mark a fundamental turning point in French, and beyond that in European, history. This transformation of all levels and all aspects of society—the "mutation of the year 1000" as historian Guy Bois described it—occurred during a period that seemed to marry disorder and creativity. During the slow and awkward consolidation of Capetian power, the lesser nobility (castellans) and their mounted warriors (*milites*) asserted their independence and power. In the long run, the resultant feuding and pillage proved a symptom of fundamental change in the basic structures of Frankish society. To many contemporaries, particularly the clerics who left written testimony, however, it seemed to mark a headlong slide into anarchy:

> With the world coming to an end, since men are driven by a briefer life, so does a more atrocious cupidity burn in them. Whence it occurs that they take away the possessions of the holy church, now by force, now by extortion, now by the claims of unjust ministers, so that only the name of the holy church remains.

Among the many responses to the perceived disorder at the turn of the millennium, one of the earliest, and perhaps the most intriguing, was the Peace of God. Rather than rely solely on the protection afforded by secular princes, ecclesiastical lords turned to their neighboring patron saints and the populace of their territories for assistance in keeping the peace. Leading regional bishops convoked councils of their fellow bishops, meetings that were also attended by the abbots of important monastic communities and by various secular leaders. Monks from the region raised up the relics enshrined in their churches and took them to the sites of the councils, where the saints could serve as witnesses and representatives of divine authority. The presence of such treasures drew large numbers of men and women from an enthusiastic *populus* [i.e., commoners]. All converged on the large open fields that were the favored sites of Peace councils. There—surrounded by clerical and lay magnates, by saints, and by their social inferiors—members of the warrior elite took oaths of peace, framed in a context that mobilized what a modern observer might call popular opinion. . . .

The Development of the Peace of God

Peace councils were first held in Aquitaine and Burgundy during the last quarter of the tenth century. In 975, Bishop Guy of Le Puy convoked a large meeting in an open field outside his episcopal city to deal with those who had pillaged the churches of his diocese. Backing his threat of excommunication with the troops of his nephews, the counts of nearby Gévaudan and Brioude, Guy forced those gathered, both knights and armed peasants, to take an oath to maintain the peace. Since he acted with secular support rather than that of his fellow bishops, he was unable to enact the formal canons or threaten the spiritual sanctions that later characterized the Peace of God. Nevertheless, the oath sworn at Le Puy serves as an important precursor of the Peace movement. Subsequent events in the Auvergne indicate that Guy and other bishops continued to call such mass gatherings and eventually began to use relics as a means of drawing larger crowds. [These] initiatives [were] undertaken by the high clergy of the Auvergne to cope with disorder in a region where no king, indeed no count, could guarantee stability.

The earliest council from which Peace canons survive was that held at Charroux in 989. According to its decree, three crimes were to be punished by excommunication: robbery of church property, assaults on clerics, and theft of cattle from peasants. The decrees of later councils, which generally followed the model laid down at Charroux, bear witness to an increasingly coherent concept of God's peace. At Le Puy in 994, the bishops opened their legislation with the statement, "Since we know that without peace no man may see God, we adjure you, in the name of the Lord, to be men of peace." They then proceeded to outlaw, in far greater detail, the same actions earlier proscribed at Charroux. On one level the bishops simply intended their decrees to be one means of reasserting the rule of law in their society. They thus hoped to protect themselves, their clerics, the property of their churches, and the productive output of their peasants from the consequences of social violence. Beyond this, the acts of these Peace councils shared the concerns of the more widely disseminated monastic and papal reform movements associated with the names of the abbey of Cluny and Pope Gregory VII.

The canons of the councils themselves provide only one lens through which to observe the Peace of God; at Charroux, in addition to the promulgated edicts, we also find the assembly of a large number of saints' relics and the enthusiastic participation of the *populus*. These characteristics also marked most subsequent councils. Narrative descriptions, such as the following from the council of Héry, allow us to observe the circumstances in which the unarmed clergy and the *populus* could extract oaths to observe God's peace from the *milites*:

> Crowds of common people without number, of every age and both genders, hurried there. In order that the devotion of these laypeople might be increased on their journey, men of faith began to bring the bodies of many saints as well. Along with such venerable relics, [the monks of Montier-en-Der] did not neglect to bring along the relics of the holy body of our patron Bercharius, which were fittingly placed for their journey on a litter. This was done, moreover, so that our leaders could make a proclamation about a certain count, Landric by name, concerning the booty he had stolen from our blessed protector.

Given the prominent role of relics at these councils, the Peace constitutes an important stage in the development of the cult of saints. . . .

At least a half dozen similar gatherings of bishops, monks, saints, and people occurred in the decade following the council at Charroux. They were scattered throughout the French Midi, from Narbonne and the Rouergue to the Auvergne and Burgundy. Perhaps the most dramatic of these early councils took place outside the walls of Limoges in 994. In response to an outbreak of ergotism—a disease known as "holy fire" and interpreted as a sign of divine wrath—the duke and bishops of Aquitaine summoned relics from monasteries at distances ranging to over one hundred kilometers. A mass healing was attributed to the miraculous powers of the relics, the most important being those of Saint Martial, an early bishop of the city. . . .

In the decades immediately following the turn of the millennium, few Peace councils were held, but the movement underwent a revival during the 1020s and 1030s. There are records of almost twenty Peace councils during these decades. Councils were held not only in Aquitaine and Burgundy, the original heartland of the Peace, but also in such other regions as Catalonia, the Narbonnais, Provence, the Berry, Flanders, Champagne, and Normandy. Territorial princes came to play an important role and "peace" ideology became the transcendant idiom; in 1024, for example, King Robert the Pious met with Emperor Henry II on the border of their lands to proclaim such a "universal peace." Writing a few years after the fact, Rodulphus Glaber noted that it was in Aquitaine in 1033 that

> bishops, abbots, and other men devoted to holy religion first began to gather councils of the whole people [*populus*]. At these gatherings the bodies of many saints and shrines containing holy relics were assembled. From there through the provinces of Arles and Lyon, then through all of Burgundy, and finally in the farthest corners of Frankland, it was proclaimed in every diocese that councils would be summoned in fixed places by bishops and by the magnates of the whole land for the purpose of reforming both the peace and the institutions of the holy faith.

But the Peace movement was changing. In 1038, for the first and perhaps only time, its adherents took arms to enforce the Peace, in the so-called Peace militia organized by Archbishop Aimon of Bourges. The creation of the Peace militia marked a major turning point in the course of the Peace movement. . . .

The Truce of God

In the 1040s, the Peace movement underwent profound changes. The Peace of God had been an attempt to protect the unarmed, particularly the clergy, at all times. What followed was the proclamation of the Truce of God, an attempt to outlaw all fighting, but only during certain periods of religious significance. The Truce first appeared in 1027 at the council of Elne (or Toulouges). It later became a dominant feature of the Peace movement at the synod of Arles (ca. 1041), where the bishops prohibited all Christians from engaging in combat from Thursday to Monday morning (in commemoration of Christ's passion), on important feast days, and in the seasons of Advent and Lent. Once again excommunication was threatened, but the importance of relics and the *populus* was considerably diminished. Unlike earlier councils, whose canons were limited to the jurisdictions of the bishops there summoned, the bishops who gathered at Arles suggested that their actions be applied throughout the kingdom of France. The idea soon spread to neighboring kingdoms, particularly by means of the efforts of Cluniac monks.

The Truce of God was both more and less ambitious in its aims than the Peace promulgated at earlier councils. The bishops of the early Peace movement had been first and foremost concerned with the unarmed. They had not punished violence perpetrated against armed men, and thus they had in essence failed to question the right of the *milites* to take up arms at will. The Truce of God, however, suggested that the very shedding of Christian blood was sinful. As a canon of the council of Narbonne (1054) phrased it, "No Christian should kill another Christian, since whoever kills a Christian doubtless sheds the blood of Christ." With such restraints on his actions within Christendom, the knight found the prospect of battle against Christ's enemies increasingly attractive, for the Truce encouraged the idea that combat pleased God only in defense of Christendom. When, at the council of Clermont in 1095, Pope Urban II called on the knights of western Europe to aid their Christian brethren in the east through the First Crusade, his first canon proclaimed the renewal of the Truce of God.

The Truce of God for the Diocese of Cologne

The Bishop of Cologne

Outbreaks of violence occurred frequently in medieval Europe, especially among the nobility. Trained to be warriors, most nobles grew restless during times of peace, and any minor slight or insult could serve as reason enough to attack their neighbors. During the eleventh century, the Catholic Church sought to stem this tide of bloodshed through the Truce of God, a pact to keep the peace on religious holidays and other specified times. The following example of a Truce of God, preserved in a letter written by the bishop of Cologne to the bishop of Münster in 1083, illustrates the typical conditions set forth in these agreements. The people of Cologne and the surrounding area consented to this truce in April 1083, and it served as a model for later enactments.

I nasmuch as in our own times the church, through its members, has been extraordinarily afflicted by tribulations and difficulties, so that tranquility and peace were wholly despaired of, we have endeavored by God's help to aid it, suffering so many burdens and perils. And by the advice of our faithful subjects we have at length provided this remedy, so that we might to some extent re-establish, on certain days at least, the peace which, because of our sins, we could

Excerpted from the Bishop of Cologne, "The Truce of God for the Diocese of Cologne," April 20, 1083.

not make enduring. Accordingly we have enacted and set forth the following: having called together our parishioners to a legally summoned council, which was held at Cologne, the chief city of our province, in the Church of St. Peter, in the 1083d year of our Lord's Incarnation, in the sixth indiction, on the XII day before the Kalends of May, after arranging other business, we have caused to be read in public what we proposed to do in this matter. After this had been for some time fully discussed "pro and con" by all, it was unanimously agreed upon, both the clergy and the people consenting, and we declared in what manner and during what parts of the year it ought to be observed:

Namely, that from the first day of the Advent of our Lord through Epiphany, and from the beginning of Septuagesima to the eighth day after Pentecost and through that whole day, and throughout the year on every Sunday, Friday and Saturday, and on the fast days of the four seasons, and on the eve and the day of all the apostles, and on all days canonically set apart—or which shall in the future be set apart—for fasts or feasts, this decree of peace shall be observed; so that both those who travel and those who remain at home may enjoy security and the most entire peace, so that no one may commit murder, arson, robbery or assault, no one may injure another with a sword, club or any kind of weapon, and so that no one irritated by any wrong, from the Advent of our Lord to the eighth day after Epiphany, and from Septuagesima to the eighth day after Pentecost, may presume to carry arms, shield, sword or lance, or moreover any kind of armor. On the remaining days indeed, viz., on Sundays, Fridays, apostles', days and the vigils of the apostles, and on every day set aside, or to be set aside, for fasts or feasts, bearing arms shall be legal, but on this condition, that no injury shall be done in any way to any one. If it shall be necessary for any one in the time of the decreed peace—i.e., from the Advent of our Lord to the eighth day after Epiphany, and from Septuagesima to the eighth day after Pentecost—to go from one bishopric into another in which the peace is not observed, he may bear arms, but on the condition that he shall not injure any one, except in self-defence if he is attacked; and when he returns into our diocese he shall immediately lay aside his arms. If it shall happen that any castle is besieged during the days which are included within the peace the besiegers shall cease from attack unless they are set upon by the besieged and compelled to beat the latter back.

Penalties for Transgressors

And in order that this statute of peace should not be violated by any one rashly or with impunity, a penalty was fixed by the common consent of all; if a free man or noble violates it, i.e., commits homicide or wounds any one or is at fault in any manner whatever, he shall be expelled from our territory, without any indulgence on account of the payment of money or the intercession of friends, and his heirs shall take all his property; if he holds a fief, the lord to whom it belongs shall receive it again. Moreover, if it is learned that his heirs after his expulsion have furnished him any support or aid, and if they are convicted of it, the estate shall be taken from them and given to the king. But if they wish to clear themselves of the charge against them, they shall take oath with twelve, who are equally free or equally noble. If a slave kills a man, he shall be beheaded; if he wounds a man, he shall lose a hand; if he does an injury in any other way with his fist or a club, or by striking with a stone, he shall be shorn and flogged. If, however, he is accused and wishes to prove his innocence, he shall clear himself by the ordeal of cold water, but he must himself be put into the water and no one else in his place; if, however, fearing the sentence decreed against him, he flees, he shall be under a perpetual excommunication; and if he is known to be in any place, letters shall be sent thither, in which it shall be announced to all that he is excommunicate, and that it is unlawful for any one to associate with him. In the case of boys who have not yet completed their twelfth year, the hand ought not to be cut off; but only in the case of those who are twelve years or more of age. Nevertheless if boys fight, they shall be whipped and deterred from fighting.

It is not an infringement of the peace, if any one orders his delinquent slave, pupil, or any one in any way under his charge to be chastised with rods or cudgels. It is also an exception to this constitution of peace, if the Lord King publicly orders an expedition to attack the enemies of the kingdom or is pleased to hold a council to judge the enemies of justice. The peace is not violated if, during the time, the duke or other counts, advocates or their substitutes hold courts and inflict punishment legally on thieves, robbers and other criminals.

The statute of this imperial peace is especially enacted for the security of those engaged in feuds; but after the end of the peace, they are not to dare to rob and plunder in the villages and houses, because the laws and penalties enacted before the institution of the peace are still legally valid to restrain them from crime, moreover because robbers and highwaymen are excluded from this divine peace and indeed from any peace.

Excommunication

If any one attempts to oppose this pious institution and is unwilling to promise peace to God with the others or to observe it, no priest in our diocese shall presume to say a mass for him or shall take any care for his salvation; if he is sick, no Christian shall dare to visit him; on his death-bed he shall not receive the Eucharist, unless he repents. The supreme authority of the peace promised to God and commonly extolled by all will be so great that it will be observed not only in our times, but forever among our posterity, because if any one shall presume to infringe, destroy or violate it, either now or ages hence, at the end of the world, he is irrevocably excommunicated by us.

The infliction of the above mentioned penalties on the violators of the peace is not more in the power of the counts, centenaries or officials, than in that of the whole people in common; and they are to be especially careful not to show friendship or hatred or do anything contrary to justice in punishing, and not to conceal the crimes, if they can be hidden, but to bring them to light. No one is to receive money for the release of those taken in fault, or to attempt to aid the guilty by any favor of any kind, because whoever does this incurs the intolerable damnation of his soul; and all the faithful ought to remember that this peace has not been promised to men, but to God, and therefore must be observed so much the more rigidly and firmly. Wherefore we exhort all in Christ to guard inviolably this necessary contract of peace, and if any one hereafter presumes to violate it, let him be damned by the ban of irrevocable excommunication and by the anathema of eternal peridition.

In the churches, however, and in the cemeteries of the churches, honor and reverence are to be paid to God, so that if any robber or thief flees thither, he is by no means to be killed or seized, but he is to remain there until by urgent hunger he is compelled to surrender. If any person presumes to furnish arms or food to the criminal or to aid him in flight, the same penalty shall be inflicted on him as on the criminal. Moreover, by our ban we interdict laymen from punishing the transgressions of the clergy and those living under this order; but if seized in open crime, they shall be handed over to their bishop. In cases in which laymen are to be executed, the clergy are to be degraded; in cases in which laymen are to be mutilated, the clergy are to be suspended from office, and with the consent of the laymen they are to suffer frequent fasts and floggings until they atone.

Papal Reform

Christopher Brooke

During the Dark Ages, the Catholic Church fell into moral decay and under the control of the nobility. In many cases, kings or powerful families determined who would be appointed pope, and they expected in return that the pope would work to further their political goals. However, the church began to free itself of secular domination during the 1000s. In the following selection from *Europe in the Central Middle Ages, 962–1154*, Christopher Brooke traces the birth of this new religious revival. The reform movement focused on establishing the supremacy of the pope over all other leaders and raising the moral standards of the general clergy, he writes.

Brooke is Dixie Professor Emeritus of Ecclesiastical History at Cambridge University in England. Among his books are *The Monastic World: 1000–1300*, *The Structure of Medieval Society*, *The Saxon and Norman Kings*, and (with his wife, Rosalind Brooke) *Popular Religion in the Middle Ages: Western Europe, 1000–1300*.

It is commonly said that the beginnings of a great religious revival can be seen in many movements of the late tenth and early eleventh centuries. In some senses this must be true. It may be that it is misleading to judge a religious movement by its outward manifestation; that what the historian can view is superficial evidence; that at a deeper level it is meaningless to say that one age is 'more religious' than another. But whether we apply the crude external test—the evidence of interest in the outward exercises of religion—or the test of maturity and subtlety in religious thought and sentiment, few historians would care to deny that a great change, a great development took place between the tenth and the twelfth centuries.

Excerpted from Christopher Brooke, *Europe in the Central Middle Ages, 962–1154*. Copyright © 1964 Christopher Brooke, © 1975 Longman Group Limited. Reprinted with permission from Pearson Education Ltd. and the author.

Its deep springs and origins, as with all such movements, lie hidden from us. We can trace many of the sources of its inspiration; why they should have bubbled over at this moment rather than at that is beyond our comprehension. The best we can do is to make some guesses, and our guesses will be wide of the mark if they do not help us to understand two facts about this movement: that it was accompanied by widespread popular enthusiasm, and that the inspiration of the movement, in its origins, was mainly monastic. It seems that the troubled conditions of the ninth and early tenth centuries had made some men long for greater peace in the world and others long for a chance to retreat from it. It appears, however, that these unsettled conditions had made it exceedingly difficult for existing communities to sustain a regular monastic life. As the tenth century proceeded, more settled conditions and royal and princely patrons made the monastic revival possible; and the urge found its means of expression. . . .

The two most influential centres of reform were the Burgundian abbey of Cluny and the abbey of Gorze in Upper Lorraine. . . .

The Origins of the Papal Reform

Cluny has been the centre of two disputes among modern historians: one concerns its relations with Gorze and the other movements of monastic reform of the tenth and eleventh centuries; the other its relation to the papal reform. It used to be the convention to call the latter the 'Cluniac' reform, as if its inspiration stemmed from Cluny; in more recent times it has been called the 'Gregorian' reform, after Pope Gregory VII (1073–85), who was its most famous, though not its first leader. The title 'Cluniac reform' gravely exaggerates the importance of Cluny; 'Gregorian reform' somewhat exaggerates the influence of Gregory. For that reason I prefer the neutral 'papal reform'. The papacy was at the centre of reforming currents from the mid–eleventh century on; and although the reform of the papal Curia was only the centre of a much wider movement—so that even the colourless label 'papal' is not free from objection—reform at the centre was the process which made possible the drastic revolution in the Church's government and outlook. . . .

The history of the papacy in the tenth and early eleventh centuries is dominated by the efforts of local factions to seize and keep control of Rome and its greatest office; efforts which might have been successful but for the incursion from time to time of an emperor determined to restore the office to a show of dignity. . . .

At the end of 1048 Henry III, the Holy Roman Emperor, nominated his cousin and friend, Bishop Bruno of Toul, in Lorraine, and Bruno's arrival and coronation in Rome as Pope Leo IX on 12 February 1049 marked the effective beginning of the papal reform.

The papal reform, whichever way one looks at it, was one of the most dramatic and startling events of the Middle Ages; the sudden emergence of the papacy, reformed, transformed, as a central organisation for the direction and improvement of the Church. . . .

The Impact of the Reformers

The reformers themselves were an oddly assorted group of men, with divergent ideas and often with divergent motives. But their impact on the contemporary world was that of a group of prophets come to make Europe live up to its spiritual vocation. It took time for this to be apparent, still longer for all the tensions they let loose to be felt; but the main ingredients were already present in the papal Curia before the death of Pope Leo IX in 1054. The second half of the eleventh century was in many ways the heroic age of papal history, the time when the medieval papacy was most evidently in touch with the roots of its inspiration. What the reformers achieved was no doubt less dramatic; but it was remarkable enough. Hitherto the papacy had been a venerable institution, the preserver of the tradition of St Peter in the Church, the custodian of his shrine and of an immeasurable treasury of relics. Rome had been a remote goal of pilgrimage, of immense prestige, to those who had lived at a distance; those who lived near had observed rather more of the difference between the Rome of legend and the papacy of present fact, the toy of local faction. The reformers brought the papacy to the notice of the whole of Europe; made an organized government out of it, which, like all effective governments, was respected, disliked, and sometimes obeyed. The reformers' work, however, went deeper than that; and [it had] numerous ramifications.

I have purposely avoided any attempt to sketch the character of the Church at large in the tenth and early eleventh centuries. Historians of the papal reform have often repeated the rhetoric of contemporaries on the depravities of the clergy of their day. It is doubtless true that the secular clergy, especially those who served the parishes, were ignorant men, with no very lofty standards of life; it may also be true that marriage or concubinage was a normal practice among them, in spite of the canons forbidding it. But both these generalisations were as true in the late twelfth as in the eleventh century, so far as the documents can inform us—and may have been largely true for centuries to come. The educated secular clergy were probably very few in number; monks were more numerous and, although the reforms of the tenth and eleventh centuries often lacked staying-power in individual monasteries, the monastic ideal was in higher repute than for many centuries before. The assimilation of clergy and laity was an abuse which stirred the reformers' anger. The German kings treated clergy as royal officers, and blurred any distinction there might have been between the spiritual and the temporal. No doubt there were objections, on any Christian standard, to a bishop whose life was spent in warfare; though before we become too censorious, let us remember, first, how much effort for the welfare of their flock as well as for their kings many of the great administrator-bishops of tenth- and eleventh-century Germany made. Let us remember, too, that Leo IX himself was a noted warrior as well as a reformer. In many ways we are very ignorant of the state of the Church in 1049; what we do know suggests that it deserves understanding as well as reproach; that it had its ideals, which were in many ways very different from those of the reformers; that there was, and remained, a wide difference of opinion; and yet that the reformers had taken on an immensely formidable task in trying to make it live up to its Christian vocation as they understood it.

In analysing the inspiration of the reformers, one can lay emphasis on their interest in the law; one can deny that they were concerned to reform, and can assert that they were first and foremost policemen, concerned to enforce an already existing law. Or again, they can be seen in a theological context, as men who had a theological vision of how the Church should be run, and were impelled to organize radical change because they were influenced by new theological trends. Finally, one can see them as practical men, with a clear vision of the specific weaknesses and specific needs of the Church of their day. None of these views, by itself, is adequate. In some of the reformers, one or another predominated; all were present to some degree in most; if we wish to give a broad analysis of the principles of the movement, we must give a large place to all three. Let us examine some of the basic principles, and see how they were related to these various springs of inspiration.

The Reformers' Objectives

All the reformers wished to see the eradication of simony and clerical marriage and incontinence, and the enforcement of the primacy of the Holy See. Simony meant the sale and purchase of offices in the Church, a practice very widespread at this time. It was contrary to canon law, the law of the Church; a formidable collection of authorities could be assembled to condemn it. An office in the Church carried with it the right to administer sacraments; and the theological development of the time was laying special emphasis on the sacraments. The right to administer them carried with it the right to mediate the gift of the Holy Ghost; and so simony was reckoned to involve the sale of the Holy Ghost, a notion so blasphemous that some of the reformers felt that those who engaged in it must be theologically unsound; hence they condemned simony not merely as a sin, but as a heresy. Simony took its name from Simon Magus, who appears from the Acts of the Apostles to have been the first Christian to attempt it. By a misunderstanding of another passage in Acts, the failure to preserve clerical celibacy was sometimes known as Nicolaism, after Nicholas the deacon of Antioch. Marriage had long been forbidden to the clergy by canon law; to mention no earlier enactments, a letter of Pope Leo I had specifically enjoined celibacy on all in subdeacon's orders or above; and this had commonly been accepted as the norm by reformers, and was to be the basis of the reformed canon law on the subject in the late eleventh and twelfth centuries. There were, however, a number of respectable authorities which suggested qualifications to this, and even some which seemed to permit clerical marriage; and the married clergy (unlike the open simonist) had several ingenious and powerful defenders in the early generations of reform. If one had to generalise on the situation before 1049, one could say that the academic tradition of the Church condemned clerical marriage; traditional practice (outside the monasteries) had made it respectable. Theological tides were running against it; the enhanced value set on the sacraments underlined the meaning of ordination, enhanced the sacredness of the person who administered the Eucharist. It was urged that he should be separated for the work, set apart from the entanglements of the world; and almost all medieval reformers inherited from St Jerome the notion that the petticoat was the supreme symbol of the snares of the world.

This separation of clergy from layfolk must of necessity be reflected, in an age so deeply conscious of hierarchy, in one's view of the Church's higher offices; above all of the papacy. The theological trend tended, therefore, to enhance the position of the pope. Even stronger was the legal support for papal supremacy. In practice, the emperors had dominated the papacy, whenever they were near enough to keep watch on the pope's activities, in the late tenth and early eleventh centuries. But the papal Curia had a tradition, never forgotten for any great length of time, of claiming independence of secular authority: of viewing the emperor as a protector, but only in the sense of a bodyguard; of claiming the ultimate supremacy of spiritual over temporal, of papacy over empire. This issue was not discussed by Henry III and Leo IX; and Leo and several of his supporters would not have thought of exerting their independence, still less their superiority, over him. But even in Leo's time there were signs that the emperor might have raised a rival to his own authority. Meanwhile, the creation of the papal monarchy as an effective organ of government was beginning; and was bound in the end to challenge the old order.

Theology and law must not be too sharply divided in this age and in this field; and they both combined to support a demand for *libertas*, which is a frequent and recurring theme. In medieval usage, *lib-*

ertas meant *privilege,* and it was normally used to cover all the special rights and privileges of the different orders of society, or of individual men, of communities, offices and institutions. The *libertas* of the Gorze monasteries meant their privilege of royal favour and patronage; the *libertas* of Cluny meant its freedom from secular entanglement. The papal reformers demanded *libertas* for the Roman Church and for all the Churches and all the clergy: freedom from secular control; independence of action; freedom to pursue a wholly spiritual vocation; in a word, disengagement.

Lifting the Church Above the World

It has commonly been argued by Christian thinkers that if the Church becomes too much concerned with the other world, it loses all contact with this; that the clergy must be worldly or they cannot mingle adequately with their lay parishioners. It seems highly probable that heretical preachers were so widely welcomed in the twelfth century because, after the first flush of the papal reform, its effect was to make the clergy more aloof, the educated segment of the clergy more removed than ever from the layfolk of Christendom. None the less, there is a reverse to this argument. If it is held that the clergy are there to set the laity a standard, to set before them the Christian life in their own lives as well as in the sacraments they perform, it clearly matters that the laity should see some distinction between layman and cleric; that the clergy should not be wholly indistinguishable in manner of life from the laity. No doubt this argument tends to give the rank-and-file clergy of the eleventh century a far more elevated moral function than they commonly performed, or than most men expected them to perform. But in some degree it clearly ran in the reformers' minds.

The human race has never been so savagely denounced as in St Peter Damian's *Book of Gomorrah*, save perhaps in the last book of *Gulliver's Travels,* which it somewhat resembles. An overwhelming sense of sin, and a sense that, under God's providence, the clergy had the vocation to attempt the superhuman task of lifting mankind from the appalling depravity of its ways, inspired Damian, and, in only a slightly less measure, his colleagues. They feared above all assimilation, since they held that if the clergy became wholly assimilated to the world, they would accept the whole gamut of the world's abominable standards. The grip of the world on a man was held to be especially symbolised by the influence of money and of the other sex. There was some humanity, but no chivalry among the reformers. At the high level, simony was part of the machinery by which bishoprics and abbeys had become largely secular offices in many parts of Europe; and if the emperor's treatment of the German Church, and of such parts of the Italian as he could control, had often been free from simony, it led no less to assimilation of the things of the world and of the Church; so that some reformers reckoned all lay interference as wicked as simony itself. At the lower level there was danger of an even more complete assimilation. The high offices of the Church were not hereditary, and it did not suit kings or princes that they should be; the higher clergy were commonly, though not invariably, celibate. Among the lower clergy the growth of the parish church which was also an *Eigenkirche* [a proprietary church] of the local lord had tended to encourage the growth of a class of clergy who were little different in manner of life from their secular neighbours. The lord of a village built a parish church on his domain; he was its owner; the priest who served it was his vassal, his servant; the lord could do what he liked with priest and altar. The system became exceedingly widespread in the century and a half after the break-up of the Carolingian Empire. These clergy seem (so far as we can tell) quite often to have married or had concubines and passed their benefices [church offices, rectories] from father to son like any other small vassal holding. Over these clerks the bishops could assert a little control, since they alone could ordain them; but because there were no seminaries or theological colleges and no means of training the ordinary parish clergy, and because many of the bishops were themselves essentially men of the world, there was little chance of new, different or higher standards passing through to the clergy. These factors encouraged the reformers to campaign for the abolition of simony and clerical marriage; and for the enforcement of the supremacy of the Holy See as the instrument for reform. They help to explain why it was these particular aspects of the law on which the reformers laid so much stress, why so much of their research into the authorities for canon law was concerned with these three points.

Such was the programme: I have given a simplified account of it; but it was in fact, like all effective programmes, a simple one. It had to be, because it was difficult enough to get the reformers to agree on anything; indeed, they fought among themselves on the definition of simony, on whether orders conferred by simoniac bishops were authentic and valid; on the influence to be allowed to the emperor in the affairs of the Church. But they agreed in the main on what we have outlined. If we analyse the writings of the reformers (which are quite voluminous) we find that with the exception of Peter Damian the bulk of what they have to say centres on these three things: the eradication of clerical marriage and simony and the establishment of the supremacy of the Holy See.

The Investiture Controversy

Joseph R. Strayer and Dana C. Munro

In 1075, as part of the ongoing attempt to lessen secular influence on the church, Pope Gregory VII banned lay investiture, the procedure by which kings and other temporal rulers appointed church officials. Henry IV, the Holy Roman Emperor, responded vehemently, asserting his right as a divinely appointed king to govern the bishops under his dominion. The pope countered by excommunicating Henry from the Catholic Church, which put Henry in jeopardy of losing his throne. In the following excerpt from *The Middle Ages: 395–1500*, Joseph R. Strayer and Dana C. Munro recount the ensuing conflict over the control of investiture and its effects on the papacy and the German monarchy.

Strayer and Munro both taught history at Princeton University in New Jersey. Strayer's books include *On the Medieval Origins of the Modern State* and *Feudalism*. Munro authored *The Kingdom of the Crusaders* and *Medieval Civilization.*

T he struggle of the Church to reform itself and to free itself from secular influences was one of the most important factors in the great revival of civilization which began in the middle of the eleventh century. The fight, begun by the monks of Cluny and taken up by the papacy under Leo IX, was to last for over two centuries. As new wealth created new temptations, as the increasing power of secular rulers threatened the independence of the clergy, the Church had to tighten its discipline, improve its organization, and stand stubbornly for its rights. Europe was boiling with new energy; every class was seeking advantages for itself; the clergy had to work furiously merely to hold its own.

But the Church was not satisfied with merely holding its own. It wanted to lead society, to fit all activities into the framework of a Christian commonwealth. Influential as it had been in the early centuries of the Middle Ages, the Church had not enjoyed a position of unquestioned leadership. It had often been dominated by secular rulers; it had had comparatively little influence on the economic and political institutions which developed during the ninth and tenth centuries. General principles could hardly be imposed on a society which was suffering acutely from localism. But now that localism was receding, now that men were learning once more how to work together, the universal Church had a great opportunity. It was the one organization which reached everywhere; it was the one organization capable of conceiving a pattern for the new civilization. During the late eleventh and early twelfth centuries it gained the leadership of society; during the late twelfth and early thirteenth centuries it fought successfully to retain its leadership. This leadership was not absolute; secular interests continued to exist, and there were always men who were little influenced by religious ideals. Yet, until 1250 at least, the Church was the final judge of what was useful to society, and all other activities conformed, at least outwardly, to its standards.

Increasing Papal Independence

The first task of the Church was to free itself from the control of the Holy Roman Empire. When Leo IX died in 1054 the emperor was still the strongest ruler in Europe, and the Empire was the one secular institution which could pretend to universal authority. If the Church could free itself from the emperor's authority, its prestige would become so great that it would have little trouble with other rulers. Conditions after 1054 were very favorable for the Church to begin such a struggle. Henry III had freed the pope from the Roman nobles, and Leo IX had greatly increased papal authority beyond the Alps. The new independence of the papacy was consolidated by a decree regulating papal elections which was drawn up in 1059 under Nicholas II. By this decree all secular influence in the choice of the pope was to be ended; neither the Roman mob, nor the local nobles, nor the German king were to intervene. The cardinals,[1] that is, the bishops of the dioceses surrounding Rome and the priests of the chief Roman churches, were to elect the pope. After their choice was announced, the Roman people were to give formal assent to the election, but no real power was left to the laity, and even the German king was given only a shadowy right of participation. This decree was somewhat modified in later years, but the basic principle was never shaken. From 1059 on, no German ruler was able to make a pope, and the cardinals' freedom of choice was interfered with only in the most exceptional circumstances. The new power given the cardinals made them an increasingly important factor in the government of the Church; they formed the papal council and headed the administrative services of the Church. Gradually, the pope began to select his cardinals from the leading clergy of all Christian countries instead of from the leading clergy of Rome, and so the College of Cardinals became a new link between the papacy and the transalpine churches.

While the papacy was thus strengthening its position, the German monarchy was suffering repeated blows. Henry III had died in 1056, leaving a six-year-old son, Henry IV, to succeed him. During the long minority the fundamental weakness of the German government became apparent. There were no institutions of central government, manned by trained officials, which could work automatically in the absence of a strong ruler. The dukes and count, who were still technically officials of the king had actually obtained hereditary rights of government. They had obeyed Henry III, but they would not obey his widow, who was acting as regent for the young king. Civil war broke out in Germany and Henry IV, kidnapped from his mother, was passed from one faction to another as the balance of power shifted. This unstable life made the boy erratic and passionate, but it also showed him what was needed if Germany was to have a really effective government. When he came of age Henry resolved to make himself independent of the magnates. He seems to have realized that this could be done only by the creation of a compact royal domain, which would be a sure source of wealth and military power, and by the creation of a royal bureaucracy, which would be devoted to his interests. For the domain he fixed his attention on the southern part of Saxony, which lay in the center of old Germany and contained important silver mines. For the bureaucracy he made increasing use of his *ministeriales*, a peculiar class of servile officials which existed only in Germany. They were definitely of unfree origin, yet they might be given very responsible positions in the administration of great estates. Henry's innovation was to use them for all sorts of public business, trusting that they could never adopt the viewpoint of the nobles from whom they were separated by a sharp class line.

Henry's plans for strengthening the monarchy were perfectly sound in principle, but he applied them rather tactlessly. He jailed the Saxon duke and confiscated Saxon lands on the slightest pretext in order to build up his domain. He filled his newly won lands with castles garrisoned with Swabian vassals who oppressed the natives.

His use of the low-born *ministeriales* infuriated the nobles, who had had a monopoly of all governmental posts for centuries. Altogether, Henry had moved entirely too fast after a long period of weak government and had alienated some of his powerful subjects. As a result, when the Saxons rebelled, neither the lay nor the ecclesiastical magnates supported their king, and Henry was forced to surrender most of his acquisitions. Under these circumstances he turned to the pope for aid, a reversal of traditional positions which shows how the situation had changed in a brief twenty years.

Henry's letter asking assistance was very humble and shows his desire to keep the good will of the Church by accepting the ideas of the reforming party. It began:

> To the most watchful and best beloved Lord Pope Gregory endowed from heaven with the apostolic dignity, Henry, by the grace of God king of the Romans, renders most faithfully due submission. Alas! Sinful and in misery, partly owing to the impulse of youthful temptation, partly owing to the freedom of our unrestrained and mighty power, partly also owing to the seductive deception of those whose plans we, too easily led, have followed, we have sinned against heaven and in your sight and are no longer worthy to be called your son. For not only have we seized ecclesiastical property, but also we have sold the churches themselves to unworthy men, although infected with the poison of simony . . . and now, because we alone without your aid cannot reform the churches, we earnestly seek your aid and advice concerning them and all our affairs; being most desirous to obey your commands in everything.

Humble as it was, this letter was sent in vain, since the reform leaders were not inclined to assist the German monarchy.

Pope Gregory VII

The pope to whom this letter was addressed was Gregory VII, one of the ablest leaders the Church has ever had. As the monk Hildebrand he had followed the reforming pope Gregory VI into exile. He returned to Rome with Leo IX and played an increasingly important rôle in the affairs of the papacy from that time on. He had spent some time at Cluny and had been impressed with the ideals of that center of reform, but his own program went far beyond a mere improvement in the morals of the clergy. There was to be a general moral reform; all Christians were to obey the decisions of the pope as to what was socially desirable; even kings and emperors could be judged and punished by the pope if they sinned. The Church, through its head, the pope, was to be the final authority in Christendom. In order to accomplish this mission the Church must be absolutely independent of any lay authority. Hildebrand aided Nicholas II to draw up the decree regulating papal elections in 1059 and he was the power behind the throne during the long pontificate of

Alexander II (1061–1073). Curiously enough, his own election to the papacy in 1073 violated the law which he had helped to make, since he was chosen by acclamation, without the prescribed formalities. Yet there was no doubt that Gregory had the support of the cardinals and Henry IV had no hesitation, as we have seen, in recognizing his authority.

Once pope, Gregory carried on the work of reform with great energy. He first attacked the marriage of priests, a custom which involved the Church in all sorts of secular affairs. He ordered all married priests to separate from their wives and children under pain of forfeiting their parishes. This decree caused many protests, especially north of the Alps, where the marriage of priests had been accepted as a normal custom. On the whole, however, public opinion accepted this reform as necessary, and lay rulers made no great difficulties in allowing the decree to be enforced.

It was otherwise when Gregory struck at the second bond between the Church and worldly affairs. If the Church were to be really free it was necessary to liberate the clergy from the control of lay rulers. So, in 1075, Gregory forbade lay investiture under pain of excommunication. Technically, lay investiture meant the conferring of the insignia of ecclesiastical authority, such as the bishop's ring and staff, by secular rulers. But the slogan, "no lay investiture," meant much more; it meant that kings and feudal lords were to have no voice in the selection of officials of the Church. This, of course, was absolutely necessary if the Church was to be an independent power, or if it was to force society to accept its standards. Yet it is easy to see the difficulties which the reform created for secular rulers. For bishops and abbots were not only ecclesiastical officials; they also held large estates, lordships, and even counties, and so had great secular responsibilities and powers. Every government was dependent, to a greater or lesser extent, on the resources and personnel of the Church. Ecclesiastical vassals often provided the military resources necessary to control rebellious lay nobles. All administrative and secretarial departments were staffed by churchmen; no one else was capable of doing the work. Churchmen were judges, ambassadors and royal councillors. It seemed hard that kings could not choose their own officials, and yet it was equally hard if the Church had to accept prelates selected for purely political reasons. The twofold duties of churchmen made a struggle inevitable, and at the same time almost insoluble, since neither pope nor king could afford to lose their services.

Of all rulers, the king of Germany had had the greatest power over the Church; of all governments his was most dependent on the aid of churchmen. Henry would have protested in any case, but Gregory's decree on lay investiture reached him just as his fortunes were taking a turn for the better. He was celebrating a great victory over the Saxons and for the moment the young king was supreme in Germany. He was not disposed to accept an attack on his authority. Henry's displeasure was increased by the tone of the letter which accompanied the papal decree. It began:

> Bishop Gregory, servant of the servants of God, greeting and apostolic benediction:—that is, if he be obedient to the apostolic throne as beseems a Christian king. Considering . . . with what strict judgment we shall have to render account for the ministry entrusted to us by St. Peter, chief of the Apostles, it is with hesitation that we have sent unto thee the apostolic benediction.[2]

The pope went on to describe Henry's sins, and to remind him that he was wholly under the authority of St. Peter and St. Peter's successor, the pope. Henry was warned not to imitate Saul in boasting of a victory won only by the grace of God.

Henry was intensely angry. Instead of negotiating and trying to win a reasonable compromise, he declared open war on the pope. In startling contrast to the humble letter of 1073 quoted above, the king's answer of January 1076 began: "Henry, king not through usurpation but through the holy ordination of God, to Hildebrand, at present not pope, but false monk." The king went on to assert that Gregory had tried to set himself up wrongfully over the whole Church and to exercise illegal authority over the German king.

> For the true pope Peter also exclaims: "Fear God, honor the king!" But thou dost not fear God, dost not honor in me his appointed one. Wherefore St. Peter, since he has not spared an angel of heaven if he shall have preached otherwise, has not excepted thee also who dost teach otherwise upon earth. For he says; "If anyone, either I or an angel of heaven, should preach a gospel other than that which has been preached to you, he shall be damned." Thou, therefore, damned by this curse and by the judgment of all our bishops and by our own, descend and relinquish the apostolic throne which thou has usurped. Let another ascend the throne of St. Peter, who shall not practise violence under the cloak of religion, but shall teach the sound doctrine of St. Peter. I, Henry, king by the grace of God, do say unto thee, together with all my bishops: Down, down, to be damned through all the ages.

As the letter indicates, Henry had forced the bishops present at his court to refuse to recognize Gregory as pope. Several of them were already under the papal ban, and all were so dependent on the king that they had to follow his policy. Thus the issues were clearly drawn. Could a German king nullify the Church's declaration of independence? Could the German bishops defy the orders of the Roman pope? Gregory was not the man to ignore an act which challenged everything in which he believed. As soon as the king's letters reached him, he excommunicated Henry and released his subjects from obedience. "Confident of my integrity and authority, I now declare in the name of the omnipotent God, Father, Son and Holy Spirit, that Henry, son of the emperor Henry, is deprived of his kingdom in Germany and Italy . . . because he has rebelled against the Church."

At the same time Gregory sought the support of the bishops and no- bles of Germany. Many of them were glad to aid the pope. The power of the magnates had been slowly growing behind the façade of impe- rial authority, and they were now ready for an open contest with the king. Henry had alarmed them by his attempts to construct a govern- ment which would not need their support, and they were determined to end this threat to their position. Papal propaganda, spread through Germany by leaders of the reforming party, also had a profound effect. The value of the recent improvements in church organization was clearly demonstrated; Gregory VII was able to influence public opin- ion north of the Alps as none of his predecessors had done. The moral prestige of the reform movement was so great that many men turned against Henry, even though they had no personal grudge against him. As a result, the king was deserted by almost all his followers, and the victorious magnates held a meeting in October 1076 to discuss his de- position. Henry was unable to oppose them, and he was ready to agree to anything which would give him a chance to save his throne. The as- sembly finally decided that Henry should live as a private citizen un- der guard at Spires, and that he was to forfeit his throne unless the pope freed him from excommunication within a year. He also had to promise complete submission and obedience to Gregory.

Showdown at Canossa

Henry's position was desperate. The pope had promised to take no action in his case until the German princes had been consulted, and it was fairly certain that they would insist on deposing him, or at least in depriving him of most of his power. But there was one weak- ness in this arrangement; the pope, as a Christian priest, could not refuse absolution to a sincerely penitent sinner who sought his pres- ence. Henry, who was always clever if not wise, saw this weakness and took full advantage of it. He escaped from Spires and rushed to Italy to intercept Gregory, who was on his way to consult the Ger- man princes. Fearing a desperate attack, the pope retired to the cas- tle of Canossa, but Henry soon showed that he was not going to add to his sins by an assault on the vicar of Christ. Instead he so hum- bled himself that Gregory was forced to forget his political plans and remember only his religious duties. The best description of the fa- mous scene is the letter which Gregory himself wrote to the German princes to excuse his violation of his oath to them:

> Finally he [Henry] came in person to Canossa, . . . bringing with him only a
> small retinue, and manifesting no hostile intentions. Once arrived, he pre-
> sented himself at the gate of the castle barefoot and clad only in a wretched
> woolen garment, beseeching us with tears to grant him absolution and for-

giveness. This he continued to do for three days, until all those about him were moved to compassion at his plight and interceded for him with tears and prayers. Indeed, they marveled at our hardheartedness, some even complaining that our action savored rather of heartless tyranny than of chastening severity. At length his persistent declarations of repentance, and the supplications of all who were there with us overcame our reluctance, and we removed the excommunication from him and received him again into the bosom of the holy mother church.

Henry had won a diplomatic victory at the price of great personal humiliation, but the moral victory won by the pope at Canossa was far more significant. The most powerful king of the West had been forced to bow before the successor of Peter. For the next two centuries no ruler was long able to withstand the opposition of the pope. For the Church, the establishment of this precedent was worth the loss of the alliance of the German princes. Later events were to show that even when the rebellious magnates remained on the pope's side long enough to place a new king on the German throne, the alliance was futile. The traditions of the office forced any king, however chosen, to oppose the papacy.

Gregory, however, wanted a political as well as a moral victory. He insisted that Henry's case was not settled, but once the excommunication had been lifted the opposition to the king was irrevocably weakened. The more stubborn princes elected an anti-king, who was pledged to respect their rights and who expressly renounced his descendants' claim to the throne. But this act, while it demonstrated the objectives of the king's opponents, was a failure politically. It merely started a devastating civil war in which Henry slowly gained the upper hand. Even a new excommunication by Gregory in 1080 had little effect; the magnates who were on the king's side felt that the pope had left them in the lurch once before and saw no reason for coming to his aid again. Henry, moreover, counterattacked by persuading his clergy to depose Gregory and elect an anti-pope. In this same year he won a significant victory: the anti-king fell on the field of battle, and many Germans felt that God had given judgment for the king. With this success Germany became obedient enough to make possible a direct attack on Gregory. Henry marched to Italy and, after a bitter struggle, succeeded in driving the pope from Rome. The anti-pope was installed in St. Peter's, and gave Henry the imperial crown on Easter Day, 1084. Gregory had to take refuge at Salerno where he died the next year. His last words were: "I have loved righteousness and hated iniquity, therefore I die in exile."

Continued Strife

This victory seemed overwhelming, but the new prestige of the papacy could not be destroyed by mere brute force. Gregory's successors carried on opposition to Henry, and so gave the German magnates justification for renewed rebellion. The magnates could not long remain loyal to the emperor; they were bound to oppose him to protect their own interests. They had made an open bid for independence, and they could not stop fighting until they were sure that Henry could not weaken their power. So once again a great rebellion broke out; the duke of Bavaria and Henry's own wife and eldest son turned against him. Once again Henry succeeded in riding out the storm; the duke of Bavaria did not receive the reward he expected and deserted his papal allies, while the rebellious son died. But once again the emperor's victory did not end the struggle; Henry was still excommunicate, and the magnates were still disloyal. There could be no peace while Henry lived; he stood for everything which the Church and the princes hated. The emperor's surviving son and heir, young Henry, king of the Romans, recognized this, and apparently felt that his father must be removed before the prestige of the monarchy was irremediably lowered. He turned against his father, allied himself with hostile magnates, and in the last civil war of the reign forced the unfortunate emperor to abdicate. Henry IV died soon after, in 1106, but even his corpse had no peace. As he had died excommunicate, his body was transferred from one temporary tomb to another, until Henry V celebrated an ephemeral victory over the papacy by solemnly burying the father whom he had hounded to death.

The reign of Henry IV showed the weakness of the German monarchy. The ruler was dependent upon the good will of the great men, who might be technically royal officials, but who were actually hereditary princes. He was also dependent upon the resources of the Church. Henry IV alienated the magnates but failed to create a bureaucracy which would take their place. He alienated the Church but failed to create a royal domain which would make up for the loss of Church wealth. During his reign the revived Empire almost came to an end because it had lost its foundations. The magnates became independent rulers, the Church withdrew its support, and the emperor had to fight frantically to preserve even his title to the throne.

Notes

1. "Cardinal" means "chief" or "important." The cardinals were the chief clergy of Rome.
2. This and other passages are from translations in E.F. Henderson, *Select Historical Documents of the Middle Ages* (London, 1896). Some slight changes in wording have been made.

The Limitations of Royal Authority

Pope Gregory VII

Prior to the eleventh century, the monarchs of western Europe exercised a significant amount of power over the Catholic Church. They frequently controlled the process by which important positions in the church's hierarchy were filled. Furthermore, the royalty did not hesitate to abuse this privilege by reserving plum appointments for their own relatives and their political cronies. Pope Gregory VII intended to stop such abuses by reasserting the authority of the papacy over the investiture of church officials. Some monarchs were resistant to Gregory's reforms, including Henry IV, the Holy Roman Emperor, whom Gregory excommunicated for the second time on March 7, 1080. In the following letter from 1081, Gregory defends his actions to Bishop Hermann of Metz in an eloquent exposition of the basis of papal authority over worldly kings.

B ishop Gregory, servant of the servants of God, to his beloved brother in Christ, Hermann bishop of Metz, greeting and apostolic benediction. It is doubtless owing to a dispensation of God that, as we learn, thou art ready to endure trials and dangers in defence of the truth. For such is His ineffable grace and wonderful mercy that He never allows His chosen ones completely to go astray—never permits them utterly to fall or to be cast down. For, after they have been afflicted by a period of persecution—a useful term of probation as it were,—He makes them, even if they have been for a time fainthearted, stronger than before. Since, moreover, manly courage impels one strong man to act more bravely than another and to press forward more boldly—even as among cowards fear induces one to flee more disgracefully than another,—we wish, beloved, with the voice of exhortation, to impress this upon thee: thou shouldst the more delight to stand in the army of the Christian faith among the first, the more thou art convinced that the conquerors are the most worthy and the nearest to God. Thy request, indeed, to be aided, as it were, by our writings and fortified against the madness of those who babble forth with impious tongue that the authority of the holy and apostolic see had no authority to excommunicate Henry—a man who despises the Christian law; a destroyer of the churches and of the empire; a patron and companion of heretics—or to absolve any one from the oath of fealty to him, seems to us to be hardly necessary when so many and such absolutely decisive warrants are to be found in the pages of Holy Scripture. Nor do we believe, indeed, that those who (heaping up for themselves damnation) impudently detract from the truth and contradict it have added these assertions to the audacity of their defence so much from ignorance as from a certain madness.

For, to cite a few passages from among many, who does not know the words of our Lord and Saviour Jesus Christ who says in the gospel: 'Thou art Peter and upon this rock will I build my church, and the gates of hell shall not prevail against it; and I will give unto thee the keys of the kingdom of Heaven; and whatsoever thou shalt bind upon earth shall be bound also in Heaven, and whatsoever thou shalt loose upon earth shall be loosed also in Heaven'? [Matthew xvi. 18, 19.] Are kings excepted here? Or are they not included among the sheep which the Son of God committed to St Peter? Who, I ask, in view of this universal concession of the power of binding and loosing, can think that he is withdrawn from the authority of St Peter, unless, perhaps, that unhappy man who is unwilling to bear the yoke of the Lord and subjects himself to the burden of the devil, refusing to be among the number of Christ's sheep? It will help him little to his wretched liberty that he shake from his proud neck the divinely granted power of Peter. For the more any one, through pride, refuses to bear it, the more heavily shall it press upon him unto damnation at the judgement.

The Primacy of the Pope

The holy fathers, as well in general councils as in their writings and doings, have called the Holy Roman Church the universal mother, accepting and serving with great veneration this institution founded by the divine will, this pledge of a dispensation to the church, this privilege entrusted in the beginning and confirmed to St Peter the chief of the apostles. And even as they accepted its statements in confirmation of their faith and of the doctrines of holy religion, so also they received its judgements—consenting in this, and agreeing as it were with one spirit and one voice: that all greater matters and exceptional cases, and judgements over all churches, ought to be referred to it as to a mother and a head; that from it there was no appeal; that no one should or could retract or reverse its decisions. . . .

Shall not an authority founded by laymen—even by those who do not know God,—be subject to that authority which the providence of God Almighty has for His own honour established and in his mercy given to the world? For His Son, even as He is undoubtingly believed to be God and man, so is He considered the highest priest, the head of all priests, sitting on the right hand of the Father and always interceding for us. Yet He despised a secular kingdom, which makes the sons of this world swell with pride, and came of His own will to the priesthood of the cross. Who does not know that kings and leaders are sprung from men who were ignorant of God, who by pride, robbery, perfidy, murders—in a word, by almost every crime at the prompting of the devil, who is the prince of this world—have striven with blind cupidity and intolerable presumption to dominate over their equals, that is, over mankind? To whom, indeed, can we better compare them, when they seek to make the priests of God bend to their feet, than to him who is head over all the sons of pride and who, tempting the Highest Pontiff Himself, the Head of priests, the Son of the Most High, and promising to Him all the kingdoms of the world, said: 'All these I will give unto Thee if Thou wilt fall down and worship me'? who can doubt but that the priests of Christ are to be considered the fathers and masters of kings and princes and of all the faithful? Is it not clearly pitiful madness for a son to attempt to subject to himself his father, a pupil his master; and for one to bring into his power and bind with iniquitous bonds him by whom he believes that he himself can be bound and loosed not only on earth but also in Heaven? . . .

The Limits of Royal Power

Many pontiffs have excommunicated kings or emperors. For, if particular examples of such princes is needed, the blessed pope Innocent excommunicated the emperor Arcadius for consenting that St John Chrysostom should be expelled from his see. Likewise another Roman pontiff, Zacchary, deposed a king of the Franks, not so much for his iniquities as because he was not fitted to exercise so great power. And in his stead he set up Pepin, father of the emperor Charles the Great, in his place—releasing all the Franks from the oath of fealty which they had sworn him. . . .

Furthermore every Christian king, when he comes to die, seeks as a pitiful suppliant the aid of a priest, that he may escape hell's prison, may pass from the darkness into the light, and at the judgement of God may appear absolved from the bondage of his sins. Who, in his last hour (what layman, not to speak of priests), has ever implored the aid of an earthly king for the salvation of his soul? And what king or emperor is able, by reason of the office he holds, to rescue a Christian from the power of the devil through holy baptism, to number him among the sons of God, and to fortify him with the divine unction? Who of them can by his own words make the body and blood of our Lord,—the greatest act in the Christian religion? Or who of them possesses the power of binding and loosing in heaven and on earth? From all of these considerations it is clear how greatly the priestly office excels in power.

Who of them can ordain a single clerk in the holy Church, much less depose him for any fault? For in the orders of the Church a greater power is needed to depose than to ordain. Bishops may ordain other bishops, but can by no means depose them without the authority of the apostolic see. Who, therefore, of even moderate understanding, can hesitate to give priests the precedence over kings? Then, if kings are to be judged by priests for their sins, by whom can they be judged with better right than by the Roman pontiff?

In short, any good Christians may far more properly be considered kings than may bad princes. For the former, seeking the glory of God, strictly govern themselves, whereas the latter, seeking the things which are their own and not the things of God, are enemies to themselves and tyrannical oppressors of others. Faithful Christians are the body of the true king, Christ; evil rulers, that of the devil. The former rule themselves in the hope that they will eternally reign with the Supreme Emperor, but the sway of the latter ends in their destruction and eternal damnation with the prince of darkness, who is king over all the sons of pride.

It is certainly not strange that wicked bishops are of one mind with a bad king, whom they love and fear for the honours which they have wrongfully obtained from him. Such men simoniacally ordain whom they please and sell God even for a paltry sum. As even the elect are indissolubly united with their Head, so also the wicked are inescapably leagued with him who is the head of evil, their chief purpose being to resist the good. But surely we ought not so much to denounce them as to mourn for them with tears and lamentations, beseeching God Almighty to snatch them from the snares of Satan in which they are held captive, and after their peril to bring them at last to a knowledge of the truth.

Seeking Worldly Glory

We refer to those kings and emperors who, too much puffed up by worldly glory, rule not for God but for themselves. Now, since it belongs to our office to admonish and encourage every one according to the rank or dignity which he enjoys, we endeavour, by God's grace, to arm emperors and kings and other princes with the weapon of humility, that they may be able to allay the waves of the sea and the floods of pride. For we know that earthly glory and the cares of this world usually tempt men to pride, especially those in authority. So that they neglect humility and seek their own glory, desiring to lord it over their brethren. Therefore it is of especial advantage for emperors and kings, when their minds tend to be puffed up and to delight in their own glory, to discover a way of humbling themselves, and to realize that what causes their complacency is the thing which should be feared above all else. Let them, therefore, diligently consider how perilous and how much to be feared is the royal or imperial dignity. For very few are saved of those who enjoy it; and those who, through the mercy of God, do come to salvation are not so glorified in the Holy Church by the judgement of the Holy Spirit as are many poor people. . . . For what emperor or king was ever so distinguished by miracles as were St Martin, St Antony and St Benedict—not to mention the apostles and martyrs? And what emperor or king raised the dead, cleansed lepers, or healed the blind? . . . Moreover, to how many kings or emperors has the holy church ordered chapels or altars to be dedicated, or masses to be celebrated in their honour? Let kings and other princes fear lest the more they rejoice at being placed over other men in this life, the more they will be subjected to eternal fires. . . . And they are about to render account to God for as many men as they have had subjects under their dominion. But if it be no little task for any private religious man to guard his own soul: how much labour will there be for those who are rulers over many thousands of souls? Moreover, if the judgement of the Holy Church severely punishes a sinner for the slaying of one man, what will become of those who, for the sake of worldly glory, hand over many thousands to death? And such persons, although after having slain many they often say with their lips 'I have sinned,' nevertheless rejoice in their hearts at the extension of their (so-called) fame. They do not regret what they have done. . . . As long as they do not repent with their whole heart, nor agree to give up what they have acquired or kept through bloodshed, their repentance remains without the true fruit of penitence before God.

Therefore they should greatly fear and often call to mind what we have said above, that out of the innumerable host of kings in all countries from the beginning of the world, very few are found to have been holy; whereas in one single see—the Roman—of the successive bishops from the time of blessed Peter the Apostle, nearly one hundred are counted amongst the most holy. And why is this, unless because kings and princes, enticed by vain glory, prefer, as has been said, their own things to things spiritual, whereas the bishops of the Church, despising vain glory, prefer God's will to earthly things? The former are quick to punish offences against themselves, but lightly tolerate those who sin against God. The latter readily pardon those who sin against themselves, but do not readily forgive offenders against God. The former, too bent on earthly achievements, think little of spiritual ones; the latter, earnestly meditating on heavenly things, despise the things of earth. . . .

Humble Obedience

Therefore let those whom Holy Church, of its own will and after proper counsel, not for transitory glory but for the salvation of many, calls to have rule or dominion, humbly obey. . . . Let them also carefully retain what God says in the gospel: 'I seek not my own glory'; and, 'He who will be the first among you shall be the servant of all.' Let them always prefer the honour of God to their own; let them cherish and guard justice by observing the rights of every man; let them not walk in the counsel of the ungodly but, with an assenting heart, always consort with good men. Let them not seek to subject to themselves or to subjugate the Holy Church as a handmaid; but above all let them strive, by recognizing the teachers and fathers, to render due honour to the eyes of the Church—the priests of God. For if we are ordered to honour our fathers and mothers after the flesh—how much more our spiritual ones! And if he who has cursed his father or mother after the flesh is to be punished with death— what does he merit who curses his spiritual father or mother? Let them not, led astray by wordly love, strive to place one of their own sons over the flock for which Christ poured forth His blood, if they can find some one who is better and more useful than he: lest, loving their son more than God, they inflict the greatest damage on the Holy Church. For he who neglects to provide to the best of his ability for such a want—and, one might say, necessity—of Holy Mother Church is openly convicted of not loving God and his neighbour as a Christian should.

For if this virtue, love, has been neglected, no matter what good any one does he shall be without any fruit of salvation. And so by humbly doing these things, and by observing the love of God and of their neighbour as they ought, they may hope for the mercy of Him who said: 'Learn of Me, for I am meek and lowly of heart.' If they have humbly imitated Him they shall pass from this servile and transitory kingdom to a true kingdom of liberty and eternity.

The Norman Conquest

Trevor Rowley

When Edward the Confessor died childless in 1066, a great dispute arose concerning the succession to the throne of England. Harold Godwinson, the powerful earl of Wessex and Edward's brother-in-law, took the crown after Edward's death—but his claim to the kingship was challenged by William, the duke of Normandy in France and Edward's cousin once removed. Enraged by what he saw as a violation of his legitimate claim to the throne, William invaded England, killed Harold, and established Norman rule over the English. Trevor Rowley describes the impact of the Norman Conquest of England in the following selection from his book *The Norman Heritage: 1066–1200*. Rowley is the deputy director of the Department for Continuing Education at Oxford University in England and the president of the Oxford Architectural and Historical Society. He is the author of *The High Middle Ages*, *Book of Norman England*, *A Traveller's Guide to Norman Britain*, and *The Normans*.

There are seldom absolute full stops in history or entirely new chapters. One event, however, which has been almost universally accepted in such terms, from the greatest scholars to the humblest schoolchild, is the Norman Conquest of England in 1066. Not only was this the last time that England was successfully invaded, but it was followed by a complete change in the ruling dynasty, the introduction of military feudalism, the reform of the church and the rapid expansion of monasticism. Such social and political changes

Excerpted from Trevor Rowley, *The Norman Heritage, 1066–1200.* Copyright © 1983 Trevor Rowley. Reprinted with permission from Taylor & Francis.

were accompanied by dramatic architectural and topographical developments: the introduction of the castle, the spread of new towns and the erection of hundreds of new ecclesiastical establishments, all executed in a new style of architecture. Whatever moral reservations must be expressed about the activities of the Normans in England there is no doubt that through their energy and administrative ability they transformed the face of town and country alike.

Two unique sources of historical evidence have contributed greatly to this impression of profound change: the Domesday Book, which was compiled some twenty years after the Norman Conquest, and the Bayeux Tapestry, which was probably completed within a decade of the Conquest. The Domesday Book (1086) provides us with the most comprehensive survey of the English landscape and society ever executed. Although doubts may be expressed about the proper interpretation of its contents, the survey represents the first historical reference to the vast majority of English settlements and therefore intrinsically it represents an historical beginning.

The Bayeux Tapestry is a confident account of the Conquest which incorporated a justification of William the Conqueror's claim to the English throne—a claim which scholars have argued about over the centuries. It seems probable that the tapestry was embroidered in England, perhaps at St Augustine's, Canterbury, for William's half brother, Bishop Odo of Bayeux, and was intended to be hung in Bayeux Cathedral. There has been considerable controversy over the dating of the tapestry, but it seems most likely that it was completed in time for the consecration of Odo's new cathedral in Bayeux in 1077. The tapestry narrates in ostensibly simple terms the events leading up to the Conquest and the story of the battle of Hastings itself. The story is quite clearly told from the Norman viewpoint and appears to be based largely on the accounts of two of William the Conqueror's contemporary hagiographers, William of Jumièges and William of Poitiers, as well as a version of the Anglo-Saxon Chronicle.

In brief the tapestry tells of [the English noble] Harold Godwinson leaving King Edward the Confessor's court and undertaking the journey to Normandy, where, after being seized by Count Guy of Ponthieu, he is taken to William's palace at Rouen. Harold then joins William in a successful campaign against the Breton border towns of Dol and Dinan. At Bayeux Harold takes an oath of obedience to William—an event which was pointedly of considerable significance in the light of subsequent events. On returning to England Edward dies and Harold accepts the crown. At this point the vision of Halley's comet which appeared that year is seen as a terrible omen. On hearing of the news of Harold's accession William prepares a fleet and then sails for England, where, after building a castle at Hastings, he goes into battle against Harold. Some of the most vivid scenes then follow, portraying aspects of the battle in considerable detail, including a brilliantly depicted cavalry attack, and Harold's death. The final section which presumably showed William being crowned at Westminster is missing. Thus the actual event which led to Norman domination in England is graphically illustrated. No other event in English medieval history received such singular treatment. . . .

William II, Duke of Normandy

Duke William II, or William the Conqueror as he was known after the battle of Hastings, was born at Falaise in 1027/8, the bastard son of Duke Robert I, or Robert the Magnificent as he was popularly known. Robert's death in 1035 while returning from a pilgrimage to Jerusalem, resulted in a politically troubled situation. William succeeded to the dukedom as a minor and there followed a period of near anarchy during which two of his guardians were assassinated. William survived this tumultuous period and formally came of age in 1044. Almost immediately he was involved in an internal revolt which was finally crushed at the decisive battle of Val-ès-Dunes in 1047.

William's long apprenticeship at the seat of power was to serve him well. In the following twenty years he consolidated his control and developed skills which he was later to apply with great success in England. Although regrettably the details are only scantily recorded in the early part of this period a strengthening of feudal ties was accompanied by a general tightening up of ducal administration most notably in the area of military service, providing the Norman duke with the strongest army in Europe. At the same time William insisted on exercising his right to garrison the castles of his strongest barons, and it was probably at this time that the castle became a particularly important element in William's military strategy.

William embarked on a series of successful and by all accounts brutal campaigns which eventually brought the whole of Maine under Norman control, and subdued Brittany over which he claimed lordship. Thus by 1066 William had established himself as master of north-west Gaul, a powerful European sovereign in all but name.

Town life flourished and in particular William deliberately fostered the development of Caen between Bayeux and Rouen on an island at the confluence of the rivers Orne and Odon. William saw Caen as a new military stronghold with the geographical advantages of Rouen, mainly access to the sea, but without Rouen's vulnerability to attack. Caen also lies in the very heart of the narrow belt of Jurassic limestone, which provided the main source of Caen stone for the construction of castles, churches and monasteries both in Normandy and England. . . .

William's claim to the throne of England lay principally through

On October 14, 1066, William the Conqueror led the Normans in defeating the English forces in the celebrated Battle of Hastings.

his grandfather's sister, Emma, who was married to two consecutive kings of England, Ethelred and Cnut. Emma who was sister to Duke Richard II (966–1026), and the mother of Edward the Confessor, was largely responsible for bringing Normans and Norman customs into the English court. Edward spent half his life in exile in the duchy and in the first years after succeeding to the throne relied on the political and military advice of his Norman comrades and generally throughout his reign maintained close personal contact with Normandy. It seems reasonably clear that Edward the Confessor had recognized William as his successor in the early 1050s, and probable that Harold's journey to Normandy in 1064 was to confirm this recognition. On hearing of Edward's death on 5 January 1066 and Harold's accession, William had no doubt about his course of action and set in motion the diplomatic and military preparations necessary for the invasion of England. . . .

William's preparation and organization, the characteristics of which were to be the hallmark of his rule as King of England, played a decisive role in his victory. Seldom can the events of one day— Saturday, 14 October 1066—have had such a profound effect on the political geography of Europe. William of Poitiers wrote that, with his success at the battle of Hastings, Duke William had conquered all of England in a single day 'between the third hour and evening'. In reality, however, although this battle saw the end of united and national resistance to William, local resistance and piecemeal risings continued and it was not until after the notorious 'harrying of the North' (1068–70) that the *pax Normanica* prevailed.

The Immediate Impact of the Conquest

The Norman occupation of England was virtually a re-run of the Scandinavian settlement in Normandy. England received a new royal dynasty, a new aristocracy, a virtually new church, a new art and architecture and, in official circles, a new language. By 1086 only half a dozen of the 180 greater landlords or tenants-in-chief were English. The Crown itself held one-fifth of the land and a considerable percentage of the remainder was held by a few of William's favourites, who had come with him from France. It has been estimated that about half the country was in the hands of ten men, most of whom were William's relatives. The power and wealth of the country was held by a small Norman elite, and as if to demonstrate the change of management castles were built throughout the kingdom. Within twenty years of the Conquest they dominated all the shire towns and within half a century sat in virtually every settlement of importance in the country. By 1090 only one of the sixteen English bishoprics was held by an Englishman and six of those sees had been moved from their historic centres to large towns where they subsequently remained. By the end of the twelfth century virtually every Anglo-Saxon cathedral had been removed and rebuilt in Anglo-Norman style, as well as hundreds of new abbeys, and parish churches.

It should, however, be remembered that Norman domination was largely confined to the upper echelons of society. Although groups of French settlers did move into England and were found in many towns particularly in the Welsh borderlands, the level of folk penetration was far less even than that perpetrated by the tenth-century Norsemen in Normandy. Indeed recent analysis of place-names in Normandy suggests that there might even have been a modest movement of English settlers into Normandy after the Conquest.

The Norman Conquest of England was in no way a folk movement to be compared with the Anglo-Saxon or Scandinavian settlements. Similarly, the place-name evidence demonstrates precisely the same pattern of hybridization that had already occurred in Normandy. Norman family names were attached to already existing Anglo-Saxon place-names and there was a considerable restyling of place-names to Norman design. Despite the use of French in polite society it never reached much beyond that, and although a considerable number of French words found their way into the English language, they did not change it profoundly. One reason for this was that the Normans transacted most of the written communication in Latin and not French, but in the process did displace Anglo-Saxon as the official language.

Norman Control of England

Once William had successfully quelled all opposition he was able to create a state in England which was far stronger and more unified than anything that had gone before. The secret of this was his complete domination of the country through feudal institutions. Before 1066 feudalism was more developed in Normandy than in England, military obligations in return for land, known as knights' service, was already a recognized institution and many feudal quotas had already been established. In the process of the Conquest, not only was the Norman model introduced into England, but it was made far more effective and systematic than it had ever been in Normandy. This was largely because, as conqueror, William quite literally claimed the whole of England as his own. He dispossessed all but a handful of English lords and gave lands to his own men, insisting that he, as king, was the only person allowed to regard land as his absolute property; everyone else was merely a tenant who paid rent, normally in the form of knights' service. This was even the case with the English bishoprics and abbeys who also became Crown tenants and had to provide service. He was therefore both king and feudal lord of absolutely all the land in his kingdom, and consequently he controlled the sole source of wealth as well as the font of justice. England became the supreme example of a feudal military monarchy. The Crown and the Norman aristocracy found themselves extremely wealthy, wealth which was rapidly translated into buildings—cathedrals, abbeys, parish churches, castles and new towns.

It is a paradox that although it was in England that the Normans achieved their greatest success in all fields, in the long run the Conquest of England turned them into Englishmen. Although the new Norman aristocracy largely despised the English and their customs, they were operating essentially within an English matrix. Because their penetration of English society was at such an elevated level it was always probable that English traditions and institutions would survive in some form, and eventually absorb the Norman masters.

William the Conqueror's Claim to the English Throne

William of Poitiers

Norman soldier and priest William of Poitiers wrote an account of the Norman Conquest shortly after the event, around the year 1071. Although he did not accompany the army that conquered England, he knew many of the participants, including William the Conqueror himself. His account of the campaign is therefore considered to be generally reliable, albeit biased due to his enthusiastic support for the Norman cause. In the following excerpt, he traces the events leading up to the Battle of Hastings. The author also defends William the Conqueror's right to rule England, listing several reasons why William's claim to the crown is legitimate.

About the same time, Edward, king of the English, who had already appointed William as his heir, and who held him in the same affection as a brother or son, gave more serious evidence of his intentions than before. He decided to anticipate the implacable decree of death, whose approaching hour this man, who aspired to

Excerpted from William of Poitiers, "Gesta Willelmi," in *The Battle of Hastings: Sources and Interpretations,* edited by Stephen Morillo. Editorial matter © 1996 Stephen Morillo. Reprinted with permission from The Boydell Press.

heaven by the saintliness of his life, now felt. In order to confirm his promise by an oath, Edward sent to William Harold, the most prominent of his subjects in wealth, honour and power, and whose brother and nephew had already been given as hostages to ensure this succession. This was a measure of the utmost wisdom because its authenticity and authority would restrain the dissensions among the whole English nation, if—as might be expected from the vagaries and perfidy of their behaviour—they had tried to rebel against it.

Ambushed and Rescued

Harold, as he was on his voyage to carry out this mission, and had already escaped the dangers of the crossing, landed in Ponthieu, where he fell into the hands of count Guy. He and his attendants were captured and thrown into prison, a misadventure which a man of his standing would willingly have exchanged for shipwreck. For the lure of gain has led certain nations in Gaul into an accursed practice, barbarous and totally foreign to Christian justice. They set ambushes for rich or powerful men, throw them into prison, and submit them to outrages and tortures. Overcome with misfortunes, and almost on the verge of death, they are only released on the payment of a huge [sum of money].

Duke William, informed of the fate of the man who had been sent to him, hastily despatched an embassy and snatched him from prison by prayers and threats, and went to meet him with due honour. Guy behaved well: without being persuaded to do so by the lure of gain or the constraint of force, he led him in person to the castle of Eu, and presented to the duke a man whom he could freely have tortured, killed or sold. As a suitable reward, William gave him vast and rich lands, and added large sums of money as well. As for Harold, William brought him into Rouen, the capital of his principality, with all honour; here his varied hospitality and attention restored and made joyful the men who had suffered such hardship on the way. William doubtless congratulated himself on having a guest of such distinction, an ambassador from his relation and dear friend: he hoped that he would be a faithful mediator between himself and the English, for whom he was second only to the king.

At a gathering at Bonneville, Harold took an oath of faithfulness to him according to the sacred rite of the Christians. And, as highly respected men of the utmost sincerity have related, who were witnesses to the event, in the last item in the oath that was drawn up, he pronounced, clearly and of his own free will, these words: that he would be the agent of duke William at the court of king Edward for as long as the king lived; that he would try with all his authority and power, to ensure for him the possession of the kingdom of England on Edward's death; and that meanwhile, he would hand over the castle of Dover, fortified under his direction and his own expense, to a garrison of the duke's knights; that he would deliver, at the same time, in various places in the kingdom, other castles to be fortified in the duke's orders; and that he would also provide abundantly for the provisioning of the garrisons. The duke, having received Harold as a vassal, and before he had taken this oath, conferred on him, at his request, all the lands he held, with full powers. For it was feared that Edward, who was already ill, would not live much longer. After this, because he knew that Harold was bold and eager for new glory, he provided him and his company with weapons, armour and the finest horses, and took them with him to fight in Brittany. He treated him as a guest and ambassador, but now made him almost one of his companions, in order to strengthen the ties between them by doing him honour. . . .

The duke, having detained his very dear guest Harold for some time, sent him home loaded with presents, worthy of the rank of the two of them, both of him on whose behalf he had been sent and of him whose honour he had thus increased. In addition, one of the two hostages, his nephew returned with him, freed as a mark of respect to his person. Thus, Harold, we address these brief reproaches to you. What inspired you to dare, after these good deeds, to despoil William of his inheritance and to fight against him, you who by a sacrosanct oath of word and hand, had recognised as master of both yourself and your nation? What you should have repressed, you wickedly encouraged. The favourable breeze which swelled your black-hearted sails on the return voyage was impious, the calm sea which bore you was impious in allowing itself to carry you to the other shore, O most shameful of men. The harbour which received you was ill-starred, you who were going to drag your country into the most disastrous shipwreck.

Preparing for War

Suddenly news came that England had lost its king, Edward, and Harold had been crowned in his place. This foolish Englishman did not await a public election, but on the day of mourning when the good king was buried and the whole nation lamented, he broke his oath and seized the throne by acclamation, thanks to the support of some iniquitous partisans. He received an unholy consecration at the hands of Stigand [the archbishop of Canterbury], who had been deprived of the office of priest by the just zeal of a papal anathema. Duke William, having consulted his men, decided to avenge this offence and regain his inheritance by force of arms, despite many who used clever arguments to dissuade him from such an arduous enterprise, as being well beyond the power of the Norman forces. . . . In the discussions, however, we know that they all yielded to the wisdom of the prince, as if he had known in advance, by divine inspiration, what needed to be done and what needed to be avoided. To those who act piously, God has given wisdom, writes a man who is learned in divine matters.

With admirable prudence, William ordered the provision of ships, arms, men and supplies, and all other things necessary for war; almost all Normandy was devoted to the task, and it would take too long to describe the preparations in detail. Equally, he made arrangements for the government and security of Normandy in his absence. Numerous soldiers from outside the duchy arrived to offer their help, partly motivated by the famed generosity of the duke, but all fully confident in the justice of his cause.

He forbade all forms of pillage, and fed at his own expense 50,000 soldiers while contrary winds detained them for a month at the mouth of the river Dives. His moderation and prudence lay in the fact that he paid most of the expenses of his soldiers and guests, and would not allow anyone to take anything whatsoever. The inhabitants of the countryside around grazed their herds of cows or sheep in safety, both in the fields and on the open pasture. The corn awaited the reaper's scythe untouched, without being trampled by the soldiers or cut down by foragers. However weak or defenceless, any man could pass through countryside, singing as he rode, watching, but not fearing, the squadrons of soldiers.

At this time the see of St Peter at Rome was occupied by pope Alexander, the most worthy of all to rule over the universal church. Whoever consulted him received a just and salutary answer. He had been bishop of Lucca, and had no ambition for a higher rank, but the urgent council of several persons whose authority was respected by the Romans, supported by the agreement of a large assembly, had raised him to his present standing as primate, to preside over, as their head and master, all the bishops throughout the world. He deserved this election by his sanctity and the purity of his teaching. In later years his virtues shone from east to west: just as the sun, by the laws of nature, follows an unchanging course, so he followed the truth throughout his life, condemning iniquity wherever he could, without compromise.

Having sought the approval of the pope and informed him of the enterprise he was undertaking, the duke received through his favour a standard, which was a sign of the protection of St Peter, as a result of which he was able to march more confidently and safely against his adversary. . . .

Harold, meanwhile, prepared to give battle by sea or land, drawing up a huge army on the shore, and sending out spies in secret. One of these was captured, and as he tried to disguise the reason for his presence using the story he had been briefed to tell, the duke showed his magnanimity in these words: 'What need has Harold to buy the devotion and labour, for gold and silver, of men like you who come to spy on us? Our determination, our preparations—are there any more certain indications he would like, other than my actual presence? Take this message to him from me: he can live for the rest of his days in peace, if within a year from now, he has not seen me in the place which he regards as his most secure refuge.' . . .

Now the whole fleet, so carefully prepared, set sail from the mouth of the Dives and neighbouring ports, where it had waited so long for a south wind in order to cross, and was carried by the west wind towards the anchorage of Saint Valéry. There too, through prayers, offerings and vows the prince entrusted himself to the assistance of Heaven; he had not been dissuaded by contrary winds, terrible shipwrecks or the cowardly desertion of several of those who had given their word. Dealing with his problems by wise behaviour, he buried those who had drowned, hiding the fact as far as possible and burying them secretly. Increasing his supplies each day, he warded off famine. By a variety of encouragements, he regained those who had been overcome with fear, and put heart into the waverers. He fought using holy prayers, and went as far as bringing the body of St Valéry, a confessor most acceptable to God, out of the cathedral in order to ensure that the contrary wind became a favourable one. All the warriors who were departing with him took part in this demonstration of humility.

At last the long-awaited breeze arose: they gave thanks to heaven with voice and hand, and all shouted together to encourage each other. They left shore as quietly as possible and set out very eagerly on this voyage whose outcome remained uncertain. . . .

The Invasion of England

Borne by a favourable breeze to Pevensey, he disembarked with ease and without having to fight his way ashore. Harold, indeed, had withdrawn to Yorkshire to fight his own brother Tostig and the king of Norway, Harold. It was hardly astonishing that his brother, driven by wrongs done to him and wishing to recover his confiscated lands, should invoke foreign aid against him; Harold's sister, too, morally quite unlike him, used vows and advice to oppose him, because he was a man soiled by luxury, a cruel homicide, proud of his wealth and plunder, an enemy of justice and goodness. This woman, as wise as any man, who recognised goodness and cherished it in her way of life, intended that the man whom her husband Edward had chosen by adopting him as his son should rule over the English: William the wise, just and strong.

The rejoicing Normans, once they had landed, occupied Pevensey, where they built their first camp, and built another at Hastings, providing a refuge for themselves and a shelter for their boats. . . . William, taking no more than twenty-five knights, boldly explored the lie of the land and its inhabitants. He came back on foot because the paths were so difficult, and laughed at having to do so; and—the reader may laugh at this—he earned yet more praise by carrying on his shoulders not only his own hauberk, but also that of one of his companions, famous for his strength and courage, William Fitz Osbern.

A rich inhabitant of these parts, Norman by birth, Robert, son of the lady Wimarc, sent a message to his lord and relative the duke at Hastings, in the following words: 'King Harold, having fought his own brother and the king of Norway, who was regarded as the most valiant warrior under heaven, has killed both of them in one battle, destroying their powerful armies. Encouraged by this success, he is returning to meet you by forced marches, at the head of a very numerous and strong army: against him, your men will be no more use, in my opinion, than as many vile curs. You are reputed to be a clever man; until now you have managed your affairs in peace and war with wisdom. Now you should act with caution, and beware of hurling yourself into a danger from which you cannot escape. I advise you to remain behind your fortifications and to refrain from giving battle for the time being.' But the duke replied to the messenger: 'Take my thanks to your master for his advice, in which he counsels prudence, though it would have been better put in less insulting words. Tell him that I will not hide behind ditches and palisades, but will engage Harold's army as soon as possible: I would not despair of crushing him and his men, with God's help, because my troops are so bold, even if I had only ten thousand warriors instead of the sixty thousand I have brought.'

One day, when the duke was inspecting the guard who protected the ships, a monk sent as an ambassador by Harold, was announced to him as he came from the ships. He went at once to find him, and cunningly said: 'There is no-one closer to William, count of the Normans, than I, his seneschal. You will have no way of speaking to him except through me: tell me what message you bring. He will be glad to learn of it through me, because no-one is dearer to him than me. Afterwards you can come and talk to him as you wish.' Once he had learnt the purpose of the embassy through what the monk told him, the duke at once made arrangements that he should be received as a guest and treated with every respect. Meanwhile, he and his men debated how to reply to the message.

The next day, seated amidst his magnates, he had the monk summoned, and said: 'I am William, by grace of God prince of the Normans. What you told me yesterday, please repeat in the presence of these men.' The messenger said: 'This is the message that King Harold sends to you. You have invaded his lands, whether from self-confidence or boldness, he does not know. He remembers that King Edward at first resolved to make you heir to the kingdom of England and that he himself gave you his pledge in Normandy. Equally, he knows that this kingdom belongs to him by right, because the same king, his lord, gave it to him on his deathbed. Now, since the time when Saint Augustine came to this land, the common custom of the nation is that a donation made by a dying man is held as valid. He therefore asks you and your men to leave the land which is his by right. Otherwise he will break the oath of friendship and the articles which he confirmed to you in Normandy, and the responsibility will be entirely yours.'

William's Challenge of Single Combat

When he heard Harold's message, the duke asked the monk if the latter would take his own ambassador safely to Harold. He promised to look after the messenger's safety just as he would his own. At once, the duke instructed a monk from Fécamp to carry a message promptly to Harold. 'It is neither boldness nor injustice, but mature reflection and the quest for justice which have led me to cross to this land, of which King Edward, my lord and relative, made me the heir, as Harold himself admits, because of the high honours and numerous benefices which I and my ancestors have conferred on him and his brother, as well as their men, and because, of all the men of his race, he believed me to be the most worthy and capable of supporting him in his lifetime, and of governing the kingdom after his death. He would not have done this without the agreement of his magnates, by the advice of archbishop Stigand, earl Godwin, earl Leofric, and earl Siward: all of them subscribed under oath that they would receive me as lord after the death of Edward and would never during his lifetime attempt to seize the kingdom by plotting against me. He gave as hostages Godwin's son and grandson. Finally, he sent Harold himself to Normandy, so that, he and I both being present, he would swear what his father and the other men already named had sworn in my absence. But, on his voyage towards me, he was in danger of being taken prisoner and I rescued him by strength and wisdom. Harold made himself my vassal by doing homage, and gave me surety in writing for my claim for the kingdom of England. I am ready to plead my case in a court wherever he pleases, either by English law or by Norman law. If, according to the verdict of law, either Normans or English decide that the kingdom belongs to him legitimately, let him possess it in peace. But if they decide that it should be restored to me, let him hand it over to me. However, if he rejects the proposal, I do not think that it is just to make my men fight his men and die as a result, because they have no part in our quarrel. I am ready to wager my head against his [in single combat] that I have a better right to the English kingdom than him.'

Such were the words of the duke: we have chosen to set them before everyone's eyes, rather than our own version, because we want to ensure for him eternal fame. It is a good illustration of his wisdom, justice, piety and boldness. The force of his argument, when considered (and Cicero, the best of the Roman orators, could not have weakened it) demolishes the arguments of Harold. In short, he was ready to abide by whatever judgment customary law decreed. He refused to condemn his enemies the English to die because of his personal quarrel. His wish was to decide the matter in single combat, at the risk of his own head.

As soon as the monk gave this message to Harold, who was approaching, he went pale with astonishment and remained silent for a long time, as if struck dumb. The messenger asked for an answer, not once but several times; at first he replied: 'We will continue our advance' and then 'We will march on to victory.' The messenger insisted on another reply, saying: 'The duke does not want the armies to be destroyed, but wishes for a single combat.' For this intrepid and good man preferred to renounce a just claim rather than cause the death of many men. He was sure that Harold's head would fall, because he was less brave and had an unjust cause. Finally Harold, raising his eyes to heaven, exclaimed: 'Let the Lord decide today between William and myself according to justice!' Blinded by his desire to rule, forgetful in his haste of the injustice of his cause, he chose, to his own ruin, his conscience as just judge.

The Normans in Italy and Sicily

C. Warren Hollister

The "other Norman conquest" of the eleventh century was almost as significant to history as William the Conqueror's invasion of England. As C. Warren Hollister relates in the following excerpt from *Medieval Europe: A Short History*, Norman adventurers began moving into southern Italy during the 1000s, working as mercenaries and seeking their fortunes. One of these Normans, Robert Guiscard, quickly consolidated his power over southern Italy and took control of important Mediterranean seaports. Along with his brothers, Robert Guiscard then conquered the nearby island of Sicily and menaced the Byzantine Empire, the author explains. A professor of history at the University of California at Santa Barbara for nearly forty years, Hollister wrote many books, including *Anglo-Saxon Military Institutions on the Eve of the Norman Conquest* and *Monarchy, Magnates, and Institutions in the Anglo-Norman World.*

Perhaps the most militant force in Europe's eleventh-century awakening was the warrior-aristocracy of Normandy. Largely Viking in ancestry, the Normans were by now thoroughly adapted to French culture. French in tongue, Christian in faith, feudal in social organization, they plied their arms across the length and breadth of Europe: in the reconquest of Spain, on the Crusades to the Holy Land, on the battlefields of England and France, and in southern Italy and Sicily.

Normandy itself was growing in prosperity and political centralization, and the pressure of an ever-increasing population drove
greedy and adventurous Norman warriors far and wide on distant
enterprises. The impression that they made on contemporaries is
suggested by a passage from an Italian chronicler:

> The Normans are a cunning and revengeful people; eloquence and de-
> ceit seem to be their hereditary qualities. They can stoop to flatter, but
> unless curbed by the restraint of law they indulge in the licentiousness
> of nature and passion and, in their eager search for wealth and power,
> despise whatever they possess and seek whatever they desire. They de-
> light in arms and horses, the luxury of dress, and the exercise of hawk-
> ing and hunting, but on pressing occasions they can endure with in-
> credible patience the inclemency of every climate and the toil and pri-
> vation of a military life.

The key figures in the Norman conquest of southern Italy were
sons of a minor baron of northwest Normandy named Tancred de
Hauteville. Tancred had twelve sons, and eight of them headed off
to Italy in the 1030s and 1040s, poor in goods but rich in ambition.
Even before the first of them arrived, other Norman adventurers had
already been drifting south to serve as hired soldiers for the Byzantine coastal cities, Lombard principalities and seaport republics that
were struggling for power in the military-political snake pit of
eleventh-century southern Italy. In the words of a contemporary observer, these Norman newcomers moved about the south Italian
countryside "hoping to find someone willing to employ them; for
they were sturdy men and well-built, and also most skilled in the use
of arms." They made their presence felt, and before long were building principalities of their own.

Robert Guiscard

In 1047 there arrived the most formidable of Tancred de Hauteville's
sons, Robert Guiscard ("the cunning"). A contemporary Byzantine
princess, Anna Comnena, describes him as a man

> of tyrannical temper, cunning in mind, brave in action, tall and well-
> proportioned. His complexion was ruddy, his hair blond, his shoulders
> broad, and his eyes all but emitted sparks of fire. His shout was loud
> enough to terrify armies . . . and he was ready to submit to nobody in all
> the world.

Robert Guiscard's wife, the Lombard princess Sichelgaita, was
equally formidable. Tall and powerfully built, she participated fully
in the wars and politics of her era. Princess Anna Comnena was
awed and terrified by Sichelgaita's military prowess: "When dressed
in full armor, the woman was a fearsome sight."

Robert Guiscard began his Italian career as a bandit leader. Swooping down from his hideaway in the barren mountains of southern Italy, he plundered villagers and travelers and terrorized the countryside. Successful at this, he expanded his activities to conquest. And demonstrating his warlike prowess with victories over his neighbors, he gradually rose to become the leader of the south-Italian Normans. In 1059 his authority over southern Italy was recognized formally by the pope himself in the Treaty of Melfi: Guiscard agreed to become a papal vassal and received in return the title of duke.

From the Treaty of Melfi onward, the conquests of the southern Normans were "holy wars," and the papacy—which was becoming increasingly hostile toward the Holy Roman Empire to its north—came more and more to depend on the military support of Duke Robert Guiscard. In 1060, with papal blessings Guiscard invaded the populous Muslim island of Sicily—driven less by Christian zeal than by Norman greed. The island was prosperous and well-defended, and its conquest consumed over thirty years. Once the invasion was well under way, Guiscard turned the campaign over to a younger brother named Roger and launched an attack against the Byzantine holdings in southern Italy. In 1071 he captured Bari, Byzantium's chief Italian seaport. Then, returning to Sicily, he combined forces with his brother Roger to seize the great Muslim metropolis of Palermo in 1072. Palermo had been one of the leading urban centers of the Islamic world. It was larger and richer than any other city in Western Christendom, and its bustling harbor was the key to the central Mediterranean. With Palermo, Bari, and all of southern Italy under his control, Guiscard was now in a position to dominate Mediterranean commerce.

His ambitions were limitless. In 1080, again with papal backing, he launched a "crusade" against the Byzantine Empire, hungering for Constantinople itself. At the crucial battle of Durazzo, Guiscard's Normans were put to flight by the Byzantines. But his wife Sichelgaita charged majestically after them, her long hair streaming out beneath her helmet, shouting in a deafening voice, "How far will you flee? Stand and acquit yourselves like men!" Seeing her approach at full gallop, spear upraised, the Normans ceased their flight, returned to battle, and won the victory.

In 1084, in the midst of his Byzantine campaign, Robert Guiscard was summoned back to Italy by Pope Gregory VII, whose conflicts with the Holy Roman Empire had brought the emperor and his army to Rome. With Pope Gregory besieged in a fortress within his own city, Robert Guiscard and Sichelgaita returned to rescue him, and the news of their coming was enough to send the emperor fleeing northward.

After a short siege, the Normans entered the ill-defended city in triumph, rescued Pope Gregory, and restored him to power. Shortly afterwards, however, simmering hostility between Guiscard's army and the Roman townspeople exploded into violence. The Normans proceeded to plunder and burn the city of Rome, causing greater devastation than the fifth-century Visigoths and Vandals. Afterwards Guiscard's followers sold a number of Rome's leading citizens into Muslim slavery.

In 1085 Robert Guiscard died, with Sichelgaita at his side, in the midst of still another campaign against Byzantium. His rags-to-riches career displays in full measure the limitless opportunities and ruthlessness of his age. His savage rescue of Pope Gregory VII was celebrated in the epitaph of his tomb in southern Italy:

> Here lies Guiscard, the terror of the world,
>
> Who out of Rome the Roman Emperor hurled. . . .

The Norman Kingdom of Sicily

In the generations following Robert Guiscard's death, his Italian-Sicilian dominions became one of the wealthiest and best-governed states in medieval Europe. The lord-vassal structure of Norman feudalism was blended with the sophisticated administrative techniques of the Italian Byzantines and Sicilian Muslims. The mixing of cultures is vividly apparent in the Capella Palatina ("Palace Chapel"), built by Norman rulers of the twelfth century in their palace at Palermo. The structural design of high nave and lower side aisles probably derives from other churches of Western Christendom; the interior glitters with mosaics in the Byzantine style; and the decor of the vaulted ceilings suggests a Muslim paradise, inhabited by djinns instead of Christian angels. The overall effect of the church, despite its diverse cultural ingredients, is one of unity—echoing the achievement of the southern Norman state in unifying peoples of many tongues and many pasts into a single, cohesive realm.

The Vikings

The Viking warriors swept down from the north like ravenous wolves, spreading terror and bloodshed wherever they went. From their Scandinavian homelands, they ranged as far south as Spain and as far east as Russia. Throughout Europe, people trembled in fear at the very mention of their name.

The Viking raids began in the ninth century, and the destruction they wrought greatly contributed to the turmoil experienced by western Europe during the Dark Ages. However, the Vikings were not merely roving pirates: They were explorers, traders, colonizers, conquerors. In the course of their expansive travels, the Vikings opened up trade routes that enabled valuable goods from the Middle East and Asia to reach the Europeans. Invaders from Denmark gained control over a large section of England—which became known as the Danelaw—and at various times during the eleventh century, the entire nation of England was ruled by Scandinavian kings. The French region of Normandy was conquered in the tenth century by Viking warriors whose descendants achieved important military victories in the 1000s, including the Norman Conquest of England in 1066 and the liberation of Sicily from the Muslims in 1091. And around the turn of the millennium, Viking sailors from Iceland discovered North America and established settlements on its coast—the first Europeans to do so.

Clearly, the exploits of the Vikings had positive effects on Europe as well as negative ones, and their accomplishments were essential in shaping the course of European history. Yet as the year 1000 dawned, the Viking age was already nearing its end. Across Scandinavia, the pagan worshipers of Odin and Thor began to convert to Christianity; as good Christians, they became reticent to attack the churches and monasteries that they had once plundered with abandon. The growth of strong centralized monarchies in Norway, Denmark, and Sweden also "ultimately resulted in taming the Viking spirit," according to historian C. Warren Hollister. "As Scandinavia became increasingly civilized," he writes, "its kings discouraged the activities of roaming warrior bands, and its social environment gave rise to a more humdrum life." By the middle of the eleventh century, the glory days of the Viking raiders had faded into twilight, never to return.

The Viking Discovery of North America

F. Donald Logan

Around the turn of the millennium, Viking explorers discovered North America—four centuries earlier than Christopher Columbus. In the following selection from his book *The Vikings in History*, F. Donald Logan presents the historical and archaeological evidence that proves Viking boats came ashore on the coast of North America. Although Leif Ericsson is often credited with the discovery, Logan maintains that another Viking named Bjarni Herjolfsson first sighted the New World and that Ericsson later retraced Herjolfsson's voyage. The author recounts the Vikings' attempts to establish a colony in America and examines various theories concerning the exact location of the Viking settlements. Logan is a Catholic priest and a former history professor at Emmanuel College in Boston, Massachusetts.

The Vikings reached North America. This is an historical fact. The evidence, written and archaeological, allows for no doubt: sometime around the millennium men whose cultural ties reached beyond Greenland and Iceland to Scandinavia arrived on the shores of North America. To deny or even to cast doubt on this would be to fly in the face of overwhelming historical evidence.

The question of the historicity of the Vikings in the New World

Excerpted from F. Donald Logan, *The Vikings in History*, 2nd edition. Copyright © 1983, 1991 F. Donald Logan. Reprinted with permission from Taylor & Francis.

arises only because it is related to the question of who actually discovered America. The fascination with the discovery of America is really a fascination, not with the discovery of the Western Hemisphere—it was discovered perhaps 30,000 years ago by Asiatics—but with its much later discovery by *Europeans*: who was the first European to sight the New World? A more significant question historically would be: what circumstances, what patterns of human development led to a European presence on the western shores of the Atlantic Ocean? The discoveries in the late fifteenth century led to European settlements and, since then, to a continuous and dominant European presence. If not Christopher Columbus, then surely someone else would have landed in America during the last decade of the fifteenth century. The person is less important than the historical forces at work which made, at least at that time, such a discovery inevitable. In the Viking age, four centuries earlier, still other forces made a landing in North America a virtual inevitability. The identity of the first Viking to sight America may never be known, perhaps with historical justice, for the first Viking to make landfall there was driven by forces spanning in distance the North Atlantic from the fjords of western and southern Norway and spanning in time several centuries of Viking explorations. . . .

The Viking Explorations

In about the year 1000 Vikings sighted, landed at, explored, and attempted to settle on the North American littoral [coast]. The earliest written source is not, as one might suspect, the saga accounts, which exist in fourteenth- and fifteenth-century manuscripts drawn from twelfth- and thirteenth-century texts. The earliest written source dates from within a few generations of the attempted Viking settlement in America: *The History of the Archbishops of Hamburg,* completed by Adam of Bremen in about 1075. Book four of this history is entitled 'A Description of the Islands of the North', which makes Adam the earliest known German geographer. Sometime during the late 1060s Adam of Bremen visited the Danish court to gather information for his history and, while there, interviewed *inter alios* [among other persons] King Svein Estrithson, nephew of King Cnut the Great.

> The king spoke about yet another island which had been discovered by many in that ocean. It is called Vinland because there grow wild in that country vines which produce fine wine. Free-growing crops abound there. I have learned this not from fanciful tales but from the trustworthy reports of the Danes.

Adam of Bremen had gathered this information in the late 1060s. King Svein, at whose court he learned these things, had been born in 1017, about the time when Vikings were attempting to colonize

Vinland. It will never be known exactly when Svein learned about this land—as king (1047–74) he seems to have been visited by the Icelander Eadwine bearing the gift of a polar bear from Greenland—but what is certain is that we are dealing here with a nearly contemporary account.

Three other early, non-saga references confirm the continued knowledge of the existence of Vinland in Iceland. A geographical treatise of the twelfth century states:

> South from Greenland there lie Helluland and then Markland and, not far beyond, Vinland.

The *Icelandic Annals* under the year 1121 record that 'Bishop Eric of Greenland set out in search of Vinland'. Iceland's first great historian, Ari Thorgilsson, writing in about 1127, indicated that he knew of Vinland and its native inhabitants from his uncle, Thorkell Gellison, who had learned about these things from one of the original settlers of Greenland. And thus, within a hundred years or so of the Vinland settlement Ari wrote about Vinland, almost incidentally, without need of explanation for none was needed.

Information from the Sagas

The sagas, arising out of a different, if kindred, tradition, support this information and add significant facts of an indisputably historical nature. Meant for entertainment, the sagas existed in oral form at first and were written down only much later. The sagas require care in the use made of them by historians: not every detail can be relied on and not every statement rejected. Sagas celebrated the great deeds of the ancestors of later Icelanders, who enhanced their own importance through the flattering descriptions of the heroic men and women from whom they claimed descent. The two sagas which describe at length the Viking experience in the New World derive from this entertainment-giving, ancestor-praising tradition of the sagas. The *Greenlanders' Saga,* the earlier of the two, was committed to writing in the twelfth century and has about it a primitive crudeness which, while not particularly attractive literarily, does add to its historical credibility. The great anthology of Icelandic material, the *Flatey Book,* compiled towards the end of the fourteenth century in northern Iceland, contains the earliest extant text of this saga. The *Eric Saga,* on the other hand, has a more polished appearance and dates, in its earliest written form, from the mid–thirteenth century, but exists only in two later medieval versions. . . . The *Greenlanders' Saga* and the *Eric Saga* tell essentially the same story, yet in some places they complement and in other places they contradict one another. It is now known that the *Greenlanders' Saga* is more reliable and its text more faithful to an oral original. Its story should be related.

The *Greenlanders' Saga* tells the Vinland story in three stages: the sighting, the exploration, and the attempted settlement of Vinland.

This land to the south and west of Greenland, according to the saga, was discovered not by Leif Ericsson but by Bjarni Herjolfsson. This Icelander was accustomed to spend alternate winters in Iceland, with his father, and Norway. One winter while Bjarni was in Norway, his father Herjolf moved from Iceland to Greenland with Eric the Red and established a homestead there at Herjolfsnes. Bjarni did not learn about this until the following summer when he arrived in Iceland. Although neither Bjarni nor any of his crew had ever previously sailed to Greenland, they set sail and headed west. Strong north winds and deep fog forced them off course. When the bad weather lifted, they hoisted their sail and headed west once again. One day later they sighted a land, which was thickly forested and had low hills. This did not tally with the description of Greenland Bjarni had been given in Iceland, and, instead of landing, he turned the prow of his ship north. The land ebbed away from his port side. Two days later land was once again sighted. This flat, wooded land was not the Greenland of the glaciers, and, against the advice of his crew, Bjarni ordered his ship to sea once again. Three days later they sighted a land, mountainous, glacier-topped, and, in Bjarni's estimate, worthless. Putting this land astern, Bjarni sailed his ship in front of strong, gale-force winds from the southwest, and four days later they sighted a fourth land. Bjarni judged this to be Greenland and landed at a promontory, which as chance would have it was Herjolfsnes. There he settled and, in time, took over his father's farm.

Some years later Eric the Red's son Leif, who, like all Greenlanders, was curious about new lands, decided to explore the places sighted by Bjarni. He bought Bjarni's ship—was there a feeling that the vessel might know its own way?—and enlisted a crew of thirty-five. The sailing plan was simply to retrace Bjarni's route. This they did successfully. They sighted, first, the mountainous, glacier-topped land, which Bjarni had sighted last. Unwilling to bear the same criticism that had been heaped on Bjarni, Leif lowered a boat and went ashore. The land was, indeed, worthless: glaciers inland and, between glaciers and the sea, slabs of rock. He called the place Helluland (i.e., Slab-land). The next land they sighted had white sandy beaches and, beyond these, flat woodlands. Leif landed, called it Markland (i.e., Forest-land), and sailed on. Two days later they caught sight of land again. To the north of this land lay an island and they landed there. They put the dew from the grass to their lips and marvelled at its sweetness. Leif now ordered his ship to go west around the promontory which lay to their south into an open sound. Not waiting for the tide to turn, they rushed ashore. Later they brought the ship up a river and anchored it in a lake at the riverhead, where they set up temporary shelters for themselves. The river had salmon bigger than they had ever seen and the plentiful grass appeared abundant for their livestock. They decided to winter there and so built houses. Leif arranged exploring parties to go out from their camp, but one of his men, a southerner (a German?) called Tyrkir, disappeared and, while Leif was preparing a search, Tyrkir stumbled into the camp, tipsy on the grapes he had found. Leif called the place Vinland (i.e., Wine-land). Night and day in this land were of more equal length than in Greenland. Leif and his crew readied a cargo of vines, grapes and timber and returned to Greenland the following summer. That was the extent of Leif's involvement in the explorations: he had retraced Bjarni's route, landed at three places, named them, and spent a winter at the third (Vinland). Thus ends the story of Leif Ericsson and the New World.

Encounters with Native Peoples

The colonizing expeditions which followed involved other children of Eric the Red: Thorvald, who died in Vinland, Thorstein, who never reached his destination, the latter's widow Gudrid and her then husband Thorfinn Karlsefni, and Eric's murderous daughter Freydis. The boat which had taken Bjarni by accident and Leif by design was sold to Thorvald Ericsson. With a crew of thirty he sailed to Vinland and found Leif's houses, where they wintered. Explorations to the west revealed attractive country of woods and sandy beaches. After another winter at Leif's houses Thorvald and his men sailed, first, eastward along the coastline and then, north, putting in at a thickly wooded promontory between two fjords. It was here that the Vikings made their first recorded contact with the native people of North America. The Vikings noticed what looked like three humps on the beach; closer inspection showed the humps to be skin boats, each covering three men. One man escaped; the other eight were captured and executed. Europe met America in unprovoked violence. Suddenly the fjord was alive with skin boats, and the Europeans fled for their lives, although Thorvald, stung by an arrow, failed to escape with his. The crew returned to Greenland without Thorvald's body but with tales of *skraelings* (uglies) on the beautiful shores of Vinland.

Thorstein, another son of Eric, went with his wife Gudrid and a crew of twenty-five in search of his brother's body so that he might bring it back to Greenland. They set out in the same ship, which had already travelled the route three times, but foul weather tossed them mercilessly until it was almost winter when they were able to land at the Western Settlement of Greenland. During that winter, sickness struck the settlement, killing Thorstein and leaving Gudrid widowed. She returned with her husband's body to Brattahlid, in the Eastern Settlement, where she buried it in consecrated ground. There she met a visiting Icelander, the wealthy Thorfinn Karlsefni, and they married. At Gudrid's urging Karlsefni agreed to undertake a colonizing expedition to Vinland. Together they sailed, taking with them a company of sixty men, five women, and a cargo of livestock of various kinds. The familiar voyage—presumably some of the men had sailed this way before—was easily accomplished. The new settlers quickly adjusted to life at the Leif site: they put their cows out to pasture, lived off the wild fruit and crops as well as the game and fish they caught. The intention was to stay and create a permanent settlement. After the first winter they encountered a large number of *skraelings,* who one day simply came out of the woods at the settlement site. The settlers' bull roared at the *skraelings* and frightened them. Soon, however, the Vikings and *skraelings* were trading: the natives' furs for the colonists' cow's milk. During that summer Gudrid gave birth to a son Snorri, the first European reported born in the Western Hemisphere. Early that next winter the *skraelings* returned to trade and, in a disagreement, a *skraeling* was killed. Battle soon followed, and the Vikings, pushing their bull ahead of them, drove their attackers away. Karlsefni decided, when spring came, to abandon the settlement. After only two winters the colonists returned to Greenland. Karlsefni, Gudrid and the young Snorri eventually settled in Iceland. After her husband's death Gudrid was to travel to Rome and, later, back in Iceland she became a nun. Among her descendants were three twelfth-century Icelandic bishops: small wonder that the twelfth-century *Greenlanders' Saga* sang the praise of this woman and her relations (Eric's family and Karlsefni).

One member of Eric's family, however, is not praised in the *Greenlanders' Saga,* and that is Freydis, Eric's daughter. In partnership with two Icelanders she sailed to Vinland and the Leif site. Disagreements broke out there, and Freydis had her partners and their men killed, she herself slaying their five women with the sharp end of an axe. This tale of the murderous Freydis ends the *Saga's* description of the attempted settlements in Vinland: three in number, all at the same site, two unsuccessful because of hostile encounters with the native people and the third unsuccessful because of a wicked woman. Nine brief chapters and the story of Vinland is told—or, at least, part of the story.

The Eric Saga tells a fuller story, repeating some of the details of the earlier saga, omitting some, changing others, and adding still others. This saga makes no mention of Bjarni and attributes the discovery of the New World to Leif Ericsson, now described as a missionary sent by King Olaf of Norway to evangelize Iceland and Greenland. Difficulties at sea threw Leif's ship off course, and he sighted a new land where there grew wild wheat, grapes and mosur (maple?) trees. Nearby he discovered and saved some shipwrecked men, and from this time he was called Leif the Lucky. After one winter there Leif made his way to Greenland to carry out his evangelizing mission. At this point, after less than a chapter, Leif disappears from the *Eric Saga*. The next voyage was led by Karlsefni and his wife Gudrid, widow of Thorstein Ericsson, and contained a company, including Freydis and Thorvald, intent upon settlement. They sighted and landed briefly at a place they called Helluland and later at a place they called Markland. Beyond a long stretch of sandy beach—they named it Furdustrand—they found inlets and after some exploration put into a fjord, where there were vines and wild wheat. The first winter proved so severe that they decided to sail further south. After sailing for a long time they came to the estuary of a river that flowed from a lake. Here there were vines and wild wheat and the sea teemed with fish. They settled here; no snow came that winter, but in the spring there came the *skraelings,* first to trade—*skraeling* pelts for Viking cloth—and later to do battle. At this point the *Eric Saga* seeks to rehabilitate the memory of Freydis and portrays her as a valiant woman who, standing her ground while men fled, pulled out one of her breasts and slapped it with a sword as the *skraelings* fled in terror. Despite her heroism the Vikings decided to return to Greenland. On the way they made several stops. At one place they met a uniped, who slew Thorvald with an arrow; at another place, Gudrid gave birth to Snorri. The saga ends by naming the three twelfth-century Icelandic bishops descended from Karlsefni and Gudrid.

What can be concluded from these saga accounts? Three facts stand out above all else as indisputable: the Vikings reached North America; they then attempted to establish a settlement at Vinland; and they abandoned their settlement after hostile encounters with the native people. Minor stories such as the tipsy Tyrkir or the breast-thumping Freydis can be placed to one side: interesting when telling a story, but not necessarily for anything else. Sagas had to be created within an historically and geographically credible context. The heroes had to be real people, their voyages true voyages, the sailing directions believable to sophisticated seafarers. Some details should be looked at. The omission, for example, of Bjarni as the discoverer of the new lands in the story as told in the *Eric Saga* is quite suspicious. That saga writer, well aware of the account of the *Greenlanders' Saga*, suppressed the Bjarni incident entirely and left it to a sea-tossed Leif to sight the new land. The *Eric Saga* throughout magnifies the families of Eric and his daughter-in-law Gudrid, and, in the case of Leif, this author attributed to him the conversion of Greenland, which we know is untrue. The conscious bypassing of Bjarni in favour of Leif fits into this general pattern. (Consider, too, the turning of the murderous Freydis into the valiant woman!) It is Bjarni Herjolfsson whom we must see in the sagas as the discoverer of North America. The references to the details of the land itself are so insistent and so much in agreement that there can be little doubt that the Vikings found a land where crops and what appeared to be grapes grew wild and where salmon ran in the rivers. This is firm ground for the historian.

Further questions impose themselves: when did these Europeans visit the New World? and where did they land there? The latter question will be dealt with presently; the other, easier question, now. Bjarni made his discovery in the year in which Eric the Red brought settlers back with him from Iceland to Greenland. There is unanimous agreement that this has to be 985 or 986. It was in the late summer that Bjarni failed to find his father in Iceland and sailed on to sight the new land. Dating Leif's voyage of exploration requires some attention. The *Greenlanders' Saga,* which generally is preferable, recounts that this voyage occurred while *Jarl* [Earl] Erik ruled in Norway (1000–14), whereas the *Eric Saga* portrays Leif as a missionary sent by King Olaf Tryggvason of Norway (995–1000). Olaf was killed and *Jarl* Erik became the ruler of much of coastal Norway in September of the year 1000. Bjarni's visit to Eric can be dated as 1001 at the earliest and as 1014 at the latest. Bjarni stayed in Norway a winter and returned to Greenland in the following summer, 1002 at the earliest and 1015 at the latest. It was at this point that Leif then sailed. Greater precision is unnecessary. The only settlement mentioned in both saga accounts was the settlement built by Thorfinn Karlsefni and Gudrid his wife; by each account it lasted three years. When did it take place? At the time of this settlement Snorri was born. We can follow his line. Snorri had a daughter Hallfrid, who gave birth to Thorlak, future Bishop of Skalhold. The Icelandic annals state that Thorlak was born in 1085. If we assume that Snorri was forty years old when he sired Hallfrid and that Hallfrid was twenty years old when she bore Thorlak, this would mean that Snorri was born in 1025. Other assumptions, of course, would lead to other conclusions. Yet it seems fairly safe to say that the Karlsefni settlement, during which Snorri was born, took place some time during the second or third decade of the eleventh century. Where he was born and where this settlement was located remain to be seen.

The Location of Vinland

The vexed question concerning the location of Vinland must be faced. One distinction should be made at the outset. The Vikings, in giving names to places, gave names to large regions (for example, Iceland, Greenland) and names to particular places (for example, Breidafjord, Brattahlid). The names Helluland, Markland and Vinland were given to large regions, to areas with hundreds of miles of coastline. Historians are virtually unanimous in locating Helluland at Baffin Island, just two hundred miles across the Davis Strait from Greenland. There the land is much as it was at the turn of the millennium: towering glaciers in the interior and stone slabs sloping from them to the sea. Markland, that thickly wooded region with miles of sandy beaches, must be seen as Labrador, for, despite intervening climatic changes, the area of Labrador south of Hamilton Inlet is still thickly forested with a strand of sandy beaches, and in Viking times the timber-line might have been as far north as Okak Bay. No mountains are to be found here, just a rolling coastal plain. It was along this coastline that Karlsefni found an extraordinary length of sandy beach, which he named Furdustrand (i.e., marvellous shore). This should be identified, it would seem, with the Porcupine Strands, which are forty-five miles of virtually unbroken beach, at most points about fifty metres wide and backed by dunes.

Vinland, the land to the south of Markland, has been located at scores of places along the eastern coast of North America, as far south even as Florida. Local pride, enthusiastic amateur archaeology, and (alas!) fraud have produced most of these claims. . . .

Serious attention in recent years has been given to two archaeological projects in Canada, one in Quebec and the other in Newfoundland; neither has arisen or taken hold from sentiments of local piety. The first was undertaken by Thomas E. Lee in northern Quebec along the western shore of Ungava Bay at two sites (Payne Bay and Deception Bay). It would not appear unreasonable that Norse Greenlanders would have sailed south of Baffin Island through the Hudson Strait into Ungava Bay. Mr Lee discovered at these sites a number of longhouses as well as stone implements, a piece of bone, and an iron axe-head, which was apparently laminated. The material objects can be dated to the Viking age, and, although some opinion held them to be Norse, a scholarly consensus considers them not Norse but Dorset Eskimo, having parallels with known Dorset-type materials found elsewhere in the Canadian Arctic.

A Momentous Discovery

Until 1960 L'Anse aux Meadows, Newfoundland, was a tiny, unknown fishing village of about seventy souls, cut off from its neighbours except by the sea. Now a road runs into that village, a national park has been opened there, and its name has been broadcast across lands and seas. L'Anse aux Meadows is the site of the well-publicized excavations which have unearthed ineluctible evidence of an early Norse settlement in the New World. In 1960 Dr Helge Ingstad, former Governor of Greenland, sailed north from Rhode Island along the northeast coast of North America in search of a Vinlandic site. At the village of L'Anse aux Meadows on the northernmost tip of Newfoundland he asked George Decker, a descendant of original English settlers, about any ruins in the vicinity. Dr Ingstad was led a short distance west from the village to the shores of Epaves Bay at Black Duck

Brook. Contours on an old beach terrace led him to believe that this might be a site worth further investigation. Behind this beach-side site rise low, rolling hills. The forests are now some distance away. The outstanding feature today is the lushness of its fields, unparalleled at this latitude in North America. Great Sacred Island stands sentry-like to the north of Epaves Bay. Dr Ingstad decided to excavate. Every summer from 1961 to 1968 the archaeologist Anne Stine Ingstad, his wife, directed the operations at the site, and in 1977 she published a scientific report of the excavations. Further work on the site was done from 1973 to 1976, first by Bengt Schonback and later by Birgitta Linderoth Wallace.

What did the Ingstads find at L'Anse aux Meadows? Quite simply, they found the remains of a small Norse community of the eleventh century. They discovered to the east of the brook three clusters of houses and to the west of the brook a smithy and a charcoal kiln. The buildings have walls constructed of horizontal layers of turf placed one on top of another. In each cluster there was a longhouse and one or more smaller, satellite houses; they were built on an ancient marine terrace which lies about 4 metres above sea level at high tide. Each of the longhouses had a side wall facing the sea. . . . In general, the buildings at this site represent Scandinavian buildings, and on the basis of the buildings themselves one has sufficient confidence to describe this as a Norse community.

The artefacts found at L'Anse aux Meadows, although not as plentiful as one would have liked, confirm the architectural evidence and point unmistakably to a Norse origin. Near the doorway to [one of the longhouses], a soapstone spindle whorl was found; it resembles very closely a spindle whorl found in Greenland—nothing of this sort can be attributed to aboriginal North Americans at this date—and indicates the presence of sheep at this Norse settlement. A small, rounded stone with a hollow was, no doubt, a lamp used to burn oil; it is very similar to Icelandic lamps of the Viking period and not similar at all to known Eskimo lamps. . . . A fragment of a bone needle had a drilled eye, a feature impossible for the Dorset Eskimoes. Of greatest significance is the ring-headed bronze pin, undoubtedly of Norse-Celtic origin. This pin, with a ring looped through a hole drilled at the top of the shank, has no ornamentation and measures 10 centimetres, and it bears a very close resemblance to pins found throughout northern Europe. Over a score of such pins from the Viking period have been found in graves in Norway alone, a half dozen or so in Iceland, and one, most recently, has been found at the site of the High Street excavations in Dublin. . . .

The age of this Norse settlement at L'Anse aux Meadows is still to be discussed. The excavators have had some of the material found at this site subjected to radiocarbon testing. . . .

The carbon-14 dating would suggest a date at the turn of the millennium. This dating is consistent with the information derived from the sagas. The conclusion is ineluctable: sometime about the year A.D. 1000 a Viking settlement was established at L'Anse aux Meadows near the northern tip of Newfoundland. . . .

Thus, the architectural and archaeological evidence is strongly supported by the carbon dating, and this evidence compels us to conclude that the Vikings reached North America. The saga evidence, as useful as it indeed is, takes second place to what was unearthed in Newfoundland. The significance of these findings can scarcely be exaggerated: the long line of Viking migration which had begun generations earlier in the fjords of western Norway had stretched all the way across the North Atlantic. The line that had reached Iceland in the 870s and Greenland in the 980s reached the shores of North America near the year 1000. . . .

Grapes, Wine, and Vinland

One worrying issue about L'Anse aux Meadows remains: the name Vinland. According to Adam of Bremen and the sagas, the land discovered by the Vikings abounded in wine-yielding grapes. No grapes now grow in this region. Inconveniently, sophisticated pollen analyses of samples taken from the site clearly show that no profound vegetational change has taken place there for the past seven-and-a-half millennia and, hence, it is highly improbable that grapes grew there during the Viking age. The climate at the time of the Viking settlement, despite an intervening cold period, was similar to the climate of today: sharp differences between winter and summer temperatures, which, in both seasons, are moderated by the Labrador Current and the Gulf Stream, thus producing much fog and a short season (about 100 days) for crops. Grapeless though this land was a thousand years ago, it did produce a wide variety of berries, some of which were 'wineberries', particularly the squashberry and both the red and the black currants; these might quite conceivably have been interpreted as grapes. Currants are still used in Scandinavia for making wine and are commonly called 'red and black wineberries' in Sweden, and elsewhere in the north (in parts of Norway and England) the red currant is known as a 'red wineberry'. . . .

Is L'Anse aux Meadows, then, Vinland? The answer has to be that L'Anse aux Meadows must have been a Viking settlement in the large region called Vinland. It would be rash, indeed, to identify this settlement with any of the settlements mentioned in the sagas, although the temptation, which must be valiantly resisted, to see this as the colony established by Thorfinn Karlsefni is strong.

It still remains for scholars to determine the extent of Vinland. How far west did it extend?—to Ungava Bay?—to Hudson Bay?

And how far south did it extend?—to Nova Scotia?—to the Maine coast?—to Cape Cod?—to Narragansett Bay or beyond? It is only archaeological evidence, perhaps accidentally found by fishermen, beachcombers, or amateur archaeologists, which will determine how far the Vikings went in the New World. . . . However far Vinland might have extended—and it remains an open question—there can be no question that the Vikings established a settlement, short-lived though it was, on the marine terraces overlooking Epaves Bay in Newfoundland.

Relations with the Native Americans

The Greenlanders' Saga

The Vikings made several attempts to settle in North America during the 1000s. The following account, taken from the twelfth-century text *The Greenlanders' Saga,* relates the events that occurred at one of these early settlements. According to the saga, Vinland—the name the Vikings gave to the new land that they had found—was bountiful in natural resources and promised a good living for the settlers. However, the territory was already occupied by Native Americans, whom the Vikings called Skraelings (a derogatory word meaning "stunted" or "shriveled up"). The Skraelings first approached the Viking encampment offering to trade goods, and the Vikings brazenly cheated them during the trading. The distrust between the two groups soon resulted in violence, and the continual threat of Skraeling attacks ultimately convinced the Vikings to abandon their efforts to colonize Vinland.

That same summer a ship arrived in Greenland from Norway. Her captain was a man called Thorfinn Karlsefni. He was a man of considerable wealth. He spent the winter with Leif Eiriksson at Brattahlid.

Karlsefni quickly fell in love with Gudrid [Leif's widowed sister-in-law] and proposed to her, but she asked Leif to answer on her behalf. She was betrothed to Karlsefni, and the wedding took place that same winter.

There was still the same talk about Vinland voyages as before, and everyone, including Gudrid, kept urging Karlsefni to make the voy-

Excerpted from Magnus Magnusson and Hermann Palsson, eds., *The Vinland Sagas: The Norse Discovery of America* (England: Penguin Books, Ltd., 1965).

age. In the end he decided to sail and gathered a company of sixty men and five women. He made an agreement with his crew that everyone should share equally in whatever profits the expedition might yield. They took livestock of all kinds, for they intended to make a permanent settlement there if possible.

Karlsefni asked Leif if he could have the houses in Vinland [that Leif had built previously]; Leif said that he was willing to lend them, but not to give them away.

They put to sea and arrived safe and sound at Leif's Houses and carried their hammocks ashore. Soon they had plenty of good supplies, for a fine big rorqual was driven ashore; they went down and cut it up, and so there was no shortage of food.

The livestock were put out to grass, and soon the male beasts became very frisky and difficult to manage. They had brought a bull with them.

Karlsefni ordered timber to be felled and cut into lengths for a cargo for the ship, and it was left out on a rock to season. They made use of all the natural resources of the country that were available, grapes and game of all kinds and other produce.

The first winter passed into summer, and then they had their first encounter with Skraelings, when a great number of them came out of the wood one day. The cattle were grazing near by and the bull began to bellow and roar with great vehemence. This terrified the Skraelings and they fled, carrying their packs which contained furs and sables and pelts of all kinds. They made for Karlsefni's houses and tried to get inside, but Karlsefni had the doors barred against them. Neither side could understand the other's language.

Then the Skraelings put down their packs and opened them up and offered their contents, preferably in exchange for weapons; but Karlsefni forbade his men to sell arms. Then he hit on the idea of telling the women to carry milk out to the Skraelings, and when the Skraelings saw the milk they wanted to buy nothing else. And so the outcome of their trading expedition was that the Skraelings carried their purchases away in their bellies, and left their packs and furs with Karlsefni and his men.

After that, Karlsefni ordered a strong wooden palisade to be erected round the houses, and they settled in.

About this time Karlsefni's wife, Gudrid, gave birth to a son, and he was named Snorri.

Violence Breaks Out

Early next winter the Skraelings returned, in much greater numbers this time, bringing with them the same kind of wares as before. Karlsefni told the women, 'You must carry out to them the same produce that was most in demand last time, and nothing else.'

As soon as the Skraelings saw it they threw their packs in over the palisade. . . .

A Skraeling was killed by one of Karlsefni's men for trying to steal some weapons. The Skraelings fled as fast as they could, leaving their clothing and wares behind. . . .

'Now we must devise a plan,' said Karlsefni,

> for I expect they will pay us a third visit, and this time with hostility and in greater numbers. This is what we must do: ten men are to go out on the headland here and make themselves conspicuous, and the rest of us are to go into the wood and make a clearing there, where we can keep our cattle when the Skraelings come out of the forest. We shall take our bull and keep him to the fore.

The place where they intended to have their encounter with the Skraelings had the lake on one side and the woods on the other.

Karlsefni's plan was put into effect, and the Skraelings came right to the place that Karlsefni had chosen for the battle. The fighting began, and many of the Skraelings were killed. There was one tall and handsome man among the Skraelings and Karlsefni reckoned that he must be their leader. One of the Skraelings had picked up an axe, and after examining it for a moment he swung it at a man standing beside him, who fell dead at once. The tall man then took hold of the axe, looked at it for a moment, and then threw it as far as he could out into the water. Then the Skraelings fled into the forest as fast as they could, and that was the end of the encounter.

Karlsefni and his men spent the whole winter there, but in the spring he announced that he had no wish to stay there any longer and wanted to return to Greenland. They made ready for the voyage and took with them much valuable produce, vines and grapes and pelts. They put to sea and reached Eiriksfjord safely and spent the winter there.

Iceland's Conversion to Christianity

Magnus Magnusson

An Icelander who has lived in Scotland for most of his life, Magnus Magnusson has translated a number of medieval Icelandic sagas into English and is the author of *Viking Expansion Westward, Hammer of the North*, and *Iceland*. He has also presented a variety of historical television series for the British Broadcasting Corporation (BBC), including *Vikings!* In the following excerpt from the companion book to the TV program, Magnusson describes the decision of the Icelandic Vikings to convert to Christianity in the year 1000. This event was unique in European history, he writes, because the Icelanders thoughtfully and peacefully chose to convert *en masse* during the proceedings of their parliament. Additionally, Magnusson traces the effects of the conversion on the Icelandic Vikings, such as a marked increase in literacy.

The so-called 'Settlement Age' in Iceland is dated to about 870–930. By the end of that period it was becoming obvious that some sort of national authority was required, some sort of *modus vivendi* [way of living] to enable neighbouring communities to deal with problems that spilled across their boundaries—straying sheep, runaway slaves, brawls, killings.

The lead in the political initiative seems to have been taken by the Reykjavík family. In the 920s a man called Grím Goat-Shoe was commissioned to reconnoitre Iceland to hold a kind of opinion poll on proposals for a National Assembly (*Althing*), and choose the most convenient site for it; meanwhile his foster-brother, Úlfljót, was sent to Norway to prepare a suitable code of laws—not for a monarchy, but for a republic.

And so, on a June day in the year 930, the people of Iceland gathered at a place called Thingvellir (Parliament Plains), fifty kilometres to the east of Reykjavík. Thingvellir is a great natural arena of lava that was formed as the earth cracked and lurched in a geological subsidence thousands of years earlier; this convulsion has left a depression forty kilometres long and ten kilometres broad, with a wall of riven lava at one side that made a splendid sounding-board for speakers' voices in those days before microphones and amplifiers were invented.

Thingvellir is a spectacular place; but it was also a spectacular enterprise that these Icelanders were embarking upon. They were meeting to create a state the like of which had not been seen before in Europe—a state without a king. A republic. What they were doing was entirely logical and consistent. They had left their homelands to get away from the power of kings. Now they formed an oligarchic commonwealth, a country without a king at a time in history when the idea of kingship, of royal authority, was becoming politically paramount. . . .

There are very few material relics left of those stirring times, apart from a small bronze crozier-head, shaped like the letter T, lost by some bishop in the eleventh century and found at Thingvellir accidentally a few years ago. It symbolises the most significant event in the early history of the Viking parliament: the Conversion of Iceland to Christianity in the year 1000, not by the sword as happened so often elsewhere, but by parliamentary decree.

We are told that King Ólaf Tryggvason of Norway (995–1000) had been putting strong pressure on the Icelanders to accept Christianity, sending missionaries and holding chieftains' sons hostage in Norway. There were far-reaching implications for both Iceland and Norway, implications that were more political than religious. Paganism in Iceland had always been rather easy-going, and some at least of the earliest settlers were already Christian, in their own way; it is said of one of them, Helgi the Lean, that he had a mixed faith—'He believed in Christ, but invoked Thór for sea-voyages and in times of emergency.' And there is a charming story in *Landnámabók* about Ingólf Arnarson's grandson, Thorkel *máni* (Moon), who was Law-Speaker at the *Althing*: 'When he was lying on his deathbed, he had himself carried out to a shaft of sunlight, and commended himself to the god who had created the sun. He had led a life as blameless as the best of Christians.'

Choosing Christianity

By the year 1000, political opinion about the potentially divisive issue of the Church had polarised into two bitterly opposed factions.
They met at the *Althing*—the new and militant Christian party who
wanted to bring Iceland into the orbit of Christian Europe, and the
old, conservative pagan party. Both sides were armed and prepared
for a showdown. Civil war seemed imminent, with the political partition of Iceland the only possible resolution. And then, in the interests of peace, the leader of the Christian party, Hall of Sítha went to
the Law-Speaker—who was a pagan—and asked him to arbitrate;
and everyone at the *Althing* swore to abide by his sole decision. The
Law-Speaker, Thorgeir Thorkelsson, retired to his tented booth,
where he lay meditating for a day and a night under a fur cloak. On
Monday, 24 June 1000, he emerged and summoned everyone to the
Law Rock to announce his momentous decision:

> He said he thought an impossible situation would arise if men did not all
> have one and the same law in Iceland, and urged people not to let that
> happen, and said that it would lead to such divisions that fighting would
> most certainly break out that would destroy the nation.
>
> 'It seems to me good sense,' he said, 'that we do not let those who wish
> conflict decide the issue, but that we should seek a middle course, so that
> we all have one law and one custom; because if we divide the law, we
> will divide the peace.'
>
> Then Thorgeir declared the law, that all unbaptised people in the land
> should become Christian and be baptised. *(Íslendingabók)*

It was a momentous and statesmanlike speech, finding compromise in the midst of imminent conflict, for certain pagan practices
were not to be banned, as long as they were carried out privately to
avoid giving offence to Christian neighbours. The actual mass baptism did not go quite so well; many people felt that the water of the
river Öxará (Axe River) that meanders through Thingvellir was too
cold, and the Northerners insisted on waiting until they were on their
way home, when they could be immersed in the lake of Laugarvatn,
which has a hot-spring warming it!

But, to me, one of the most telling moments in the historic con-
frontation at the *Althing* had come a little earlier, before the Law-
Speaker's decision. During the passionate arguments that were rag-
ing in the parliament, a breathless messenger came running into the
arena with the news that a volcano was erupting near the home of
one of the leading Christians. 'Aha!' said the pagans. 'That proves
that the gods are angry at all the blasphemies they have been hearing.' Whereupon a wise old chieftain, Snorri Thorgrímsson, one of
the leading pagans, turned and looked at the great volcanic cliff behind him and remarked wryly, 'At what were the gods angry when

that lava flowed?' There was no answer to that; and so realism, political pragmatism, and downright common sense won the day, and Iceland remained a united nation.

The Effects of Conversion

The Conversion to Christianity had a profound effect on Iceland, socially, politically and culturally. Chieftains who had been in charge of pagan ceremonies now built churches whose tithes would add to their wealth and power. Within no more than fifty years, the Church established itself as a potent new power factor, trafficking not just in men's souls but also in their lands and ancient authorities.

In 1056, a native Icelandic bishopric was established at Skálholt, a manor-farm in the south-west that had belonged to one of the leaders of the Christian party, Gissur the White; it was his son, Ísleif Gissurarson, who now returned from lengthy education abroad in Westphalia to become Iceland's first bishop. But the really important impact of the Church was that it made Iceland literate; it brought her into the mainstream of European culture and learning. The Vikings in Iceland had their runes, of course, for inscriptions, but by 'literate' I am referring specifically to the use of the Roman alphabet, which was brought to Iceland by English missionary bishops early in the eleventh century. The *lingua franca* of Europe at that time was Latin; but through its church schools, the Icelandic Church also encouraged the use of Icelandic, translating edifying books into the vernacular so that the rural folk in their remote and scattered farmsteads could read the good news. And thus the Icelanders learned to write for themselves as well.

The first great scholar of the early Icelandic Church we know of was Saemund the Learned (1054–1133), who wrote a Latin history (now lost) of the kings of Norway. He was followed by Iceland's first vernacular historian, Ari the Learned, who wrote *Íslendingabók* (*Book of Icelanders*) around 1130. Simultaneously, he and other erudite scholars were busy compiling the first version of Iceland's Domesday Book—*Landnámabók*, the *Book of Settlements*, a systematic account of the first four hundred settlers in Iceland, their land-takes and their descendants. *Landnámabók* reflected the decisive break that Iceland had already made by opting for a republic: the history of Iceland was not the story of a single royal line, but the story of *all* Icelanders. And with that, a latent national genius for story-telling was unleashed, and the literature of the Icelandic Sagas was born.

Saga-writing became a great industry in Iceland. Sagas were regarded as 'serious entertainment', not only immensely popular but functionally important as well, for they enshrined genealogical memories that had peculiar significance in a country whose social fabric was woven on the loom of family kinships. They were written on calfskin (vellum), penned by the sharpened quill-feathers of swans or ravens, using a glossy ink distilled from bear-berry plants. The vellums were expensive to make, yet Sagas and other learned works poured out in their thousands. What is more, they never became the exclusive possession of any one social class; they were available to all, and treasured by all. Even after Saga-writing had reached its apogee in the thirteenth century, the old Sagas were cherished as family heirlooms.

The Viking Rulers of England

Frank R. Donovan

In the following excerpt from his book *The Vikings*, author Frank R. Donovan provides an overview of the Scandinavian kings who conquered England in the early 1000s. He writes that during the end of the tenth century
and the beginning of the eleventh, England suffered repeated attacks by
Viking raiders. One of these Vikings, Sweyn Forkbeard, eventually
wrested control of England from its weak king, Ethelred the Unready, and
established himself as the ruler of England. According to Donovan, Sweyn
Forkbeard's son Canute ruled England wisely and well for many years,
bringing peace to the country and halting the Viking raids. The author also
examines the last great battle between the English and the Viking invaders
in 1066, which occurred just a few days before the Norman Conquest.

The voyage of Leif Ericson in the year 1002, which opened the
New World to Viking exploration, coincided with the beginning
of the end of the Viking Era in the Old World. By this time the
Vikings who had established the kingdom of the Rus had become
more Russian than Scandinavian. The Vikings who had ravaged
France had become the Christian feudal dukes and nobles of Normandy and were now vigorously upholding the Church of which
their forebears had been the scourge. Their descendants would later
be numbered among the most pious of the Crusaders. . . .

Excerpted from Frank R. Donovan, *The Vikings* (New York: American Heritage Publishing Co.,
1964).

Viking Incursions

The Viking Era lasted longest in England. There, in the year 1000, the weak King Ethelred the Unready held the throne but hardly ruled. In the last twenty years of the tenth century the country was wracked by repeated large-scale raids. The first were led by Olaf Tryggvesson, who had been brought up in Novogorod and whose ninety-three ships were probably manned by Swedish Vikings from Russia. Ethelred bought him off with Danegeld [a monetary tribute], baptized him, and Olaf returned to become the zealous Christian king of Norway.

Next came Sweyn Forkbeard, who was already king of Denmark. Year after year he attacked in a different section of England. Each time he was bribed to go home with larger Danegeld, only to return the following year.

In the year 1002 Ethelred once more paid Danegeld to rid himself of the Vikings. But, on hearing of a plot against his life, he unwisely broke the truce and ordered the slaughter of all Danes in England. The bloody massacre was carried out on St. Brice's Day of that same year, and among the victims was Gunhild, Sweyn's sister.

The enraged Danish king intensified his raids to avenge the death of his sister. The greatest attack took place in 1012 when Sweyn sent the Jomsvikings [an order of Viking knights] into England under their chief Thorkel the Tall and young Olaf Haroldson of Norway. This time Ethelred bought the Vikings off with the tremendous Danegeld of 48,000 pounds of silver. He also hired Thorkel, Olaf, and some of the Jomsvikings to remain in his service.

The loss of his lieutenants—and of the forty-five of his ships that they kept—persuaded Sweyn to change his tactics. He attacked England with a great army, rallied the Danes in the Danelaw [an area in the northeast of England settled by Danish Vikings], and swept through the land, subduing section after section whose lords usually submitted to his overpowering force without a struggle. This was a new type of Viking invasion—whereas Ivar the Boneless and the chiefs of the Great Army had been content to let the English rule while they plundered, Sweyn was bent on national conquest. Before he died in 1014 he had overrun all of England, and Ethelred had fled to Normandy.

After the Danish king's death, the English recalled the unready Ethelred from his refuge with the Duke of Normandy and hailed him as king. Sweyn's twenty-year-old son Canute returned to Denmark for a larger army and came back the next year. Canute faced Ethelred's determined son Edmund Ironside, but the fierce young English patriot was defeated and forced to flee to stubbornly defended London. Here Ethelred, who had been too ill to fight, died, and Edmund was chosen king. After several more defeats, Edmund finally came to terms with

Canute. The kingdom was divided into two uneasy parts, Canute receiving the larger share, including London. When Edmund died in 1016, the nobles turned to the remaining strong man and crowned Canute undisputed king of all England.

This was the peak of triumph of the Viking Era. The Viking leader Rollo had gained a province in France in the early 900s. Other Viking chiefs had ruled as kings in cities of Ireland and in sections of England. But Canute ruled an entire country—and for twenty years he ruled it well. To consolidate the kingdom and ally himself with the powerful Normans across the Channel, he married Ethelred's widow, Emma, great-aunt of Duke William of Normandy. He declared he did not want England to be regarded as a colony, and to show his confidence in his new subjects he sent the Danish army home, keeping only a bodyguard of housecarls in England.

Canute's reign lasted until 1035. He was already king of Denmark, and he added the throne of Norway to his dominions. Scotland submitted to him and also the northern islands. This Viking king was an astute statesman as well as an able and just ruler. His reign was peaceful and constructive. Although he had been brought up among the Vikings, he permitted no Viking raids while he was king—and, with one important exception, there were no more Viking raids after he died.

The exception was in the year 1066. England was then ruled by Harold Godwinson, whose mother was half Danish and whose father had dominated Canute's successor, Edward the Confessor. Harold was a mighty figure, but he was plagued by his disloyal brother, Tostig, who felt he had an equal right to be king. Seeking support for his claim, Tostig journeyed among his mother's people in the Northland.

He found a ready ear in Harold Hardrada, the king of Norway, who was not loath to take the crown of England away from its rightful owner—to put it on his own head, not Tostig's. Tostig was willing to take second place, and he told Harold that he could induce several of the English earls to declare for him if he landed with a sufficiently strong army. Harold called out half of the Viking host and sailed for England with two hundred ships, picking up reinforcements from the Scottish isles on the way.

The Battle at Stamford Bridge

After winning a few skirmishes along the coast, Harold sailed up the Humber to attack York. First he won an easy battle outside the city, then Tostig induced the garrison to surrender. It was arranged for the Vikings to take possession of the castle the next day. They returned to their ships and celebrated. The next day dawned clear and hot; so hot in fact that two thirds of the men that Harold took toward York with him did not wear their armor. They expected to do some drinking and perhaps some plundering but no fighting.

   The Vikings did not know that the situation in York had changed during the night. Harold of England had arrived with his host and entered the city. As the Vikings marched casually toward their goal, a cloud of dust advanced from the city to meet them. Through it they could see the glint of sun on armor. Tostig advised retiring to the ships; Harold, who had never been defeated by Slavs or Saracens, Greeks or Sicilians, would have no part of this cautious advice. The two kings deployed their forces at Stamford Bridge—the half-Danish Harold of England faced the Norwegian Viking. Before the battle, twenty armored knights rode forward from the English line, and the leader called to Tostig, saying that his brother offered him the earldom of Northumbria if he would make peace.

   "And what," said Tostig, "does my brother offer my ally, Harold of Norway?"

   "To Harold of Norway, Harold of England will give seven feet of English ground, or as much more as he may be taller than other men," was the reply.

   When battle was joined, it was a hard and bloody one. The English charged the Viking shield wall and were repulsed, but when the Vikings broke the wall to pursue, their unarmored bodies were soft targets for English arrows. As they fell around him, the giant Harold of Norway seemed to go berserk and charged forward, cutting a swath through the enemy with great sweeps of his broadsword. His men rallied behind him, and the English started to fall back in confusion.

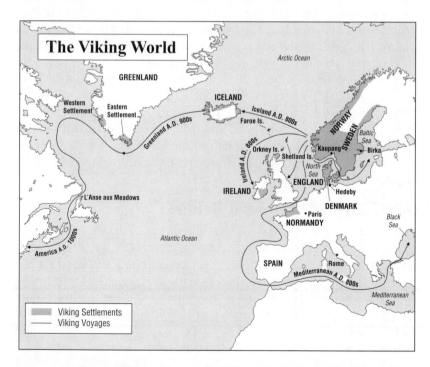

Then an arrow found its mark in Harold's unprotected throat, and he fell to win his seven feet of English ground, the last true Viking chieftain to die on foreign soil.

Harold of England's triumph was short-lived. An even more dangerous enemy was approaching to the south—Duke William of Normandy, great-great-grandson of the Viking Rollo. Harold hastened to face him with his depleted, battle-weary army, and a few days later, he fell with an arrow in his eye at the Battle of Hastings.

This famous battle of the Norman Conquest was no Viking affair, but, in a sense, it was an outcome of the Viking movement. Had there been no Vikings, there would have been neither a William the Conqueror nor a Harold of England, for Viking blood flowed strongly in the veins of both; and many of the men who fought with them on both sides could trace descent from the followers of Rollo in France and Ivar the Boneless in England and to the many Vikings who had later swelled the settlements in both countries.

The End of the Viking Age

Michael Gibson

The following piece, taken from Michael Gibson's book *The Vikings,* traces the events that led to the end of the Viking era during the middle of the eleventh century. In Gibson's view, social and political changes— both in the Scandinavian world and in Europe at large—reduced the incentives for Vikings to go on raids. For example, he writes, the western European countries that had once been easy prey for the Vikings had grown stronger and began to fiercely resist the Scandinavian invaders. The spread of Christianity throughout the Viking lands also contributed to the end of the raiders' lifestyle, he maintains. Gibson is the author of numerous histories and biographies, an editor, and an amateur archaeologist.

B y about 1066, the great days of the Vikings were over. The raids continued for some time, but were increasingly ineffective. What had happened?

Changes in the Viking World

Important social changes had taken place in the Scandinavian communities. In early Viking times there had been many petty kings whose power was confined to their immediate estates. But as the years passed, effective kingdoms were created by strong men like Olaf Tryggvason and Swein Forkbeard. The chieftains, who had played one king off against another, and gone raiding whenever they chose, found themselves reduced to the status of the king's representatives.

The struggle between the kings and the chieftains usually coincided with the battle between paganism and Christianity. Denmark was the first Scandinavian kingdom to be converted. Harald Bluetooth (945–985) was convinced of the power of Jesus by a brave little priest called Poppo who, according to *Olaf Tryggvason's Saga,* "picked up red hot iron bars and showed his unscorched hands to the King. Thereafter, King Harald and the whole Danish army were baptised."

King Hakon (945–960) was the first Christian King of Norway. But he had to tread carefully: "He was a good Christian when he came to Norway," says *Hakon the Good's Saga,* "but all the land was heathen and as he needed the help and friendship of the people, he decided to conceal his Christianity. When he had established himself in the land and fully subjected it to himself, he sent to England for a bishop and other priests." Norway's conversion was completed by Olaf Tryggvason (995–1000) and St. Olaf (1014– 30) who used terrorist methods.

The Swedes clung tenaciously to the old faith. An Anglo-Danish monk wrote gloomily at the beginning of the twelfth century: "As long as things go well, Svear and Goter seem willing to honour Christianity, but when they go wrong and there are bad harvests, droughts, storms, enemy attacks or outbreaks of fire, they persecute the Church they nominally support, not only with words but in deeds. They revenge themselves upon the Christians and seek to chase them right out of the country." Gradually, the Christian priests won and the old religion disappeared. Scandinavia was divided up into bishoprics and parishes and the bishops and priests supported the kings who were their protectors and kept law and order.

The great overseas migration of the Vikings was over. There was nowhere left to colonize—the Western Islands, Iceland and Greenland were fully settled. However, Scandinavian farming methods had improved and more land was brought under cultivation. At last they were able to satisfy their own needs.

Meanwhile, the Norse colonists in Ireland, the English Danelaw, Normandy and Russia were being absorbed by the native populations. They married the local girls and accepted the religion, language and customs of their adopted countries.

Raiding became more difficult: the rulers of Western Europe were stronger in the eleventh century than they had been in the ninth. Everywhere, Viking armies were being bloodily defeated. One of the most celebrated of these defeats took place at Clontarf in Ireland at the hands of the aged Brian Boru in 1014. The following description of the battle is from the medieval text *The War of the*

Gaedil with the Gaill: "On one side of the battle were the shouting, hard hearted, murderous Vikings. They had sharp, poisoned arrows which had been dipped in the blood of dragons, toads, scorpions and venomous snakes of all kinds. They were equipped with fine quivers and polished, shining yellow bows and strong spears. They wore heavy coats of mail of double refined iron and carried stout swords.

"On the other side were the brave Irishmen—the lions, wolfhounds and hawks of Ireland. They had spears and shields, broad axes and swords. They wore golden crested helmets and fine cloth tunics and shirts of many colours.

"When the battle began, Brian had his cushions spread upon the ground, opened his prayer book, put his hands together and prayed. The fighting continued from sunrise to sunset. . . . At the end of the day, the Irish gathered themselves for one last great effort and swept the Vikings from the field. In the excitement, the King's guards rushed off and joined in the killing.

"Then, three Vikings led by Earl Brodir approached the King. Brian arose and unsheathed his great two-handed sword. Brodir carried a gleaming battleaxe in his hand. He passed Brian without noticing him, but one of his men called out, 'This is the High King.' 'No,' said Earl Brodir, 'no, that is not he, but a noble priest.' 'By your leave,' insisted the soldier, 'that is Brian the High King.' At that, Brian struck Brodir with his sword and cut off his left leg and right foot. At

Viking raiders in their dragonships could not survive the changes of time.

the very same moment, the Viking dealt Brian a blow with his axe which cut off the King's head. Both fell dead to the ground."

The Viking Legacy

What had the Viking peoples achieved? Traditionally, historians have followed contemporary chroniclers and described them as barbarians who robbed, raped and murdered their way across Europe, wantonly destroying fine buildings and beautiful works of art. The Vikings did these things, but so did the other Europeans when they were fighting among themselves. What marked the Vikings out for special treatment by the chroniclers was their paganism.

On the credit side, the Vikings stimulated trade wherever they went and founded or developed thriving towns. Often, they taught the local people new skills like shipbuilding and coin making. The Vikings developed a distinctive art style, as anyone who looks at their swords, wood carvings and metal work can see. They produced a fine heroic literature—the Sagas—which forms part of our cultural heritage in the West.

Even their attacks had some value, since they forced their victims to stand together. For example, the Viking raids provided the stimulus for the conquest of England by the kings of Wessex and for the unification of the Slav tribes by the Rus.

Lastly, wherever they settled, they kept alive their own sense of personal freedom—when the Franks asked the Vikings who their leader was, they answered proudly, "We have no lord, we are all equal."

For two and a half centuries, the Vikings had terrorized Europe, but now people suddenly asked:

What has become of the warrior?
What has become of the steed?
What has become of the seats at the banquet?
Where are the joys of the hall?
O for the bright cup.
O for the mailclad warrior.
O for the glory of the prince.
Now that time has passed away
And grown dark under the cover of night
As if it had never been.

The First Crusade

The city of Jerusalem is holy to three religions: Judaism, Christianity, and Islam. Originally a Jewish city, Jerusalem came under Christian control during the Roman Empire. After the empire disintegrated in the fifth century, the Greek Christians of the Byzantine Empire governed Jerusalem and maintained the sites sacred to Christianity. The Islamic religion arose at the beginning of the seventh century, and the Muslims conquered Jerusalem in the year 638.

For several centuries, the Muslim rulers of Jerusalem cultivated a congenial relationship with the Christians, allowing them unhindered access to their sacred places and welcoming continual pilgrimages from Europe. Then in 1071, the Seljuk Turks wrested control of Jerusalem away from the Egyptian caliph. Unlike the Egyptian Muslims, the recently converted Seljuks were not inclined to practice religious tolerance toward the Christians. Pilgrims from western Europe could no longer obtain safe passage on the Seljuk-controlled routes to the Holy Land, and pilgrimages to the sacred sites drastically decreased.

In the same year, the Seljuks also scored a decisive victory against the Byzantine army at the Battle of Menzikert, allowing them to easily overrun much of the Byzantine Empire during the following decade. The Muslim incursions into the land of the Greek Christians concerned the western Europeans as much as the loss of Jerusalem, so when the Byzantine emperor appealed to Pope Urban II for help in fighting the Seljuks, the pope lost no time in deciding to call for a holy war—a crusade—to aid the Byzantines and to liberate Jerusalem.

The response to Urban's call was overwhelming. Thousands of nobles and knights pledged to free Jerusalem and began making preparations for their military campaign. Unexpectedly, the poor peasants also heeded Urban's appeal; thousands of commoners headed off to the Holy Land with sickles, pitchforks, and faith as their only weapons. A wave of religious fervor washed over Europe, making the impossible seem possible. This belief would sustain the crusaders through three long years of fighting in foreign and inhospitable lands, until they did in fact achieve the seemingly impossible: In July 1099, the crusader army entered the gates of Jerusalem in victory and claimed the city for Christianity.

The Origin of the First Crusade

Robert Payne

In the following selection from his book *The Dream and the Tomb: A History of the Crusades*, Robert Payne traces the events that led up to the First Crusade. Payne writes that in the middle of the eleventh century, the Seljuk Turks swept over much of the Muslim world. After converting to Islam, the Turks continued to expand their territory, conquering the holy city of Jerusalem and menacing the Christian rulers of the Byzantine Empire. The Byzantine army was routed by the Turks in the Battle of Menzikert in 1071, the author explains, and during the following years the Muslims continued to steadily chip away at the borders of the Byzantine Empire. Finally, Payne relates, the Byzantine emperor appealed to his fellow Christians in the West for aid in defending his territory against the Muslim invaders.

A t the beginning of the eleventh century, the Arab empire extended halfway across the known world from the Pyrenees to Persia. It had made inroads into India, and Arab armies were breaking through the Asiatic outposts of the Byzantine empire. The Muslims regarded Constantinople, the capital of the Byzantine empire, as the eastern gateway to Europe: it must be captured and all Europe must fall under their sway. . . .

It was as though Christianity and Islam were meant to engage in a death struggle, which would end only when one submitted to the other. Yet there were long periods when there was a kind of peace between them. Jerusalem, captured very early by the Arabs, was permitted to retain a Christian community, and the Church of the Holy Sepulchre remained untouched. . . . Throughout the ninth century, relations between Christians and Muslims were fairly amicable. The Christians demanded only that Jerusalem should be accessible to them, and that pilgrims to the Church of the Holy Sepulchre should be treated reasonably. And so it continued for another century. Even after the destruction of the church by the mad Caliph Hakim in 1009, there was peace, for the church was quickly restored. The pilgrims continued to come to Jerusalem, worshipping at the altars in the Church of the Holy Sepulchre, passing freely in and out of the city. It was as though the two religions had reached an accommodation, as though nothing would interrupt the continual flow of pilgrims.

The Seljuk Turks

In the middle years of the eleventh century there occurred an event that would cause a drastic change in the military posture of the Muslims in the Near East. The Seljuk Turks, advancing from Central Asia, conquered Persia. Converted to Islam, they moved with the zeal of converts, prosetylizing all the tribes they came upon in their lust for conquest. They had been herdsmen; they became raiders, cavalrymen, living off the earth, setting up their tents wherever they pleased, taking pleasure in sacking cities and leaving only ashes. The once all-powerful Caliph of Baghdad became the servant of the Seljuk Sultan Alp Arslan. In August 1071, the Seljuk army under Alp Arslan confronted the much larger army of the Byzantine Emperor Romanus IV Diogenes near Menzikert north of Lake Van in Armenia. Romanus was an emperor with vast military experience, brave to excess, commanding a hundred thousand well-trained troops, including many Frankish and German mercenaries. There was, however, treachery among his officers; orders were not obeyed. The lightly armed Seljuk cavalry poured thousands of arrows into the tight formations of the Byzantine army, and when the emperor ordered a retreat at the end of the day, his flanks were exposed, his army began to disintegrate, and the Turks rushed in to fill the vacuum created by his retreating troops. Romanus fought bravely; he was seriously wounded in the arm and his horse was killed under him. Captured, he was led to the tent of Alp Arslan in chains. There he was thrown to the ground, and Alp Arslan placed his foot ceremonially on the emperor's neck. The Seljuk sultan half-admired the broad-shouldered Byzantine emperor, and two weeks later the emperor was allowed to go free. Still the defeat was so decisive, so shattering, that the emperor fell from grace in the eyes of the Byzantines, who had no difficulty deposing him. When he returned to Constantinople, he was blinded, and in the following year he died either from the injuries caused by the blinding or of a broken heart.

Although Alp Arslan himself, and his son Malek Shah, had no thought of conquering the Byzantine empire, the chieftains who served under them had different ideas. They poured into the undefended provinces of Anatolia. While the Christians remained in the towns, the invading Turks ravaged the countryside. Gone were the days when the Byzantine empire stretched from Egypt to the Danube and from the borders of Persia to southern Italy. The Turks advanced to Nicaea, less than a hundred miles from Constantinople, and occupied the city, making it the capital of the sultanate that ruled over Asia Minor. The Turks were spreading out in all directions. In the same year that saw the Byzantine defeat at Manzikert, they captured Jerusalem from the Arabs of Egypt on behalf of the Caliph of Baghdad. In 1085 Malek Shah captured Antioch from the Byzantines. Malek Shah himself came to the Palestinian shore and dipped his sword in the waters of the Mediterranean, a ceremony by which he asserted that the Mediterranean itself belonged to him. . . .

Christendom was reeling from the Turkish invasions. In a single generation Asia Minor had fallen into their hands. The Byzantine empire had lost the sources of its greatest wealth. Christians could no longer be assured that they could journey to Jerusalem without being arrested or sold into slavery or ill treated in other ways. The Turks were fanatical Muslims, determined to exact the last ounce of power from their victories. But their survival as a united people depended on their leader, and when Malek Shah died in 1091, the empire was divided up among his sons and nephews, whose hatred for one another contributed to the early success of the Crusaders when at last they made their way across Asia Minor in order to recover Jerusalem.

An Appeal from Constantinople

In 1081, Alexius Comnenus, who had served in the army of Romanus IV Diogenes as a general fighting against the inroads of the Turks, came to the throne at the age of thirty-three. He was an able commander in the field and uncompromising in his determination to regain the lost provinces of his empire. . . . He reigned for thirty-seven years, recaptured some of the lost provinces, and there were few Byzantine emperors who reigned so long or fought so well.

When Alexius Comnenus came to the throne, the empire was in disarray. . . . He was confronted with dangers along the long Danube border from the Oghuz, Kuman, and Pecheneg Turks, half brothers to the Turks in Asia Minor, and from Slavs and Bulgars. Only a few coastal cities in Asia Minor remained in his hands. It was necessary at all costs to push back the frontiers of the sultanate of Roum. He appealed for military assistance to the pope and to the Western princes who might be sympathetic to his cause. They were asked to raise armies, to march to Constantinople and to join forces under the banner of Christendom against the infidels. He recounted the atrocities committed by the enemy and pointed to the peculiar sanctity of Constantinople as the guardian of so many relics of Christ. Constantinople and the Byzantine empire must be saved, Jerusalem must be reconquered, and the *pax Christiana* [Christian peace] must be established in the Near East. A copy of his letter to Robert, Count of Flanders, a cousin of William the Conqueror, has been preserved. The emperor speaks with mingled anguish and pride, despair and humility. . . .

Mingling allurements and enticements with intimations of the final disaster that would overwhelm the community of Christians if the Turks and Pechenegs succeeded in conquering what was left of the Byzantine empire, Alexius Comnenus appealed to Robert of Flanders to come to his aid. The letter contained admissions of terrible defeats and was sustained by a vast pride, but it also provided a picture of the world as he saw it, with its pressing dangers and wildest hopes. Two images prevailed: the atrocities committed by the enemy, and the spiritual and material wealth of Constantinople, last bastion against the Turks.

The letter was addressed not only to Robert of Flanders but to Western Christendom. Pope Urban II read it and was deeply moved. . . . And now very slowly and with immense difficulty there came into existence the machinery that would bring the armies of the West to Constantinople and later to Jerusalem.

Pope Urban's Call for the First Crusade

Antony Bridge

Antony Bridge is a professional painter, an ordained minister, and the author of several histories and biographies. In the following excerpt from his book *The Crusades*, Bridge describes the background and character of Pope Urban II, the architect of the First Crusade. According to Bridge, Urban was a gentle man who was greatly disturbed by accounts of the Turks' brutal treatment of the Eastern Christians. However, Bridge notes, Urban was also a dynamic, forceful leader who possessed the ability to sway hearts and minds. Urban's decision to call on the Western Christians to aid the Byzantines and liberate Jerusalem was the spark that ignited the First Crusade, the author concludes.

T he Pope to whom the Byzantine Emperor appealed for help was Pope Urban II. He was an impressive man, who had been born in Châtillon-sur-Marne of a noble French family. He had become a monk at Cluny before he was thirty years old and Cardinal Bishop of Ostia before he was forty; then, in March 1088, when he was about forty-six, he had been made Pope.

Restoring Power to the Papacy

He could not have ascended the throne of St Peter at a more difficult time; the Papacy and the German Emperor had been locked in a power struggle for years, and at the time of Urban's election the Emperor Henry IV was having very much the better of it. There had been a celebrated incident, in the days of one of Urban's predecessors when the Emperor had been forced to wait humbly, bare-foot and dressed in the clothes of a penitent, in the courtyard of the Castle at Canossa in order to receive absolution from Pope Gregory VII, who had excommunicated him; but those days were gone, and the tables had been turned with a vengeance. Henry was triumphant everywhere; he was supported by an anti-Pope (a failed candidate in the papal elections) who reigned supreme in the city of Rome itself, and he had no patience with Urban, whom he regarded as an obstinate man. Indeed, it had not been long since he had imprisoned him in Germany for his stubborn support of Pope Gregory.

Now Gregory was dead, and Urban brought to the task of reasserting the power of the Papacy a formidable array of talents which were destined to redress the balance between himself and the German Emperor. He was gentle, firm, courteous and peace loving; he hated bloodshed, avoided controversy, and won people's hearts by a combination of forbearance and innate authority, so that he had not been Pope for five years before he was acknowledged by everyone to be the spiritual leader of western Christendom. Having won the western Church, he turned eastwards in an attempt to improve the strained relations which existed with the Byzantines. Emperor Alexius responded warmly, and it was not long before the two men were, at least by correspondence, firm friends. As a result, Byzantine ambassadors were despatched by Alexius to Urban's first great Council, which was held at Cremona in March 1095, and there they explained on the Emperor's behalf the plight of Christians in the East under Turkish domination. The assembled bishops were deeply shocked, and so was Urban. It is almost certain that it was at Cremona that he first began to think of calling upon the Christians of the West to rally to the aid of their eastern brothers and sisters in Christ, but for the moment he did nothing. He was a cautious man, and he needed time to develop the idea which had occurred to him.

By November of the same year, he had made up his mind. He travelled in a leisurely way through France, occupying himself with various affairs of the Church which needed his attention, and eventually he summoned the bishops of France and its neighbouring countries to a Council at Clermont. Over three hundred bishops assembled there on the eighteenth of the month, and for the first few days they concerned themselves with routine business of one kind or another: King Philip of France was excommunicated for adultery and the Bishop of Cambrai for simony, the Truce of God was reaffirmed and urged on everyone, and the seniority of the See of Lyons over two rival Sees was established. Then, just before the Council was about to end, Urban let it be known that he wanted to make an important announcement before everyone went home, and that he would do so in public session on Tuesday, 27 November.

Proclaiming the Crusade

The crowds which assembled that day to hear what the Pope might have to say were so great that room could not be found for them in the Cathedral where the Council had met hitherto, and a platform for the Pope to stand on was erected in a field outside the eastern gate of the city. Amongst his many talents, Urban had a gift for oratory, and on this occasion he used it to the full; his audience listened to him spellbound. Christians in the East had appealed to him for help, he told them; the Turks were advancing into Christian lands, maltreating innocent men and women and desecrating their churches. This was bad enough, but the desecration of Jerusalem with its multitude of holy places and the appalling indignities and brutalities to which pilgrims to the Holy Land were being subjected, was even worse. It was time for Christians in the West to rise up in righteous wrath and march to the rescue; let them stop making war on each other at home and wage a holy war against God's enemies instead. God himself would lead them, and give them the victory, and to all who died in battle he, Pope Urban, promised there and then absolution and remission of all their sins. Why were they wasting their lives in sin and misery here, when they could be finding happiness in this world and salvation in the next as soldiers of Christ in the land where Christ had lived and died? There must be no delay; the time was ripe for action, and when the summer came, the armies of Christ must be mobilised and ready to move.

It was heady stuff, and the response was immediate and overwhelming. There were cries of *'Dieu le volt'*—'God wills it'—as people gave vent to the emotions which Urban had aroused in them. The Bishop of Le Puy, a man named Adhemar, fell on his knees before the Pope and begged to be allowed to join the expedition to the Holy Land; a Cardinal began to say the *Confiteor* in a loud voice and thousands joined in, and when it was over Urban gave them absolution, and told them to go home and pray about what he had told them, dismissing them with his blessing. Nor was their departure the signal for a return to normal life and the end of their enthusiasm; on the contrary, the Pope had started something even greater than he could have expected, and great waves of enthusiasm spread out from Clermont across the whole of France to spill over into all the western European countries and set their people alight. Everywhere, bishops, priests and monks began to preach a holy war against the Turks in order to liberate the Holy Land.

The Speech at Clermont

Pope Urban II

Pope Urban II was perhaps the most dynamic of the reforming popes of the eleventh century. Like his predecessors, Urban concentrated on establishing the authority and effectiveness of the Catholic Church through a series of reforms. He also used his considerable diplomatic skills to repair papal relations with secular monarchs and nobles, which had been weakened during the investiture controversy. His ability to inspire and mobilize popular support is most clearly seen in the overwhelming response to his proclamation of the First Crusade. Urban's speech at the Council of Clermont is extant in several different versions. The following excerpt is taken from the version written around 1107 by a monk known as Robert of Rheims, who most likely was present at the Council of Clermont.

Oh, race of Franks, race from across the mountains, race chosen and beloved by God—as shines forth in very many of your works—set apart from all nations by the situation of your country, as well as by your catholic faith and the honor of the holy church! To you our discourse is addressed and for you our exhortation is intended. We wish you to know what a grievous cause has led us to your country, what peril threatening you and all the faithful has brought us.

From the confines of Jerusalem and the city of Constantinople a horrible tale has gone forth and very frequently has been brought to

Excerpted from Pope Urban II, speech given at the Council of Clermont, version given by Robert the Monk, in *Translations and Reprints from the Original Sources of European History,* edited by Dana C. Munro.

our ears, namely, that a race from the kingdom of the Persians, an accursed race, a race utterly alienated from God, a generation forsooth which has not directed its heart and has not entrusted its spirit to God, has invaded the lands of those Christians and has depopulated them by the sword, pillage and fire; it has led away a part of the captives into its own country, and a part it has destroyed by cruel tortures; it has either entirely destroyed the churches of God or appropriated them for the rites of its own religion. They destroy the altars, after having defiled them with their uncleanness. They circumcise the Christians, and the blood of the circumcision they either spread upon the altars or pour into the vases of the baptismal font. When they wish to torture people by a base death, they perforate their navels, and dragging forth the extremity of the intestines, bind it to a stake; then with flogging they lead the victim around until the viscera having gushed forth the victim falls prostrate upon the ground. Others they bind to a post and pierce with arrows. Others they compel to extend their necks and then, attacking them with naked swords, attempt to cut through the neck with a single blow. What shall I say of the abominable rape of the women? To speak of it is worse than to be silent. The kingdom of the Greeks is now dismembered by them and deprived of territory so vast in extent that it can not be traversed in a march of two months. On whom therefore is the labor of avenging these wrongs and of recovering this territory incumbent, if not upon you? You, upon whom above other nations God has conferred remarkable glory in arms, great courage, bodily activity, and strength to humble the hairy scalp of those who resist you.

Let the deeds of your ancestors move you and incite your minds to manly achievements; the glory and greatness of king Charles the Great, and of his son Louis, and of your other kings, who have destroyed the kingdoms of the pagans, and have extended in these lands the territory of the holy church. Let the holy sepulchre of the Lord our Saviour, which is possessed by unclean nations, especially incite you, and the holy places which are now treated with ignominy and irreverently polluted with their filthiness. Oh, most valiant soldiers and descendants of invincible ancestors, be not degenerate, but recall the valor of your progenitors.

The Glories of Jerusalem

But if you are hindered by love of children, parents and wives, remember what the Lord says in the Gospel, "He that loveth father or mother more than me, is not worthy of me." "Every one that hath forsaken houses, or brethren, or sisters, or father, or mother, or wife, or children, or lands for my name's sake shall receive an hundredfold and shall inherit everlasting life." Let none of your possessions detain you, no solicitude for your family affairs, since this land which you inhabit, shut in on all sides by the seas and surrounded by the mountain peaks, is too narrow for your large population; nor does it abound in wealth; and it furnishes scarcely food enough for its cultivators. Hence it is that you murder and devour one another, that you wage war, and that frequently you perish by mutual wounds. Let therefore hatred depart from among you, let your quarrels end, let wars cease, and let all dissensions and controversies slumber. Enter upon the road to the Holy Sepulchre; wrest that land from the wicked race, and subject it to yourselves. That land which as the Scripture says "floweth with milk and honey," was given by God into the possession of the children of Israel.

Jerusalem is the navel of the world; the land is fruitful above others, like another paradise of delights. This the Redeemer of the human race has made illustrious by His advent, has beautified by residence, has consecrated by suffering, has redeemed by death, has glorified by burial. This royal city, therefore, situated at the centre of the world, is now held captive by His enemies, and is in subjection to those who do not know God, to the worship of the heathens. She seeks therefore and desires to be liberated, and does not cease to implore you to come to her aid. From you especially she asks succor, because, as we have already said, God has conferred upon you above all nations great glory in arms. Accordingly undertake this journey for the remission of your sins, with the assurance of the imperishable glory of the kingdom of heaven.

The Peasants' Crusade

Martin Erbstösser

Pope Urban II intended the First Crusade to be a military expedition of knights, nobles, and trained military men. However, while the crusader army was still making preparations for the march to Jerusalem, thousands of peasants banded together and set off to liberate the Holy Land in what became known as the Peasants' Crusade. According to Martin Erbstösser, a professor at the University of Leipzig in Germany, the participants in the Peasants' Crusade were not only motivated by religious fervor; they also desired to escape their impoverished lives, made worse during the final years of the 1000s by frequent famines and plagues. These ill-prepared crusaders ravaged the countryside for food and terrorized Jewish communities before meeting their doom at the hands of the superior Seljuk army, he relates. Erbstösser is the author of *The Crusades*, from which the following piece is taken.

It was not the clergy who laid the groundwork for the Peasants' Crusade and even the Pope had not thought of a direct mobilization of the common people, even though he would have probably welcomed the spirit that a general movement of this kind would have inspired. It was rather the case that the wave of agitation emanated from a particular group of preachers. Traditionally and to a certain extent in respect of some of the individually involved, too, it followed a socio-religious movement which had achieved a certain success in various regions of France in the last years of the 11th century. This was the movement of the "itinerant preachers". Priests and monks had retired to woods and other lonely spots and lived there in extreme poverty, in accordance with the precept that in this way they were closest to the ideals of Christ. In their sermons, they not only lauded this way of life but also violently attacked the wealthy Church which had moved away from the tenets of the Early Church in every respect. Their followers were peasants, charcoal burners and those who had lost their homes and sought refuge in the woods where they cleared the land and found a new life. The common people listened to the words of these itinerant preachers with enthusiasm. They respected these men since in their way of life and in what they preached they saw, above all, a kind of Christianity which was very close to their own miserable condition and contrasted with the material prosperity of the clergy. This movement was one form of opposition to the feudal Church among the ordinary people and, in a specific historical context, it supported the policy of the reform papacy against the wealthy priests with their worldly outlook.

Peter the Hermit

It was from this band of itinerant preachers that the principal voice of the Peasants' Crusade came—Peter the Hermit. In all likelihood a member of a knightly family of Picardy, he was a well-known and beloved itinerant preacher even before the Crusade movement. In appearance he was an impressive sight. He was of small stature and his skin was dark brown in colour and covered with dirt. It was said that his face resembled that of the donkey on which he rode. Peter went barefoot, ate neither bread nor meat and apparently lived mainly on fish and wine. This is precisely the characteristic of the itinerant preacher living in poverty.

Peter's power of suggestion must have been tremendous. Chroniclers depict him as a passionate zealot of extraordinary eloquence. An abbot characterized his activities in the following words: "Of that which he received, he gave generously to the poor. He did not send wenches to their future husbands without a dowry. In feuds and quarrels he established peace everywhere with remarkable authority." All this endeared him to the peasants and explains the popularity of Peter. He was venerated as an apostle of peace and a saint and people crowded around him, trying to touch him or his donkey or to get hairs from his steed as relics.

Not very much is known of what he said in the sermons he held immediately after the Council of Clermont in Central France, to begin with, and then in Champagne and Lorraine. We may be sure that he spoke of a heavenly message which promised that the Christians, with divine help, would succeed in freeing Jerusalem from the heathens without difficulty. According to versions from other chroniclers in which he preached the same message, he related, as divine evidence, a vision which came to him at the Sepulchre of Christ on the occasion of his pilgrimage to Jerusalem. . . .

The Peasants' Motives

The peasants who followed Peter the Hermit and the other Crusade preachers were attracted by the idea of the Crusade because the objective social circumstances had caused an exceptionally severe deterioration in their economic situation. Their material basis, which had been precarious enough before, became significantly worse in 1095 in the centres of the Peasants' Crusade movement, this being due to floods, famine and epidemics. For economic reasons, the even more extreme impoverishment which followed made it easier for the peasants to leave the soil, which was not their property anyway. The result of years of famine such as these was that increasing numbers of peasants were to be found wandering around the country since they had lost their means of livelihood and had been obliged to leave the area where they had spent their lives. In this situation, they made their way to the towns, provided additional labour for clearing new land or wandered through the countryside as beggars. All this made the work of the Crusade preachers relatively easy. A chronicler revealed a very perceptive appreciation of these less obvious factors when he wrote: "The West Franks can be easily persuaded to abandon their land since Gaul has been plagued for some years by discord among the people, famine and many deaths."

The columns which followed the preachers accordingly did not resemble organized military detachments so much as a legitimate flight from misery. The few material possessions which the people could not take with them were hurriedly sold. Entire families set off with their domestic utensils and agricultural implements.

> Poor people shoed their oxen with iron like horses, harnessed them to two-wheeled carts, loaded them with their few provisions and young children and walked behind them; and as soon as the young children caught sight of a castle or a town, they asked if this was Jerusalem.

This is how the scene was recorded by a historian. Only a few of these peasants possessed weapons in the military sense or knew how to use them.

What the peasants on the move actually expected was of a highly imaginative character. They looked forward to the second coming of Jesus Christ who they hoped would put an end to the actual misery of the ordinary people on earth. Jerusalem was not simply regarded as a worthy place of pilgrimage but took on supernatural features. For many of the people of the time, the earthly and heavenly Jerusalem were the same place, the journey to this holy place was the beginning of the final period of the World and the return of the state of paradise on Earth was believed to be imminent. Many of Peter's flock believed that the journey to Jerusalem would take them to the land of milk and honey described in the Bible when the legions of the Anti-Christ had been vanquished.

All unusual phenomena of Nature such as locust plagues or the appearance of shooting stars were regarded not only by the participants but also by the general public as signs of God indicating that a Crusade should be undertaken. The chroniclers of the time report numerous interpretations of this kind, occasionally not without highly sarcastic comments.

The Peasants' Crusade was a spontaneous happening. Peter, the mainspring of it, travelled from village to village, from town to town, and his adherents followed him. It was a similar story with other preachers. In all, according to the unreliable statistics, some fifty to seventy thousand people took part in the Peasants' Crusade. They consisted of a number of groups which set out in the direction of Jerusalem from Central and Eastern France, the Netherlands and the Rhineland. The historical sources record that they included not only peasants and artisans but also beggars, thieves and tricksters. Apart from Peter the Hermit, their leaders are said to have been Walter the Penniless (Sans-Avoir), a French knight, a certain Gottschlak from the Rhineland, a man known as Volkmar and finally the knight Emicho of Leiningen. There will be further mention of the evil role played by the latter.

Peter the Hermit and Walter the Penniless were the leaders of the French groups while the others mainly looked after the people from the Rhineland although they, too, benefited from the rousing effect of the sermons that Peter had delivered in the cities of the Rhineland in support of the Crusade.

Peasants' Crusade, 1096
Route of Peter the Hermit

Violence Against the Jews

The departure of the individual contingents was associated with the first pogroms of the Jews in mediaeval Europe. Relatively large Jewish communities had become established in the flourishing trading cities. Not being allowed to work as artisans, they traded with the Orient and also handled money transactions, benefitting from the fact that Christians were not permitted to charge interest on loans. In addition, they had made a name for themselves in the thriving cities through their skills in the sphere of medicine where their abilities far surpassed the general standards in Europe. The Jews had no rights as citizens but they were respected and prosperous. They dwelt in separate districts of the cities and as communities led a very active intellectual and religious life. Of profound religious convictions, each community possessed a synagogue of its own. Close relations were maintained between the individual communities. Thus Metz in the 11th century was the intellectual centre of all the Jewish communities in the cities of the Rhineland and Lorraine.

Almost all the Jewish communities of the Rhineland cities in particular experienced trials and tribulations of a horrifying nature as the individual bands of peasants passed through. Extortion, plundering and mass-murder were the loathsome results. The Jewish colonies in Metz, Speyer, Worms, Mainz, Cologne, Neuss, Xanthen and Trier were exposed to this terror in one form or another. There is also evidence of a whole series of persecutions even in smaller places. Bamberg and Prague also suffered in the further course of the expedition. Contemporary reports of the situation in French cities are unclear. It is known for certain that the Jews of Rouen were subjected to extortion but there is no other information in the old accounts. . . .

Research has shown that the encouragement for the Jewish pogroms came from the ranks of the Church reformers. . . . The reformers did not hesitate to direct the anger of the people against the "murderers of Christ" and to stir up hatred. Time and again, we hear of preachers who adroitly aroused feelings against the Jews. In Rouen, words of the following tenor were used: "We have a long way to go against the enemies of God but his worst adversaries, the Jews, stand before us. Is it not precipitate to overlook them.". . . However, there were also other factors which became apparent in the course of the terror and plundering and caused a further deterioration in the state of affairs.

In the first phase, the Crusaders only indulged in extortion, as in Rouen and Trier where the peasants led by Peter the Hermit demanded money from the Jews, to buy equipment for their journey to the Orient. Indeed, the peasants were in no position to feed and arm themselves during the journey by legal means so that they were only too ready to heed the whisperings of the reformers. In Hungary and the Balkans, they made the same material demands on the Christian population and again underlined their demands by plundering. This method of enrichment rapidly became a habit. Peter showed the Jewish communities of the Rhineland a "letter of introduction" from French Jews in which they were urged to give the Crusaders material assistance on their journey. Peter had quickly learned to exploit the possibilities of extortion.

The deciding phase of the pogrom began with the organization of the "German contingents" and the groups led by Emicho of Leiningen in particular were notorious for their bestial cruelty. A vivid account of what happened in Mainz has survived. Emicho laid siege to the city and demanded a ransom from the Jews in return for sparing their lives. Having received the money, he nevertheless stormed the city. The archbishop, who happened to be a relative of Emicho, left the Jews who had sought refuge in his palace to their fate. It was a hopeless situation. The oldest people were first killed. At the same time, the Jews themselves now began to kill their own people in ritual form. Women killed their sons, husbands their wives and each neighbour killed the other. Only a few fell into the hands of their enemies. They were given the choice of baptism or death. The Jews of Mainz refused to be baptized and were murdered.

In the second phase of the pogrom, more importance was attached to the baptism of the Jews. Thus members of both the Trier and Bamberg congregations, for example, physically survived the second phase of the terror by allowing themselves to be converted, they nevertheless suffered severe financial losses. The desire, born from religious fanaticism, to convert the Jews by force was a consequence of the ideology of fighting against the enemies of Christ, against the Anti-Christ. However, this seems only to have been a front for the greed of especially those people around Emicho of Leiningen who is known to have considered the acquisition of personal wealth to be a matter of prime importance. He deliberately organized a series of pogroms under this pretext. For him, the heady sentiment of his followers was only a means to an end. . . .

The Demise of the Peasants' Crusade

The peasant bands of the first Crusade marched upstream along the Rhine, the Neckar and the Danube in separate groups with the intention of reaching Constantinople via the Balkans. Only the first two groups, the French peasants under the leadership of Walter the Penniless and Peter the Hermit, succeeded in reaching this intermediate station after many difficulties. On the way there, plundering and violence had become a habit. What the Jews of the Rhineland had been forced to give was now taken from the Christian population. The inhabitants of the Hungarian villages were particularly hard-hit in this respect. Granaries were taken by storm, livestock driven from the fields and the population of the various regions mistreated. The news of the preparations in Europe had already reached Byzantium and the emperor, as a precaution, had stocks of food placed in readiness. Nevertheless, the population of the country were shocked at the sight of the hordes of peasants. The groups were escorted to Constantinople. Here, too, the bands of Walter and Peter began to plunder. Public buildings were ransacked and lead panels ripped from the roofs and sold. Without losing much time, the Byzantine emperor had the Crusaders taken over to Asia Minor in August 1096. The column did not get very far. Untrained in the handling of weapons and without experience in military tactics, they were totally at the mercy of the Seljuks. To begin with, one group was surrounded and cut off. Not possessing any reserves of water, they suffered such thirst that they opened the arteries of the donkeys and horses that they had brought with them. On 21 October, the main group was ambushed by the Seljuks at Civetot and killed to the last man. The knights of the first Crusade passed by the great piles of bones, the mortal remains of the first two groups. . . .

The bands of German peasants did not reach Constantinople at all. Some groups under the leadership of the knights contented themselves with persecuting Jews. The columns under Volkmar and Emicho got as far as Hungary. Plundering began already in the border districts with the result that Kolman, the Hungarian king, sent his army out to meet the bands of peasants who were defeated after a few skirmishes. The great majority of them were killed, while other members of the Peasants' Crusade had already turned back or found new homes en route.

And so the Peasants' Crusade ended long before it had even reached Jerusalem.

A Byzantine's View of the First Crusaders

Anna Comnena

Most historians agree that although Alexius Comnenus, the Byzantine emperor, did appeal to western Europe for military aid, he did not expect the massive armies that arrived at Constantinople, much less the ragged and unruly rabble of the Peasants' Crusade. Alexius was especially alarmed by the presence of Bohemund and his Norman troops from southern Italy, old enemies who had previously attacked the Byzantine Empire. The emperor's daughter, Anna Comnena, was a teenager during the First Crusade and later wrote *The Alexiad*, which recounts the events of her father's reign. In the following excerpt, Anna depicts the crusaders as uncivilized and untrustworthy barbarians.

The Emperor heard a report of the approach of innumerable Frankish armies. Now he dreaded their arrival for he knew their irresistible manner of attack, their unstable and mobile character and all the peculiar natural and concomitant characteristics which the Frank retains throughout; and he also knew that they were always agape for money, and seemed to disregard their truces readily for any reason that cropped up. For he had always heard this reported of them, and found it very true. However, he did not lose heart, but prepared himself in every way so that, when the occasion called, he would be

Excerpted from Anna Comnena in *The Alexiad of the Princess Anna Comnena,* translated by Elizabeth A.S. Dawes (New York: Barnes & Noble, Inc., 1967).

ready for battle. And indeed the actual facts were far greater and more terrible than rumour made them. For the whole of the West and all the barbarian tribes which dwell between the further side of the Adriatic and the pillars of Heracles, had all migrated in a body and were marching into Asia through the intervening Europe, and were making the Journey with all their household. The reason of this upheaval was more or less the following. A certain Frank, Peter [the Hermit] by name, nicknamed Cucupeter [Peter of the Cowl], had gone to worship at the Holy Sepulchre and after suffering many things at the hands of the Turks and Saracens who were ravaging Asia, he got back to his own country with difficulty. But he was angry at having failed in his object, and wanted to undertake the same journey again. However, he saw that he ought not to make the journey to the Holy Sepulchre alone again, lest worse things befall him, so he worked out a cunning plan. This was to preach in all the Latin countries that 'the voice of God bids me announce to all the Counts in France that they should all leave their homes and set out to worship at the Holy Sepulchre, and to endeavour wholeheartedly with hand and mind to deliver Jerusalem from the hand of the Hagarenes [the Muslims].' And he really succeeded. For after inspiring the souls of all with this quasi-divine command he contrived to assemble the Franks from all sides, one after the other, with arms, horses and all the other paraphernalia of war. And they were all so zealous and eager that every highroad was full of them. And those Frankish soldiers were accompanied by an unarmed host more numerous than the sand or the stars, carrying palms and crosses on their shoulders; women and children, too, came away from their countries. And the sight of them was like many rivers streaming from all sides, and they were advancing towards us through Dacia generally with all their hosts. . . .

A Horde of Locusts

The incidents of the barbarians' approach followed in the order I have described, and persons of intelligence could feel that they were witnessing a strange occurrence. The arrival of these multitudes did not take place at the same time nor by the same road (for how indeed could such masses starting from different places have crossed the straits of Lombardy all together?) Some first, some next, others after them and thus successively all accomplished the transit, and then marched through the Continent. Each army was preceded . . . by an unspeakable number of locusts; and all who saw this more than once recognized them as forerunners of the Frankish armies. When the first of them began crossing the straits of Lombardy sporadically the Emperor summoned certain leaders of the [Byzantine] forces, and sent them to the parts of Dyrrachium and Valona with instructions to offer a courteous welcome to the Franks who had crossed, and to collect abundant supplies from all the countries along their route; then to follow and watch them covertly all the time, and if they saw them making any foraging-excursions, they were to come out from under cover and check them by light skirmishing. These captains were accompanied by some men who knew the Latin tongue, so that they might settle any disputes that arose between them.

Let me, however, give an account of this subject more clearly and in due order. According to universal rumour Godfrey [the count of Bouillon], who had sold his country, was the first to start on the appointed road; this man was very rich and very proud of his bravery, courage and conspicuous lineage; for every Frank is anxious to outdo the others. And such an upheaval of both men and women took place then as had never occurred within human memory, the simpler-minded were urged on by the real desire of worshipping at our Lord's Sepulchre, and visiting the sacred places; but the more astute, especially men like Bohemund [the son of Robert Guiscard] and those of like mind, had another secret reason, namely, the hope that while on their travels they might by some means be able to seize the capital itself, looking upon this as a kind of corollary. And Bohemund disturbed the minds of many nobler men by thus cherishing his old grudge against the Emperor. [In the early 1080s, Robert Guiscard and Bohemund had fought Alexius in an attempt to conquer the Byzantine Empire.] Meanwhile Peter, after he had delivered his message, crossed the straits of Lombardy before anybody else with eighty thousand men on foot, and one hundred thousand on horseback, and reached the capital by way of Hungary. For the Frankish race, as one may conjecture, is always very hotheaded and eager, but when once it has espoused a cause, it is uncontrollable.

The Emperor, knowing what Peter had suffered before from the Turks, advised him to wait for the arrival of the other Counts, but Peter would not listen for he trusted to the multitude of his followers, so crossed and pitched his camp near a small town called Helenopolis. After him followed the Normans numbering ten thousand, who separated themselves from the rest of the army and devastated the country round [the Muslim-controlled town of] Nicaea, and behaved most cruelly to all. For they dismembered some of the children and fixed others on wooden spits and roasted them at the fire, and on persons advanced in age they inflicted every kind of torture. But when the inhabitants of Nicaea became aware of these doings, they threw open their gates and marched out upon them, and after a violent conflict had taken place they had to dash back inside their citadel as the Normans fought so bravely. And thus the latter recovered all the booty and returned to Helenopolis. Then a dispute arose between them and the others who had not gone out with them, as is usual in such cases, for the minds of those who had stayed behind were aflame with envy, and thus caused a skirmish after which the headstrong Normans drew apart again, marched to Xerigordus and took it by assault. When the Sultan heard what had happened, he dispatched Elchanes against them with a substantial force. He came, and recaptured Xerigordus and sacrificed some of the Normans to the sword, and took others captive, at the same time laid plans to catch those who had remained behind with Cucupeter. He placed ambushes in suitable spots so that any coming from the camp in the direction of Nicaea would fall into them unexpectedly and be killed. Besides this, as he knew the Franks' love of money, he sent for two active-minded men and ordered them to go to Cucupeter's camp and proclaim there that the Normans had gained possession of Nicaea, and were now dividing everything in it. When this report was circulated among Peter's followers, it upset them terribly. Directly they heard the words 'partition' and 'money' they started in a disorderly crowd along the road to Nicaea, all but unmindful of their military experience and the discipline which is essential for those starting out to battle. For, as I remarked above, the Latin race is always very fond of money, but more especially when it is bent on raiding a country; it then loses its reason and gets beyond control. As they journeyed neither in ranks nor in squadrons, they fell foul of the Turkish ambuscades near the river Dracon and perished miserably. . . .

The Battle on Good Friday

Now Count Godfrey crossed about this time, too, with more Counts, and an army of ten thousand horsemen and seventy thousand foot, and on reaching the capital he quartered his army near the Propontis, and it reached from the bridge nearest to the monastery of Cosmidium right up to the church of St. Phocas. But when the Emperor urged him to cross the straits of the Propontis, he let one day pass after another and postponed doing so on one pretext after another; the truth was that he was awaiting the arrival of Bohemund and the rest of the Counts. For although Peter for his part undertook this great journey originally only to worship at the Holy Sepulchre, yet the rest of the Counts, and especially Bohemund, who cherished an old grudge against the Emperor, were seeking an opportunity of taking their vengeance on him for that brilliant victory he had gained over Bohemund when he engaged in battle with him at Larissa. The other Counts agreed to Bohemund's plan, and in their dreams of capturing the capital had come to the same decision (which I have often mentioned already) that while in appearance making the journey to Jerusalem, in reality their object was to dethrone the Emperor and to capture the capital. But the Emperor, aware of their rascality from previous experience, sent an order by letter that the auxiliary forces with their officers should move from Athyra to Phileas (a seaside town on the Euxine) and station themselves there by squadrons, and watch whether any messenger came from Godfrey to Bohemund and the other Counts behind, or contrariwise one from them to him, and if so, to prevent their passage. But in the meantime the following incident occurred. The Emperor invited some of the Counts with Godfrey in order to advise them to suggest to Godfrey to take [an] oath [of loyalty to the Emperor]; and as time was wasted owing to the long-winded talkativeness of the Latins, a false rumour reached the others that the Counts had been thrown into prison by the Emperor. Immediately numerous regiments moved on Byzantium, and to begin with they demolished the palace near the so-called Silver Lake. They also made an attack on the walls of Byzantium, not with siege-engines indeed, as they had none, but trusting to their numbers they actually had the impudence to try to set fire to the gate below the palace which is close to the chapel built long ago by one of the Emperors to the memory of Nicolas, the greatest saint in the hierarchy. Now it was not only the promiscuous mob of Byzantines, who were utterly cowardly and unused to war, that wailed and howled when they saw the Latin troops, and beat their breasts, not knowing what to do for fear, but the loyal adherents of the Emperor. . . . All who had military knowledge rushed helter-skelter to the palace. But the Emperor did not trouble to arm himself, did not even put on his corselet of scale-armour, nor take shield or spear in hand, nor gird on his sword, but sat firmly on his throne and with cheerful countenance encouraged and inspired confidence in them all, while deliberating with his kinsmen and generals, about the action to take. To begin with he insisted that not a single person should go out of the city to fight the Latins, firstly, because of the sacredness of that day (for it was the Friday of the greatest and holiest week, the day on which our Saviour suffered an ignominious death for us all) and secondly, because he wanted to avoid civil strife. So he sent frequent messengers to persuade the Latins to desist from their undertaking; "Reverence," he said, "the God who was slain for us all to-day, who for the sake of our salvation refused neither the Cross nor the nails nor the lance, things fit only for malefactors. But if you really desire war, we shall be ready for you the day after our Lord's resurrection." Not only did the Latins not obey him, but they even placed their troops more closely and sent such heavy showers of darts that one of the men standing by the Emperor's throne was hit in the chest. Seeing this most of those who were standing on either side of the Emperor proceeded to draw back. But he sat on unmoved, consoling and gently chiding them in a way; this demeanour filled all with amazement. However, when he saw that the Latins approached the walls quite shamelessly and would not listen to sensible advice, he sent first for his son-in-law, Nicephorus, my Caesar. Him he ordered to take stout soldiers, skilled archers, and station them on the top of the wall,

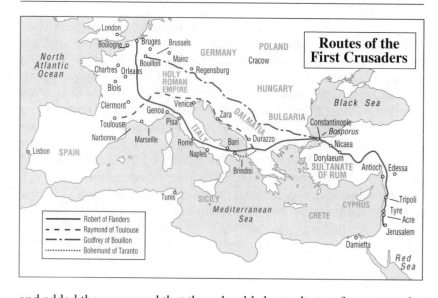

Routes of the First Crusaders

Robert of Flanders
Raymond of Toulouse
Godfrey of Bouillon
Bohemund of Taranto

and added the command that they should shoot plenty of arrows at the Latins without taking aim, but should rather miss, so as to terrify them by the frequency of the darts, but by no means to kill. For, as I said above, he respected the sanctity of the day and did not wish for civil war. Then he bade others of the nobles, most of whom carried bows, and others wielding long lances, to throw open the gate of St. Romanus and make a display of a violent assault upon them. They were to draw themselves up in this order, . . . each of the spear-bearers was guarded by two peltasts [shield-bearers] on either side; then in this order they were to proceed at a slow pace, but send a few skilled archers ahead to shoot at the Franks from a distance, and to keep turning about from one side to another. And as soon as they saw only a narrow space left between the armies, they were to give the order to the archers accompanying them to direct a shower of arrows at the horses, not the riders, and to dash at full speed against the Latins, partly to break the violence of the Franks' onrush by wounding the horses so that they could not ride against the Romans, and secondly, which was more important, to prevent any Christians being killed. The nobles joyfully fulfilled the Emperor's bidding; threw open the gates, and now galloping at full speed against the enemy, and now checking the horses, they killed many of them while only a few of their own party were wounded on this day. I leave them to their perdition.

My lord, the Caesar, took, as I have said, the experienced archers and stood on the towers shooting at the barbarians. And all aimed well and shot far; for all these young men were . . . skilled . . . in the use of the bow. But the Caesar's bow was in very deed the bow of Apollo; . . . provided he willed it, he never missed the mark at which he aimed. For on other occasions during the time of strife and battle, he invariably hit whatever object he proposed himself, and whatever part of a man he aimed at, that part exactly he always struck. . . . But although he was so skilful, he respected the sanctity of the day and took the Emperor's injunction to heart, and when he saw the Latins recklessly approaching the walls while protecting themselves with shield and helmet, he did indeed stretch his bow and fix the arrow to the string, but purposely shot without aim, launching them sometimes short of the foe, and sometimes beyond. Even though on that day he only pretended to aim properly at the Latins, yet if a reckless and impudent Latin not only aimed several arrows at them up above, but also seemed to be shouting out insults in his own tongue, then the Caesar did indeed stretch his bow at him. And the arrow did not leap from his hand in vain, but pierced through the long shield and the corselet of mail and pinned the man's arm to his side. And he, as says the poet, at once lay on the ground speechless. And the cry went up to heaven of our men congratulating the Caesar and of the Latins lamenting over the fallen. As our cavalry was fighting bravely outside, and our men on the walls equally so, a serious and severe battle was kindled between the two armies. Finally the Emperor threw in his own troops and drove the Latins into headlong flight. . . .

[On the following day, the Emperor] sent a selected few of the generals with their troops, and enjoined them again to advise, nay even to compel, Godfrey to cross the straits. Directly the Latins caught sight of them, without waiting even a minute or asking what they wanted, they betook themselves to battle and fighting. A severe battle arose between them in which many fell on either side. . . . As the imperial troops fought very bravely, the Latins turned their backs. In consequence Godfrey shortly afterwards yielded to the Emperor's wish. He went to the Emperor and swore the oath which was required of him, namely, that whatever towns, countries or forts he managed to take [from the Muslims] which had formerly belonged to the [Byzantine] Empire, he would deliver up to the Governor expressly sent by the Emperor for this purpose. After he had taken this oath, and received a large sum of money, he was invited to the Emperor's hearth and table, and feasted luxuriously, and afterwards crossed the straits and encamped near Pelecanus. Thereupon the Emperor gave orders that abundant supplies of food should be conveyed to them. . . .

Bohemund's False Oath

Now when Bohemund reached Apros with the other Counts, he reflected that he was not sprung from the nobility, nor was he bringing a large force owing to his poverty, but he was anxious to win the Emperor's goodwill and at the same time conceal his own designs against him, so leaving the other Counts behind he rode ahead with only ten Franks and hastened to reach the capital. As the Emperor knew his machinations and had been long aware of his treacherous and scheming nature, he desired to talk with him before the other Counts arrived, and to hear what he had to say, and to persuade him to cross into Asia before the others in order that he might not join those who were on the point of arriving, and corrupt their minds also. So when Bohemund entered, he smiled at him cheerfully and asked him about his journey and where he had left the Counts. All these things Bohemund explained clearly as he thought best, and then the Emperor joked and reminded him of his former daring deeds at [the battle of] Dyrrachium and his former enmity. To this the other replied, "Though I was certainly your adversary and enemy at that time, yet now I come of my own free will as a friend of your Majesty." The Emperor talked of many things with him, and lightly sounded his feelings, and as he perceived that he would agree to take the oath of fidelity, he dismissed him saying, "You must be tired from your journey and must go and rest now; tomorrow we can talk of whatever we like.". . . .

The Emperor sent for Bohemund [the next day] and requested him to take the customary oath of the Latins. And he, mindful of his own position, namely, that he was not descended from illustrious ancestors, nor had a great supply of money, and for this reason not even many troops, but only a very limited number of Frankish retainers, and being moreover by nature ready to swear falsely, yielded readily to the Emperor's wish. . . . For by nature the man was a rogue and ready for any eventualities; in roguery and courage he was far superior to all the Latins who came through then, as he was inferior to them in forces and money. . . . He was sad in mind as he had left his country a landless man, ostensibly to worship at the Holy Sepulchre, but in reality with the intent of gaining a kingdom for himself, or rather, if it were possible, to follow his father's advice and seize the [Byzantine] Empire itself. . . . But the Emperor, who understood his melancholy and ill-natured disposition, did his best cleverly to remove anything that would assist him in his secret plans. . . . Further, he did not want Bohemund to have the slightest suspicion that he was already detected. . . . After bestowing gifts and honours of many kinds on them, the next day he took his seat on the imperial throne and summoned Bohemund and all the Counts. To them he discoursed of the things likely to befall them on their journey, and gave them useful advice; he also instructed them in the Turks' usual methods of warfare, and suggested the manner in which they should dispose the army and arrange their ranks, and advised them not to go far in pursuit of the Turks when they fled. And after he had in this way somewhat softened their savage behaviour by dint of money and advice, and had given them good counsel, he suggested their crossing into Asia. . . .

The Crusaders Depart

Now the Emperor desired to march against the barbarians [the Muslims] with the Franks, but their countless masses terrified him. So he decided it would be wise to go to Pelecanus and stay there, so that being close to Nicaea he could learn how the Franks fared and hear also about the Turks' expeditions outside the city and the state of affairs within. For he considered it would be a pity if in the meantime he did not succeed in some military exploit and he aimed at capturing Nicaea himself, if the occasion seemed propitious, and not receiving it from the Franks in accordance with their pledged word. He kept this plan to himself and the arrangements he made, and the reason for them only he himself understood, and Butumites who was his sole confidant. Him he sent to win over the barbarians inside Nicaea partly by promising them complete immunity beside many other things, and partly by warning them that they would endure terrible sufferings and fall a prey to the sword if the city were taken by the Franks.

Victory and Atrocities: The Conquest of Jerusalem

Karen Armstrong

The crusading army spent three difficult years fighting its way to Jerusalem and experienced several miraculous victories in the face of certain defeat. Fearsome stories of the crusaders spread throughout the region, and many Muslims considered them invincible. By the time the crusaders reached the gates of Jerusalem in June 1099, they believed they were under the protection of divine forces. According to theologian Karen Armstrong, these and other factors contributed to the fall of Jerusalem to the crusaders. In particular, she maintains that the crusaders were in the grips of a mass religious hysteria, which led them to brutally massacre the Muslim and Jewish inhabitants of the city. Armstrong's books include *The Battle for God* and *Holy War*, from which the following is excerpted. She teaches comparative religion at Leo Baeck College in London.

O n 13 May 1099 . . . the Crusaders began their march towards Jerusalem. [During the last three years as they conquered Muslim cities on their route] the Crusaders had won a formidable reputation for themselves. They were held to be unbeatable and wild stories circulated of their ferocity and apparently miraculous survival. These iron-clad giants from the West looked like monsters to the Turks and Arabs. . . . The amirs and rulers of the cities granted them free passage and supplies, begging only that they might be spared. The Holy Journey had . . . become a triumphal procession. There were visions: St George and other saints appeared to Crusaders with detailed instructions for finding their relics along the route. As their relic collection increased, the Crusaders felt a new power and mastery, and as they talked over their experience it seemed more and more incredible. Everything now seemed a miracle, even natural phenomena. The light wind that had sprung up when the Crusaders had entered Antioch and had muffled the noise they had been making was now seen to have been sent by God; when they had sallied forth to fight the Turkish Emir of Mosul, Qawam ad-Daula Kerbuqa, it had been God who had sent the light rainstorm that had refreshed them. If a Muslim carrier-pigeon were intercepted it showed that even the birds of the air obeyed them. They were now walking in a holy atmosphere where everything seemed divine.

This sense of the divine naturally increased when they arrived in Palestine and the Crusade took on even more the spirit of the pilgrimage. On 23 May they passed Tyre, a place that Jesus himself had visited. The Crusaders truly felt that they were standing on holy ground. The places became even more familiar as they passed through Galilee, Caesarea and what they took to be Emmaus. When they reached Ramleh, the administrative capital of Muslim Palestine, they had a breakthrough. The garrison and the townspeople fled in terror when they saw the fearful Christian army approaching and the Crusaders were able to occupy it without fighting. They had their first foothold in the Holy Land. At Ramleh they found the tomb of their new friend and patron St George; at once they created a bishopric of Ramleh in his honour and the shrine was solemnly venerated by the whole army.

The Battle for Jerusalem

Finally on 7 June 1099 the Crusaders arrived outside the walls of Jerusalem. Their first sight of the Holy City was marked by a new outburst of extraordinary fervour. After the agonies of the last three years, they had finally reached their goal, and in their highly-strung and exalted mood some may have felt that they were gazing at the Heavenly Jerusalem described in Revelation. The whole army wept and shouted aloud, gripped by a sudden mass hysteria. But their cries were probably cries of pure rage. Then as now the imposing city in the hills with its powerful walls was dominated by the great mosques of al-Aqsa and the Mosque of Omar. The power and majesty of these buildings—so very much more imposing than almost anything in Western Christendom at this time—must have seemed an affront to God and to the true faith. . . . The Crusaders had been told that Muslims occupied the Holy City, but now they could see it with their own eyes. They could hear the call to prayer echoing through the surrounding hills and valleys and it must have seemed a deliberate insult and deeply threatening to their whole enterprise on which they had staked their souls. These Muslims with their mysterious and false religion were polluting the Holy Ground. . . .

As usual the Crusaders adopted both a pious and a practical policy. They started to build two siege towers from which to attack the city walls and at the same time consulted a hermit about the best way to take the city. Following his instructions, the whole army processed seven times round the city walls, singing hymns and walking barefoot. They stopped at their holy places outside the city: there was Mount Zion where Jesus had eaten the Last Supper with his disciples, the Garden of Gethsemane where he had prayed in agony af-

After three years of hardships and battles, the crusaders were overwhelmed by the sight of Jerusalem.

terwards and the place on the Mount of Olives whence he had ascended into heaven. At these places, pregnant with divine power, they listened to sermons preached by Peter the Hermit and the other leading prelates. Finally the whole army flung itself on the city walls, convinced in their exaltation that they could conquer it by a miracle of prayer and fasting. The city remained proof against their prayers, however, and as the Crusaders walked back to their camp, listening to the hoots and jeers of the Muslims, who had been watching all this incredulously from the city walls, these loud insults seemed directly aimed against Christ himself. They vowed vengeance.

On 15 July 1099 the Crusaders forced an entry to the city and conquered it. For two days they fell upon the Muslim and Jewish inhabitants of Jerusalem. 'They killed all the Saracens and the Turks they found,' says the author of the *Gesta Francorum*, 'they killed everyone whether male or female.' The day after the massacre, Crusaders climbed to the roof of al-Aqsa and in cold blood they killed a group of Muslims [who] had [been] granted sanctuary. The Muslims were no longer respected enemies and a foil for Frankish honour. They had become the enemies of God and were thus doomed to ruthless extermination. They were polluting this Holy City and had to be eliminated like vermin, and from this point in the jargon of crusading the word given to Muslims is 'filth'. The famous eyewitness account of Raymund of Aguiles shows the spirit in which this massacre was accomplished:

> Wonderful sights were to be seen. Some of our men (and this was more merciful) cut off the heads of their enemies; others shot them with arrows, so that they fell from the towers; others tortured them longer by casting them into the flames. Piles of heads, hands and feet were to be seen in the streets of the city. It was necessary to pick one's way over the bodies of men and horses. But these were small matters compared to what happened at the Temple of Solomon, a place where religious services are normally chanted. What happened there? If I tell the truth it will exceed your powers of belief. So let it suffice to say this much, at least, that in the Temple and porch of Solomon, men rode in blood up to their knees and bridle reins. Indeed it was a just and splendid judgement of God that this place should be filled with the blood of the unbelievers since it had suffered so long from their blasphemies.

This killing was not just an ordinary battle of conquest; the Crusaders had fallen upon the Muslims of Jerusalem and slain them like the avenging angels of the Apocalypse. It was a judgement of God himself. It was a salvation like the salvation that God had effected at the Red Sea when he slaughtered the whole army of the Egyptians, a violent and ruthless separation of the just and the unjust. The Crusade had indeed become a holy war. The Holy Journey had ended in a righteous battle against evil in which the soldiers of Christ killed some 40,000 Muslims in two days.

Celebration and Solidification

With tears of joy coursing down their cheeks the leaders of the Crusade processed into the Holy Sepulchre. It was a profound psychic encounter with the origin of their faith when they entered the holy atmosphere of the tomb from which Christ had risen from the dead. To celebrate the return of the faith to its most holy and powerful centre they sang the office of the Resurrection. Echoing the cadences of the Easter liturgy, which celebrates a new era that has broken upon the world, Raymund of Aguiles wrote:

> A new day, new joy, new and perpetual gladness, the consummation of our labour and devotion, drew forth from all new words and new songs. This day, I say, will be famous in all future ages, for it turned our labours and sorrows into joy and exultation; this day, I say, marks the justification of all Christianity, the humiliation of Paganism, the renewal of our faith.

This glorious day happened also to be the feast of the Dispersal of the Apostles, who, according to an old tradition, had left Jerusalem to bring the gospel to the rest of the world. The Crusaders naturally saw this as far more than a coincidence. As Raymund explained: 'On this same day the children of the apostles regained the city and fatherland for God.' The new chosen people were thus caught up in the drama of salvation history. The ancient home of the Jews had now become their own fatherland. They had conquered it by divine right in one of those dramatic events in which God had intervened in human history and used his holy people to save the world.

But the Crusaders knew that they had to establish themselves practically in the country and not get carried away by the thrill of victory. First, they needed a king for their Christian kingdom, and a week after the victory the electors, who were probably the higher clergy and some of the nobler knights, offered the crown to Godfrey of Bouillon. Although Godfrey was in some ways a weak and unintelligent man, he had the advantage of embodying the piety and values of most of the Crusaders. . . . Godfrey refused the title of king: he would not wear a crown of gold, he said, in the place where his Saviour had worn a crown of thorns. He would be called the Defender of the Holy Sepulchre and was solemnly invested with this title in the ancient Church of the Nativity in Bethlehem. Godfrey managed to establish the new Frankish state on a secure basis when he defeated an invading Egyptian army at the battle of Askelon on 12 August. . . . The great task had been achieved.

Pope Urban II had died two weeks after the victory, but he would have been horrified by the massacre in Jerusalem. He had imagined an orderly war of liberation whereby the Western Church would have extended its frontiers and gained the prestige of conquering the Holy City. . . . It seems that many Christians were initially shocked by news of the massacre, which would never be forgotten by the Muslims of the Near East. When later, wiser Christian rulers tried to secure their kingdom by making overtures to the Muslims, the memory of the cruel bloodbath always stood in the way of true friendship. But in general the news of the conquest of Jerusalem was greeted ecstatically by the Christians of Europe. The new Pope, Paschal II, seems to have been caught up in the general euphoria, and wrote that the Crusaders had fulfilled the ancient biblical prophecies. . . .

Returning Home

After the state had been put on a secure military basis, most of the Crusaders returned home, as they had always intended, leaving only a few hundred knights behind. This alone shows that land-hunger was not a motive for the majority of the Crusaders. It is unlikely that any of them returned home rich men. Though much booty had been taken in Jerusalem and Askelon, large sums of money and treasure were given by the Crusaders to the churches in the Holy Land or were donated to the new Latin kingdom. In his exhaustive research on the matter, Professor Jonathan Riley-Smith found only one Crusader who was reputed to have been made rich by the First Crusade. In fact, some of them were worse off. Many of them returned home with damaged health after the traumas of the campaign. Some of them arrived home to face great difficulties that had developed while they were away. Flanders, for example, was in considerable disarray during Count Robert's absence in the East; other Crusaders found that people who had stayed at home had profited by their absence and seized their lands or titles. The most dramatic example of this was, of course, William Rufus' seizure of the throne of England while the rightful heir, Robert of Normandy, was on the Crusade. . . . Crusading offered spiritual rather than material riches and some of the Crusaders seemed to have come home with deep religious convictions: some actually became monks, others gave donations to churches or built churches at home to commemorate the victory and very many arrived home with relics, the true riches of crusading, which they donated to monasteries and priories, bringing some of the holiness of the East back to the West. Many of the Crusaders seem to have been venerated for the rest of their lives. . . .

Indeed, instead of recoiling in horror from the massacre of Jerusalem, people in Europe were gripped by a new passion for crusading. The conquest of the Holy City stirred them as deeply as it had stirred the conquerors themselves, and Jerusalem and the Latin kingdom in the Holy Land became as important to the Christians of the West as the State of Israel is to many Jews in the diaspora today. The euphoria that gripped Europe after the victory of 1099 saw this as just the first in a series of new victories against Islam. As early as September 1099 Raymund of St Gilles and Bishop Daimbert of Pisa, in their joint letter describing the Crusade, wrote that 'the power of the Muslims and the devil has been broken and the kingdom of Christ and the Church now stretches all the way from sea to sea.' There was talk of conquering Egypt, Asia, Africa and Ethiopia. There seems also to have been an apocalyptic spirit abroad that saw the conquest of Jerusalem as a prelude to the Last Days.

The Muslim Perspective on the First Crusade

Carole Hillenbrand

Carole Hillenbrand examines the Muslim response to the First Crusade in the following article. During the 1090s, she writes, the Islamic world was wracked by internal religious disputes between Sunni and Shi'ite Muslims that spilled over into armed conflict. At odds with each other, the Muslim leaders did not initially view the crusaders as a serious threat, nor were they much concerned with protecting Jerusalem. If this disunity among the Muslims had not kept them from forming a united front against the crusaders, the author argues, the First Crusade would most likely have ended in failure. Hillenbrand is the head of the department of Islamic and Middle Eastern studies at the University of Edinburgh in Scotland. Her books include *The Crusades: Islamic Perspectives.*

It is a truism of crusader history that the warriors of the First Crusade succeeded because of Muslim disunity and weakness. Had the First Crusade arrived even ten years earlier, it would have met strong, unified resistance from the East under Malikshāh, the last of the three so-called Great Seljuq sultans. To what extent was the Islamic world bereft of unity and weakened by a complete lack of powerful overall leadership and by religious schism? First, the issue of leadership. It has often been said that the centrifugal forces at the heart of the Seljuq government machine all worked towards the fragmentation of the once unified Seljuq empire after 1092. Thus the crusaders found in Syria and Palestine small territorial units under the nominal suzerainty of the Seljuqs but ruled by mutually hostile Seljuq princelings and military commanders.

Seljuq weakness should be further contextualised and emphasised. In the space of less than two years, beginning in 1092, there was a total sweep of *all* the major political pieces on the Islamic chessboard from Egypt eastwards. In 1092 the greatest figure of Seljuq history, the vizier, Nizām al-Mulk, the *de facto* ruler of the Seljuq empire for over thirty years, was murdered. A month later, Malikshāh, the third Seljuq sultan, died in suspicious circumstances, after a successful twenty-year reign, followed closely by his wife, grandson and other powerful political figures. In the ensuing turbulence, Seljuq pretenders fought fratricidal and familial struggles to gain supreme power, struggles which monopolised their energies and military resources. The medieval Muslim sources view the year 1094 as even more doom-laden, for in this year yet another era was brought to an end with the death of the Fātimid caliph of Egypt, al- Mustansir, the arch-enemy of the Seljuqs, who had ruled for fifty-eight years. His death was closely followed by that of *his* vizier, Badr al-Jamālī. Also in 1094 the Abbāsid Sunni caliph, al-Muqtadī, died. As the medieval chronicler, Ibn Taghribirdī, put it: 'This year is called the year of the death of caliphs and commanders'. This succession of deaths in both the key power centres of the Islamic world, the Seljuq and Fātimid empires, occurring at exactly the same time, must have had the same impact as the disintegration of the Iron Curtain in recent years: known political entities and certainties gave way to disorientation and anarchy. The timing of the First Crusade could not have been more propitious. Could one suggest that the Europeans had somehow been briefed that *this* was the perfect moment to pounce?

Religious Divisions Among the Muslims

Religious schism was not removed by the deaths of the major political figures of the time. It permeated Islamic life at every level of society and was indeed exacerbated by the political vacuum which developed in the years 1092–4. As 'good Sunni Islamic rulers' the Seljuqs had pursued a vigorous foreign policy in the period 1063–92, the main thrust of which had been to wage war but not against Byzantium or the Christian kingdoms of the Caucasus, although such initiatives did occur. The prime Seljuq obsession on the military front had been the 'heretical' Fātimid Shi'ite caliphate of Cairo and a protracted struggle was fought out in Syria and Palestine. The ideological and political enmity between Fātimid Ismaili Shi'ites and the Seljuq Sunnis died hard. Indeed, the crusaders, once they were established in the Levant, would prove, for a while at least, preferable as allies for both Sunnis and Shi'ites; it was almost unthinkable to form a united Islamic front against the outside invaders, as might have been expected, for example, at the siege of Antioch. As for Jerusalem itself, in 1095 it was not the cynosure of Muslim eyes that it was to become in the build-up to its reconquest by Saladin in 1187. The concept of *jihād* [holy war], sharpened in the tenth and eleventh centuries on the frontiers with the nomadic Turks of Central Asia in the east and with Byzantium in the west, was flagging now, a rhetorical term rather than a politico-religious rallying-cry.

The same disunity characterised other areas of the Islamic world. The Turks of Asia Minor were the first Muslim foe to be encountered by the crusaders. The information in Muslim sources on their activities is scattered in the chronicles of the Seljuqs of Iraq and Iran and in Ayyūbid and Mamlūk histories written from the vantage point of Syria and Egypt. The battle of Manzikert in 1071 is usually taken as a convenient date to symbolise the beginning of a gradual but steady process by which diverse groups of nomadic Turks infiltrated the Byzantine empire, pursuing their time-honoured lifestyle of pastoralism and raiding. We do not know how numerous these groups were: some were authorised to raid by the Seljuq sultans, others progressed unchecked by any allegiance, even nominal, to a supra-tribal authority. The Seljuq ruler of western Asia Minor, Qilij Arslan (ruled 1092–1107), called 'sultan' retrospectively in the sources, came from a renegade branch of the great Seljuq family, and even though he was far from Iran he was still attached emotionally to his tribal heritage in the east. In the political instability of the post-1092 period he interfered whenever possible in the affairs of the Seljuq sultanate in the east, to exploit its weakness and to gain territory for himself. This was of far greater moment to him than to contemplate campaigns across the mountains into Syria and Palestine to fight the crusaders. Even within Asia Minor there was no semblance of overall political unity between the disparate nomadic Turkish groups vying for territory there in the aftermath of the battle of Manzikert in 1071. The Danishmendids, who held sway in central Anatolia, between Sivas and Malatya, did, it is true, form a temporary alliance with the Seljuqs of western Anatolia [against the crusaders] for the battle of Dorylaeum (July 1097), but such alliances were always ephemeral. Any concerted Turcoman initiative into Palestine or Syria was inconceivable.

As for the Fātimids of Egypt, they are portrayed most unfavourably by the great Sunni historians of the Islamic Middle Ages, for the Fātimids had begun life as a secretive, esoteric, extremist Ismaili Shi'ite sect and they had become the major enemies of the

Seljuqs who presented themselves as the 'defenders of Sunni Islam'. At the time of the First Crusade, the Fātimids were experiencing difficulties. Their religious persuasion usually cut them off from alliances with neighbouring Sunni Muslim powers. Their *de facto* ruler, the vizier al-Afdal, chose to rule through young puppet caliphs. Al-Maqrīzī, the great Mamlūk historian, wrote a complete history of the Fātimids. For the period of the First Crusade it is noteworthy that he mentions that Egypt was laid low by famine and plague, in 1096–7 and especially in 1099–1100. He also stresses further religious schism with the formation of the breakaway Fātimid group, the Assassins, after al-Mustansir's death in 1094. In these difficult circumstances it is hardly surprising that the Fātimid war effort against the crusaders was to prove less than creditable. . . .

The Seljuqs' Lack of Concern

What of the eastern perspective after 1092? The Seljuqs, and especially two sons of Malikshāh, Barkyaruq and Muhammad, were locked in a protracted military conflict which lasted until Barkyaruq's death in 1105. This conflict gobbled up almost all the available military resources. It was fought out in western Iran, but its repercussions were felt in Iraq, the traditional seat of the Sunni caliph, in eastern Iran and Central Asia, and, by default, in distant Syria and Palestine, earlier a centre of Seljuq activity. Most Sunni Islamic sources try to whitewash Seljuq indifference to the loss of Jerusalem and the Syrian ports and they stress the fact that some campaigns were sent out under the auspices of the Seljuq sultan to wage *jihād* against the crusaders.

An exception to this approach is the historian, Ibn al-Jawzī. Writing from the vantage-point of Baghdad, he notes as early as 1097–8, that is, *before* the fall of Jerusalem: 'There were many calls to go out and fight against the Franks and complaints multiplied in every place'. He records that on the orders of the Seljuq sultan, Barkyaruq, commanders assembled: 'But then his resoluteness fizzled out'. Ibn al-Jawzī also notes succinctly that after the fall of Jerusalem, when a Syrian delegation came to ask for military assistance, the sultan's army held themselves aloof, or to render the Arabic text more closely, they remained sitting on their backsides.

The implications of Seljuq political weakness and lack of concern for the plight of the Muslims of Syria and Palestine were far-reaching. It has often been pointed out that it was the Turkish warriors, not the Fātimid armies, who posed a military threat to the crusaders. Only the Seljuq armies could seriously have arrested Latin Christian expansion in the Levant. Whilst the Seljuq sultans, first Barkyaruq and then his brother Muhammad, paid lip service to the cause and sent some armies to fight the Frankish settlers in the period 1100–18, neither sultan took the field himself at the head of an army, as Alp Arslan had done at the battle of Manzikert in 1071. Neither dared to leave his power base in the east undefended. And that was the territory that counted for them, not Palestine. The fate of Jerusalem was sealed, therefore, in Isfahān. The disparate nature of the Seljuq army—composed as it was of the standing troops, provincial contingents under local commanders, and groups of nomadic Turcomans organised on tribal lines—necessitated strong military leadership, epitomised in the figure of the sultan. Otherwise, and this often proved the case, there was dissension and defection and the Turcomans would disappear as soon as they had been paid.

Confusion About the Crusaders

Historian Philip Hitti speaks of the Crusaders as 'a strange and unexpected enemy'. This is an apt description of the initial reaction of the Muslims most in the firing line of the First Crusade. . . . As the First Crusade unfolded, waves of fear, shock and incomprehension spread from the areas most affected across the whole Islamic world. But the impact of the catastrophe diminished the further afield the news of it spread. The waves became ripples. There was confusion in Baghdad about the identity of the enemy: al-Abīwardī, the Seljuq poet, writing a lament after the fall of Jerusalem, calls the malefactors *al-Rūm*, the usual Arabic term for the Byzantines, and Ibn Shaddād also confuses Byzantines and Franks in his geography of northern Syria. This is not surprising, since the Muslims' centuries-old struggle with their close neighbours, Byzantium, had been waged in the very same frontier areas now penetrated by the crusaders.

Nor is this the only evidence that the Muslim world as a whole failed to grasp what was happening. It is especially noticeable that the Islamic sources, with a few exceptions, do not evince any curiosity as to the motivation for the Latin Christian presence in Muslim territory. The correlation of the concepts of crusade/*jihād* never crosses the mind of the medieval Muslim chronicler. Crusader activities are narrated as an inevitable fact of life in the Muslim context from the First Crusade onwards, but occasion little or no special comment or digression. There is no sense that the crusaders are an unusual kind of enemy, with a fundamentally new agenda.

The Expansion of the Islamic World

PREFACE

At the beginning of the eleventh century, the Islamic world was one of the mightiest and most prosperous civilizations in existence. Venturing out from their homelands in the Middle East, the Muslim peoples had greatly expanded their dominions, conquering and settling territory in southern Europe, North Africa, the Near East, and India. Within these realms, they commanded all the important trade routes, both by land and by sea.

This expansion was unprecedented for its day: The Muslims were the only members of the Old World who maintained direct contact with every other major civilization of the region, including China and the kingdom of Ghana in sub-Saharan Africa. In fact, as historian Archibald R. Lewis notes, the Islamic world of the early eleventh century "formed the largest expanse of territory yet to appear in which goods could flow relatively freely over vast distances." The profits from these lucrative trade routes enabled the Muslims to build magnificent cities, to cultivate the arts, and to sponsor both religious and scientific scholarship. These accomplishments were all the more remarkable in light of the fact that Islam had only arisen four short centuries before.

Yet for all its power and scope, the Islamic world cannot be accurately spoken of as an empire because it was not unified under a single ruler or government. Instead, the people of the various Islamic countries were united by their culture and their faith. Under Islam, adherents shared not only certain beliefs and religious practices but also a standard legal system based on the tenets of the Koran (the holy book of Islam). The government bureaucracies of the Islamic nations also tended to be structured similarly. Arabic, the language of the Koran, was employed as a *lingua franca* throughout Islamic civilization, especially in religious, academic, governmental, and business circles. Arabic served much the same function as Latin did in western Europe during this era, simplifying business transactions between disparate groups and enabling the rapid spread of scientific knowledge and literary works.

While many factors worked to unify Islamic civilization in the 1000s, there were also serious disagreements among the Muslims that threatened their strength. Ethnic divisions played a role: Islam had originated among the Arabs, but by the eleventh century Egyptians, Persians, and Turks also constituted a significant part of the Islamic world. Most important, however, was the long-standing controversy between the two main branches of Islam, the Sunni and the Shi'ites (or Shias). This conflict began shortly after the death of Muhammad, the founder of the religion, when his followers selected a caliph (literally, "successor") to head their community in both spiritual and temporal matters. The first two caliphs ruled with little difficulty, but trouble broke out during the reign of the third caliph: Among other charges, he was accused of showing undue favoritism to his family, the Umayyads, who had at one time been bitter enemies of Muhammad. The third caliph was assassinated in 656, and Ali, the son-in-law of Muhammad, was chosen as the fourth caliph. The Umayyads fomented an uprising against Ali and installed one of their own family members as caliph. From this point on, Islam has been divided between the Shi'ites, who believe the Umayyads usurped the caliphate from its rightful heirs (Ali and his descendants), and the orthodox Sunni, who accept the historic succession of the caliphs.

Despite the split of Islam into two branches, for some time the Umayyads managed to keep the Muslim world unified under one caliph. In the early 700s, they attacked the kingdom of the Visigoths in Spain and conquered most of the peninsula, which they called al-Andalus. In the 750s, when the Abbasid dynasty initiated a bloody overthrow of the Umayyads, one Umayyad prince escaped to al-Andalus and established a separate caliphate in Cordoba. The Abbasid caliphs ruled the rest of the Muslim world from their capital in Baghdad. But they were not strong leaders for the most part, and by the middle of the 800s, the caliph held only nominal authority in the outlying districts of the Islamic territories. In the early 900s, the Fatimids, who led a radical Shi'ite sect known as Ismailism, took control of Egypt and set up a third independent caliphate in Cairo. A few decades later, the Shi'ite Buyids conquered Baghdad and reduced the Sunni Abbasid caliph to a puppet. As the Abbasid caliphate weakened, minor dynasties in outlying regions, such as the Sunni Samanids, began to exercise semi-autonomous power in their own principalities.

Thus, at the beginning of the eleventh century, the Islamic world was divided into three separate caliphates headed by mutually antagonistic families. Destabilized by factional strife and a lack of centralized power, the Muslim realm suffered some significant setbacks during the course of the 1000s, such as the loss of Jerusalem to the crusaders. Overall, though, the Islamic world remained strong and continued to expand its borders of control and influence. In particular, the recently converted Seljuk Turks embarked on a new wave of expansion through conquest that reestablished the reputation of the Muslims as a force to be feared and obeyed.

The Turks' Rise to Power

J.J. Saunders

The Turks, who were relatively new converts to Islam, conquered vast sections of the Near East during the eleventh century. Their dominion stretched over much of the Islamic world and extended into parts of India and the Byzantine Empire. In the following passage from his book *A History of Medieval Islam,* J.J. Saunders explores the political, cultural, and religious impact of the Turkish ascendancy in the Near East. Saunders taught history for many years at the University of Canterbury in Christchurch, New Zealand. His books include *Muslims and Mongols: Essays on Medieval Asia* and *Aspects of the Crusades.*

The entry of the Seljuk Turks into Western Asia in the second half of the eleventh century forms one of the great epochs of world history. It added a third nation, after the Arabs and Persians, to the dominant races of Islam; it prolonged the life of the moribund Caliphate for another two hundred years; it tore Asia Minor away from Christendom and opened the path to the later Ottoman invasion of Europe; it allowed the orthodox Muslims to crush the Isma'ilian heresy, and provoked in reprisal the murderous activities of the Assassins; it put an end to the political domination of the Arabs in the Near East, it spread the language and culture of Persia over a wide area from Anatolia to Northern India, and by posing a grave threat to the Christian Powers, it impelled the Latin West to undertake the remarkable counter-offensive of the Crusades.

The Land of the Turks

The Turkish family of nations first emerged into the light of history in the mid–sixth century, when they built up a short-lived nomad empire in the heart of Asia, the steppes which have ever since borne the name Turkestan, the land of the Turks. When it broke in pieces, in the manner of such confederacies, fragments of the Turkish race, under a bewildering variety of names, were scattered over a vast area, from the Uighurs, who once dwelt in Mongolia, to the Polovtsians of the Russian steppes. Despite the wide differences between them—some came under Chinese, others under Persian influence; some were pure nomads, others were settled agriculturists—they all spoke dialects of the same tongue; they possessed common folk memories and legends; in religion they were shamanists, and they reckoned time according to a twelve-year cycle named after animals, events being placed in the Year of the Panther, the Year of the Hare, the Year of the Horse, and so on.

The Oxus was the traditional boundary between civilization and barbarism in Western Asia, between Iran and Turan, and Persian legend, versified in the eleventh-century poet Firdawsi's great epic, the *Shah-namah* [*Book of Kings*], told of the heroic battles of the Iranians against the Turanian king Afrasiyab, who was at last hunted down and killed in Azerbaijan. When the Arabs crossed the Oxus after the fall of the Sassanids, they took over the defence of Iran against the barbarian nomads and pushed them back beyond the Jaxartes. The Turkish tribes were in political disarray, and were never able to oppose a unified resistance to the Arabs, who carried their advance as far as the Talas river. For nearly three centuries Transoxiana, or as the Arabs called it, Ma Wara al-Nahr, 'that which is beyond the river', was a flourishing land, free from serious nomadic incursions, and cities like Samarkand and Bukhara rose to fame and wealth.

From the ninth century onwards the Turks began to enter the Caliphate, not in mass, but as slaves or adventurers serving as soldiers. They thus infiltrated the world of Islam as the Germans did the Roman Empire. The Caliph Mu'tasim (833–842) was the first Muslim ruler to surround himself with a Turkish guard. Turkish officers rose to high rank, commanding armies, governing provinces, sometimes ruling as independent princes. . . . The disintegration of the Abbasid Empire afforded ample scope for such political adventurism, but so long as Transoxiana was held for civilization, the heart of Islam was safe from a massive barbarian break-through. When the Caliphs ceased to exercise authority on the distant eastern frontier, the task was shouldered by the Samanids, perhaps the most brilliant of the dynasties which took over from the enfeebled Abbasids.

In the end it proved too heavy a burden, and the Samanid collapse at the end of the tenth century opened the floodgates to Turkish nomad tribes, who poured across both Jaxartes and Oxus into the lands of the Persians and Arabs.

The Turks Seize Power

Despite their brief rule of little more than a hundred years, the Samanids had much to their credit. Of Persian origin, they set up a strong centralized government in Khurasan and Transoxiana, with its capital at Bukhara; they encouraged trade and manufactures; they patronized learning, and they sponsored the spread of Islam by peaceful conversion among the barbarians to the north and east of their realm. . . . About 956 the Seljuks, destined to so glorious a future, embraced Islam, and in 960 the conversion of a Turkish tribe of 200,000 tents is recorded: their precise identity is unspecified. Thus the tenth century witnessed the islamization, under Samanid auspices, of a large section of the Western Turks, an event of great significance.

Notwithstanding the prosperity of their kingdom, the Samanids failed to keep the loyalty of their subjects. . . . They surrounded themselves with Turkish guards, whose fidelity was far from assured. In 962 one of their Turkish officers, Alp-tagin ('hero prince'), seized the town and fortress of Ghazna, in what is now Afghanistan, a wealthy commercial centre whose inhabitants had grown rich on the Indian trade, and set up a semi-independent principality. He died in the following year, and after an interval another Turkish general, Sabuktagin, won control of Ghazna in 977 and founded a dynasty which gained immortal lustre from his son Mahmud. The Samanid kingdom fell into anarchy; the Kara-Khanids, a Turkish people of unknown antecedents (they may have been the tribe converted to Islam in 960), crossed the Jaxartes and captured Bukhara in 999, while Mahmud of Ghazna, who had succeeded his father Sabuktagin two years earlier, annexed the large and flourishing province of Khurasan. Thus Persian rule disappeared along the eastern marches of Islam, and Turkish princes reigned in Khurasan and Transoxiana. Barbarians though they might be, they found a certain favour with their subjects: they stood for order, they allowed Persian officials to run the government, they protected trade, they were orthodox Sunnite Muslims, and they professed themselves ardent champions of the faith against heretics and unbelievers.

The fame of Mahmud of Ghazna rests upon his expeditions into India. In the thirty years between 1000 and his death in 1030 he led some seventeen massive raids into the Indus valley and the Punjab. Ghazna was an admirable base for such attacks; the vast Indian subcontinent was a mosaic of principalities great and small; no strong

State existed capable of throwing back the invader, and there was no trace of national consciousness. Mahmud's motives were a mixture of cupidity and religious zeal: when he was looting Hindu shrines he could claim to be destroying idolatry in the name of God and his Prophet, and he received congratulations and honours from the Caliph for his services to the faith. He fought not only against the unbelievers of Hindustan but against the Isma'ili heretics, among them the Muslim ruler of Multan. His most celebrated exploit was the capture of Somnath in Gujarat in 1025, where he stormed the temple of Shiva, one of the most richly endowed in India, and levelled it to the ground amid frightful carnage. Ghazna was flooded with Indian plunder, and the multitude of prisoners was such that they were sold as slaves for two or three dirhams apiece. Some of the wealth was used to promote art and learning, and the court of Mahmud was adorned by such notabilities as Firdawsi, Persia's greatest epic poet, Biruni, the most distinguished scientist of the age, and Utbi, the historian of the reign. . . .

The preoccupation of Mahmud and his son and successor Mas'ud with their Indian campaigns left them little time or opportunity to observe and check the steadily mounting pressure of Turkish nomads along the Oxus. While their backs were turned, so to speak, the Seljuks rose to prominence and power in their rear and became the masters of all Western Asia.

The pasture-lands to the north of the Caspian and Aral Seas had long been the home of a group of Turkish tribes known as the Ghuzz

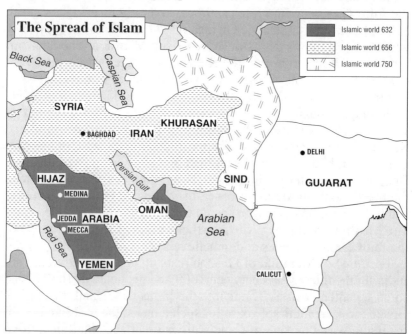

or Oghuz, later styled Turkomans. About 950 a number of clans withdrew from the Ghuzz confederacy, and settled in and around Jand, along the lower reaches of the Jaxartes, under a chief named Seljuk. A few years later they abandoned their ancestral shamanism for Islam, a change of faith as momentous for the future of Asia as the conversion of Clovis and his Franks to Catholicism in 496 was to Christian Europe. Seljuk is a semi-legendary figure who is said to have lived to the patriarchal age of 107, but he seems to have been an able leader, who welded his people into a first-class fighting force and by adroit diplomacy played off one neighbouring prince against another. He supported the Samanids against the Kara-Khanids; his son Arslan ran into trouble with Mahmud of Ghazna, to whom he boasted that he had 100,000 bowmen under his command, where-upon Mahmud's minister advised his master to have these men's thumbs cut off, so that they could no longer draw the bow! However, Mahmud contented himself with holding Arslan as a hostage for the good behaviour of his people, some of whom he brought into Khurasan and settled in widely-separated areas in the hope that they could thus be kept under control. The hope was vain: the tribesmen began raiding all over northern Persia and holding towns to ransom. After Mahmud's death in 1030, the rest of the tribe, led by Arslan's nephews Tughril-Beg and Chaghri-Beg, after encamping for a time in Khwarazm, along the lower Oxus, pushed their way into Khurasan and in 1036 seized Merv and Nishapur. Mahmud's son Mas'ud, at-tempting to bar their path, was routed with heavy loss at Dandankan near Merv in 1040, and retreated on Ghazna. From this battle dates the foundation of the Seljuk Empire.

The Seljuks now moved westwards into the disintegrating realm of the Buyids. Conditions in Persia and Iraq favoured their inter-vention. Political power had been split up among the various members of the Buyid family. The semi-feudal practice had grown up of paying high officials out of the taxes of certain fiscal districts: hence there was a serious loss of control by the central government. The Fatimid policy of diverting trade with the East from the Persian Gulf to the Red Sea had impoverished the Buyid State. Isma'ilian propaganda helped to undermine its authority. It had no outlet to the Mediterranean since the Byzantines and the Fatimids had divided Syria between them. The urban merchant class resented the loss of trade and the arrogance of the military aristocracy. Local dynasties, some Arab, some Kurdish, sprang up and drained the strength of the regime. Orthodox Muslims chafed under the rule of Shi'ites, especially those unable to maintain peace and order. The Abbasids, humiliated by their impotence, yearned for deliverance from their heretic masters, and entered into negotiations with Tughril. One by one the towns of Persia fell into Seljuk hands. In Iraq power was held by the Buyid general Basasiri, who asked for help from Cairo in order to stop the advance of the Seljuks by declaring for the Fatimids. An extraordinary struggle ensued. . . . Finally in 1060 the Seljuks fought their way into Baghdad; Basasiri was killed, and Tughril replaced the Abbasid on his throne. . . .

The fall of the Buyids and the coming of the Seljuks registered a great triumph for Sunnite orthodoxy: the power of the State could now be employed to put down Shi'ism of all kinds and Isma'ilism in particular. The Abbasid Caliphate was restored to some sort of life and independence, but its character was changed, and a new institution —the Sultanate—was created in an endeavour to re-establish the political unity of Islam. . . .

Two enemies were obviously marked out for attack by the new protectors of Sunnite Islam: the Byzantines and the Fatimids. In the previous age the former had thrust deep into the heart of Islam, had conquered a good deal of Syria and annexed Armenia to the Empire. But the Byzantine revival had now spent itself: the vigorous Macedonian dynasty was no more; the central government was in conflict with the great landed families of Asia Minor, and in order to reduce their power, had cut down the military establishment, thereby rendering the Empire defensively weak against the new assault from the East. The Turks drove towards the Byzantine frontiers, partly by design, partly by accident. Their coming had produced something of a social crisis in the Persian and Arab lands. In a society where the fundamental distinction was between believer and unbeliever, the fact that the Turks were Muslims counted for much; but even so, the educated city-dweller could scarcely avoid a feeling of disgust at the presence of these coarse and uncouth sons of the steppes. . . . To make matters worse, once the barrier of the Oxus was down, the regular Seljuk forces, cavalrymen of slave origin, were followed by swarms of 'Turkomans', free and undisciplined nomads seeking pasture and plunder, who raided estates, destroyed crops, robbed merchant caravans, and fought other nomads, such as Kurds and Bedouin Arabs, for the possession of wells and grazing-lands. Many of them poured into Azerbaijan, a fertile province of orchards and pastures which in a few generations became mainly Turkish-speaking, and from there began raiding Byzantine territory. When Tughril died childless in 1063, the Sultanate passed to his nephew Alp Arslan ('hero lion'), Chagri's son, who was probably anxious to divert the stream of nomadic violence away from the lands of Islam towards Christendom and at the same time to win glory as a *ghazi*, or champion of the faith. His armies pushed into the valleys of Armenia and Georgia, while the Turkomans plunged deeper and deeper into Anatolia. An appeal from the enemies of the Fatimids then diverted him into southern Syria, but his plans for an invasion of Egypt were abandoned at the news of an impending massive Byzantine counter-stroke.

The Emperor Romanus Diogenes had resolved on a desperate effort to clear the Turkish raiders out of his dominions, and at the head of a motley army of mercenaries, including Normans from the west and Pechenegs and Uzes (Turkish tribes) from southern Russia, he marched eastwards into Armenia. Alp Arslan, hurriedly returning, met him at Manzikert, near the shores of Lake Van. The Normans started a quarrel and refused to fight for the Emperor; his Turkish mercenaries, perhaps unwilling to face their kinsmen, deserted, and this, combined with Romanus's bad generalship, produced (August 1071) a catastrophic Byzantine defeat. For the first time in history, a Christian Emperor fell a prisoner into Muslim hands.

Alp Arslan stands out a not unattractive figure, his name indissolubly connected with the momentous battle which turned Asia Minor into a Turkish land. We picture him as an impressive soldier in his thirties, his long moustaches tied over his tall Persian cap to prevent them interfering with his shooting. . . . He treated the captive Emperor with courtesy, and when the ransom money was paid sent him home with a Turkish escort. Perhaps he hardly grasped the significance of his victory. He had no plans to conquer Asia Minor and destroy the Byzantine State; he was soon called away to deal with a Kara-Khanid invasion from Transoxiana, and in 1073, while interrogating a rebel chief, the man suddenly sprang at him and stabbed him dead. In fact, Manzikert struck a fatal blow at Christian and imperial power in Anatolia. With the Byzantine field-army gone, the Turks spread over the central plateau, so well adapted for pastoral settlement; in the struggles for the throne which now ensued, rival pretenders hired Turkish troops, and in this way the nomads got possession of towns and fortresses they could never have taken otherwise. The Greek landlords and officials fled; the peasants, deprived of their natural leaders, in time adopted the religion of their new masters, and the faith of Muhammad was taught in the lands where St. Paul had proclaimed the gospel of Christ. With Asia Minor, its principal source of soldiers and revenue, lost, menaced by the aggression of the Normans from Italy and the Pechenegs from across the Danube, the Byzantine Empire faced total ruin, and appeals for help to the Pope and the Latin world went out from Constantinople which produced twenty-five years after Manzikert the preaching of the First Crusade.

On the murder of Alp Arslan, he was succeeded as Sultan by his son Malik-Shah, a youth of eighteen whose twenty years' reign (1073–1092) marked the fullest expansion of Seljuk power. Malik-Shah was a more cultivated man than his father and great-uncle, who were essentially rough tribal chiefs, and he wisely entrusted the civil administration to the great Persian minister usually known by his title Nizam al-Mulk, 'order of the kingdom'. A just and humane ruler, he received the praise of Christian and Muslim historians alike. His suzerainty was recognized from Kashgar to the Yemen. . . .

Successes and Failures

The Seljuks rendered notable service to Islam, but their successes were balanced by many failures. They brought a new vigour and unity into Western Asia and put an end to the decadent regime of the Buyids. They dealt a staggering blow to Byzantine power by winning Asia Minor for Islam, a feat the Arabs had never been able to achieve, thereby breaking down the last defences of Christendom on the Asiatic continent, and opening up this ancient land to Turkish colonial settlement. Their vehement orthodoxy checked the spread of Isma'ilism, which was in future able to operate only as an underground terrorist movement whose agents became notorious as the Assassins. Under Seljuk protection the champions of Sunnite Islam launched a strong propaganda drive against heretics and deviators from the true faith: *madrasas* or 'college-mosques' were founded in the principal cities for the instruction of students in *fikh* (Islamic jurisprudence), according to the teaching of the four orthodox schools. The best known of these institutions was the Nizamiya Madrasa in Baghdad, named after Nizam al-Mulk and dedicated by him in 1067. . . .

On the other hand, the Seljuks proved unable to create a strong, durable and centralized Empire or to destroy the Fatimid Anti-Caliphate in Egypt. Their conceptions of government were primitive, and despite the efforts of Nizam al-Mulk to instruct them in the principles of ancient Persian despotism, which he regarded as the only satisfactory form of rule, they treated their realm as family property to be divided up among sons and nephews, who if minors were entrusted to the care of *atabegs* ('father-chiefs'), usually generals of servile origin who governed their appanages until their wards came of age and who often became hereditary princes in their own right. Until the death of Malik-Shah in 1092 some degree of unity was preserved, but under the fourth Seljuk Sultan Berkyaruk (1095–1114) the Empire was changed into a kind of federation of autonomous princes, not all of them Turks, for in certain localities Buyid and Kurdish chiefs held sway while admitting only a vague Seljuk suzerainty. Incessant struggles for the succession further weakened the Empire and gave the Abbasid Caliphs a chance to recover some of their power by playing off one candidate for the Sultanate against another. . . . By 1100 the best days of the Seljuks were over, and it was precisely at this juncture that the Franks chose to launch against Islam the strange Christian counter-offensive which we know as the Crusades.

The Reign of the Mad Caliph

Al-Maqrizi

For several centuries, the city of Jerusalem was controlled by the Muslims. These rulers tended to be open-minded, treating their non-Muslim subjects well. However, in the early 1000s, the caliph al-Hakim began to persecute both Christians and Jews. He ordered the destruction of many churches and monasteries, including one of the most sacred shrines of Christendom, the Church of the Holy Sepulchre. At the same time, al-Hakim instituted strict enforcement of Islamic dictates, such as the ban on imbibing alcohol. His rule was marked by extreme and often capricious acts of cruelty, which led many of his subjects to believe that he was insane. The following description of al-Hakim's troubled reign is taken from *The Book of Proceeding to the Knowledge of the History of the Kings* by the medieval Islamic scholar Al-Maqrizi.

Al-Ḥākim bi-amr Allāh Abū 'Alī Manṣūr, the son of al-'Azīz billāh Nizār . . . , was born in the palace in Cairo on the night of Thursday, 23 Rabī'I of the year 375 of the Hijra [August 14, 985], at the ninth hour of the day, at the moment when the 27th degree of the sign of Cancer was ascending. He was hailed as Caliph in the town of Bilbays after the hour of noon on Tuesday, 20 Ramadan 386 [October 7, 996]. On the Wednesday he went to Cairo with the whole court. The body of his father al-'Azīz, in a covered litter, was carried before him on a she-camel. Al-Ḥākim wore a plain cloak and a jeweled turban. He had a lance in his hand and a sword hung on a baldric. No unit of the army was missing. He entered the palace before the hour of the sunset prayer and arranged the funeral and burial of his father al-'Azīz billāh. The following day, Thursday, the whole court attended in the early morning at the palace. A golden throne had been set up for al-Ḥākim in the main hall, with a gilded mattress. He came out of his palace on horseback, wearing a jeweled turban. Those present were standing on the floor of the hall. They kissed the ground before him and walked in front of him until he seated himself on the throne. Then those whose rule it was to stand, stood, and those whom usage allowed to sit, sat, and all of them hailed him as Imam [spiritual leader; one of the titles of a caliph]. The regnal title chosen for him was Al-Ḥākim bi-amr Allāh [he who governs by the order of God]. He was then eleven years, five months, and six days old. . . .

In the year 391 [1000–1001], al-Ḥākim went riding every night through the streets and alleys, and people outdid themselves with torches and decorations. They spent much money on food, drink, music, and entertainment and enjoyed themselves in this way beyond all limits. Al-Ḥākim therefore forbade women to go out at night, and then he also forbade men to sit in shops. . . .

In the year 395 [1004–1005] al-Ḥākim ordered the Jews and Christians to wear sashes round their waists and distinguishing badges on their clothes. He also forbade people to eat [certain types of herbs and shellfish], or to slaughter a cow free from defect except for the feast of sacrifices. He forbade outright the sale and making of beer. He gave orders that no one should enter the public baths without wearing a loincloth, that women should not uncover their faces in the street or in a funeral procession and should not bedeck themselves, and that no fish without scales should be sold or caught by any fisherman. He enforced all these rules with the utmost rigor, and many persons were flogged for disobeying his orders and prohibitions. . . .

Al-Ḥākim also caused notices to be placed on the doors of the mosques, on the doors of shops, barracks, and cemeteries, abusing and cursing [certain] early Muslims [who were disliked by the Shi'ite branch of Islam]. He forced his subjects to write and inscribe these curses in different colors in all these places. . . .

Al-Ḥākim forbade people to go out into the street after sunset or appear there to buy or to sell. Thus the streets became empty of passersby. Everywhere the wine jars were broken and the wine was spilt. People were seized with terror, horror increased, and alarm became general. A number of secretaries and other persons assembled under the palace walls, shouting and begging for mercy, and many letters of safe-conduct were written for all the personnel of the court as well as for shopkeepers and other people.

Al-Ḥākim also gave orders that dogs should be killed, and innumerable dogs were killed so that none were to be seen. A House of Wisdom was opened in Cairo. Books were brought there and the public entered. Al-Ḥākim was particularly severe against the stirrup-holders who were employed at the stirrup. He put many of them to death, then pardoned the survivors and gave them safe-conduct. He gave orders that no person whatsoever was to enter the gates of Cairo mounted. He did not allow anyone to pass by his palace, even on foot. The chief Qāḍī [magistrate] Ḥusayn b. al-Nuʿmān was put to death and thrown into a fire, and a large number of people were killed and decapitated. . . .

Hard Times

Prices rose high in 398 [1007–1008]. . . . Al-Ḥākim confiscated all goods belonging to churches and placed them under sequestration. He burned many crosses by the gate of the Fusṭāṭ Mosque and sent orders to all the provinces to do the same thing. . . .

The Nile flood having ceased, public prayers for water were held twice, and the Caliph abolished several taxes. Bread became so dear and so scarce that it was difficult to find. . . . Al-Ḥākim forbade people to hold public musical performances or to indulge in trips on the river. He prohibited the sale of intoxicating drinks and forbade anyone whatsoever to go out into the streets before daybreak or after nightfall. Times were very hard for everybody, because of the great fear which came upon them, in addition to the high prices and the spread of disease and death among people.

In the month of Rajab [March 1009] food prices fell. . . .

Sicknesses spread, deaths increased, and medicines became scarce. Taxes which had been abolished were reimposed, the churches which were on the Makas road were destroyed, as was also a church which was in the street of the Greeks in Cairo, and its contents were pillaged. Many eunuchs, scribes, and Slavs were put to death, after some of the scribes had had their hands cut off from the mid-arm with a chopper on a block. . . .

On 11 Ṣafar [400; October 4, 1009], . . . IbnʿAbdūn the Christian scribe was appointed . . . as secretary to al-Ḥākim and as intendant [an administrative official]. He [al-Ḥākim] wrote, ordering the destruction of the church of the Resurrection [the Church of the Holy Sepulchre]. . . . Sickness increased, and medicines grew scarce. Several people found in possession of beer . . . were publicly reviled and flogged. He destroyed [the monastery known as] Dayr al-Qaṣr and strictly enforced the rule against Christians and Jews, requiring them to wear the special mark. . . . The ban on intoxicants was more strictly enforced, and many scribes, eunuchs, and servants were put to death. . . .

On 4 Muḥarram 401 [August 18, 1010], al-Kāfī ibn ʻAbdūn was dismissed both as intendant and as secretary and was replaced in both positions by the scribe Aḥmad ibn Muḥammad al-Qashūrī [who], after holding his posts for only ten days, was dismissed and decapitated. . . .

Al-Ḥākim forbade people to sail on the canal on boats and had the doors and windows of houses overlooking the canal blocked up. . . . Many people were flogged and publicly reviled for selling . . . scale-less fish and wine. Music and games were forbidden, as also were the sale of singing-girls and pleasure parties in the desert. . . .

In the year 402 [1011–1012] the sale of dried grapes was forbid-den, and written orders were sent out to prevent their import. A large quantity of these dried grapes was thrown into the Nile or burned. Women were forbidden to visit graves and not a single woman was henceforth seen in the cemeteries on public holidays. It was also for-bidden to foregather on the banks of the Nile for amusement. It was forbidden to sell fresh grapes except in quantities of four raṭls or less, and it was also forbidden to squeeze out the juice. Large quan-tities of grapes were thrown into the streets and trampled underfoot or thrown into the river. The import of grapes was forbidden, all the vines of Jīza were cut down, and orders were sent to all parts to do the same thing.

In the year 403 [1012–1013] food prices rose, and the people jos-tled to get bread. . . . The Christians were ordered to dress in black and to hang wooden crosses from their necks, one cubit long, one cubit wide, weighing five raṭls, and uncovered so that people could see them. They were forbidden to ride horses and allowed to ride only mules or donkeys, with wooden saddles and black girths with-out any ornament. They had to wear [sashes] and could not employ any Muslim or buy any slave of either sex. These orders were strictly enforced, so that many of them became Muslims. . . .

Several people were flogged for playing chess. Churches were de-stroyed and their contents pillaged, as also were their tenement houses and the houses pertaining to them. Orders to this effect were written and sent to the provinces, and churches there were also de-stroyed. . . . Al-Ḥākim gave orders that no one was to kiss the ground in front of him, nor kiss his stirrup nor his hand when greeting him in public processions, because bowing to the ground before a mor-tal was an invention of the Greeks; that they should say no more than "Greeting to the Commander of the Faithful, and the mercy and blessings of God be upon him"; that in addressing him, whether in writing or in speech, they should not use the formula "May God pray for him," but that in writing to him they confine themselves to these words, "The peace of God, His favors and the abundance of His blessings upon the Commander of the Faithful"; that only the customary invocation should be used for him, and no more. . . .

In the year 404 [1013–1014] he compelled the Jews to wear bells round their necks when they entered the public baths, and the Christians to hang crosses from their necks. He forbade people to talk about the stars, and astrologers disappeared from the streets. They were pursued, hid themselves, and were banished. Al-Ḥākim gave many gifts, much charity, and freed many slaves.

He ordered the Christians and the Jews to leave Egypt and go to the land of the Greeks or elsewhere. . . .

In Rabī' II [October–November 1013] he had both hands of Abu'l-Qāsim al-Jarjarā'ī, who had been the secretary of the ʠa'id [military leader] Ghayn, cut off. He had Ghayn's remaining hand cut off, so that he lost both hands. Then, after cutting off his hands, al-Ḥākim sent him a thousand pieces of gold and garments, but later he also had his tongue cut out. He abolished a number of taxes, had all the dogs killed, and rode much by night. He forbade women to walk in the streets, and no woman was seen in the streets at all. The public baths for women were closed, the shoemakers were forbidden to make women's shoes, and their shops fell into disuse.

The rumor grew that many would perish by the sword. People therefore fled. The markets were closed, and nothing was sold. . . .

The Caliph Disappears

Al-Ḥākim rode more and more often, going out six times a day, sometimes on horseback, sometimes on a donkey, sometimes carried in a litter on men's shoulders, sometimes in a boat on the Nile, always without a turban. . . .

Two days before the end of the month of Shawwāl of the year 411 [February 13, 1021], al-Ḥākim disappeared. It was said that his sister had killed him, but this is untrue. He was thirty-six years and seven months old and had reigned for twenty-five years and one month. He was generous but a shedder of blood, who killed numberless victims. His way of life was the strangest that can be. . . . He studied the sciences of the ancients and observed the stars. He made astronomical observations, and he had a house on Mount Muqaṭṭam, to which he used to retire alone for this purpose. It is said that he was afflicted with a dryness in his brain and that this was the cause of his many contradictions. It was well said of him that, "His actions were without purpose and the dreams of his imaginings without interpretation."

The Culture and Society of Muslim Spain

Bernard F. Reilly

Bernard F. Reilly is a professor of medieval history at Villanova University in Villanova, Pennsylvania. His books include *The Medieval Spains*, *The Kingdom of León-Castilla Under King Alfonso VI, 1065–1109*, and *The Contest of Christian and Muslim Spain, 1031–1157*, from which the following selection is taken. Reilly provides a portrait of life in Muslim Spain during the eleventh century, focusing on both its rural and urban societies. According to the author, the culture and economy of Islamic Spain were far more advanced than in the rest of Christian Europe. He also explores the differences and similarities between the three main populations of Islamic Spain: the Muslims, the Jews, and the Christians.

Muslim Spain, like all societies of any size before the nineteenth century, was agricultural. At the same time, despite the fact that most of its inhabitants were essentially subsistence farmers who lived by eating what they themselves raised, it should be noted that it was the most advanced agricultural society in Europe during the 11th Century. Of course, in Roman times, Iberia exported wheat and olive oil, but even during the Muslim period material improvements had been made on the level of the Romans. Hard wheat and sorghum were introduced from North Africa, and their superior resistance to heat and drought increased both productivity and living standards. Bread and rice were the staples of the diet, supplemented above all by the olive and the grape. Again, the latter two vines were known in Roman times, but their cultivation seems to have increased under Islam, perhaps with a contraction of the land under wheat, for the same fields were suitable for either purpose. Indeed, wheat was imported from North Africa from the period of the caliphate.

Much of the change in agriculture under Islam is to be associated with the rise of irrigation. To be sure, Roman Iberia had known irrigation, but most of it had been based upon gravity flow canals, a method possible only in severely limited areas. Muslims introduced the *noria,* or water-driven wheel, which could raise the level of water flow significantly, and also the animal-driven, geared waterwheel, which could do the same and was even more adaptable to a large variety of small streams and springs.

Such innovation was responsible for the success of the new rice crop, introduced during the Muslim period. Rice took its place alongside wheat and sorghum as a staple food in areas amenable to its cultivation. But the increased efficiency in the use of available water supplies made possible a major extension of the cultivation of fruits, beyond the olive and the grape. The fig, the apricot, the lemon, the orange, and the grapefruit all came to supplement the already cultivated apple, cherry, and pear, and these newcomers were largely dependent upon irrigation in the peninsular climate. In this connection one should also mention the introduction of sugarcane, although its dietary significance was relatively minor. Rather more important than sugar were humbler new crops such as the carrot, parsnip, eggplant, and artichoke. These were further additions to the vegetable sustenance foods of beans, lentils, and chickpeas cultivated since antiquity.

The Urban Elite

During the Roman period Iberia had been an urban society in the sense that political, economic, and social life had had their seat in the cities and were directed by an essentially urban class. The new prosperity of agriculture in Muslim Spain made the urban character of society even more marked. The urban elite not only monopolized the government but also owned much of the land, especially that belt surrounding the cities and specializing in garden produce for their markets. Advantageous leaseholds, as well as the manipulation of taxes, made it possible for that class to consume cheaply the products of the countryside and also to reclaim part of the price paid for that very produce in the form of government revenue.

Under these conditions, something like 5 per cent of the population of Islamic Spain were able to reside permanently in cities of

5,000 or more. Out of a total population of some six million, the size of major cities could reach as high as 90,000, for Córdoba; 52,000, for Sevilla; 21,000, for Badajoz; 20,000, for Granada; 17,000, for Murcia; 17,000, for Zaragoza; 28,000, for Toledo; and even 24,000 in Jerez de la Frontera. By comparison, in the society of the Christian north, also agricultural if in a different sense, the sum total of the inhabitants of all of its cities over 2,000 in population in A.D. 1031 would not have equaled that of Muslim Zaragoza.

These Islamic cities lived not solely from the proceeds of government and rents. They were also centers for the processing of agricultural products, for manufacturing, and for trade. If it imported wheat from North Africa, Spanish Islam also exported olive oil, raisins, figs, and almonds to the remainder of the dar-al-Islam ["the abode of Islam"; i.e., other Islamic countries] in substantial quantities. It probably exported all of the above, in addition to wine, to the Christian north during the 11th Century as well. From the fields of the countryside came cotton, silk, and flax, introduced into the peninsula from the Levant; and from the cities they went out of the peninsula as cotton, silk, and linen cloth. Even southern Iberia was then still well supplied with forests, whose timber was shipped to North Africa where it had become scarce indeed. . . .

Pottery was widely produced for both domestic and foreign markets. Fine cabinetry of an advanced sort, various objects of worked leather, and weapons of a very good steel found an internal as well as an external market. . . .

Commercial life still flowed in good measure along the routes of the old Roman roads. . . . The most important of these routes, that which led from Cádiz through Sevilla and Córdoba and then northeast through Toledo and Medinaceli and ultimately to Zaragoza and Barcelona, remained heavily trafficked. . . .

The land routes were supplemented by the sea-lanes that ran from Lisbon south to Cádiz, through the Straits to Algeciras, thence east to Málaga, Almería, and north to Cartagena, Denia, Valencia, Tortosa, and the Balearics. This was coastal traffic, of course, but fairly considerable fleets operated out of Almería, Tortosa, and the Balearics in trade that reached to North Africa, Sicily, and Egypt.

Peoples of Muslim Spain

The society of Islam in Iberia at this time was fundamentally divided into three distinct parts along religious lines—Muslims, Jews, and Christians. All other divisions were superficial by comparison. The Muslim community itself was fairly homogeneous, although it did not always think of itself as being so. In strictly religious terms it was solidly Sunnite without even a tincture of Shias. . . .

The major distinctions between Muslim inhabitants were those that derived from social and economic status. The older Muslim immigrants to the peninsula had come initially as conquerors, and it was to be expected that they—and their descendants, generally speaking—would occupy the chief positions of political and economic privilege. The newer immigrants . . . managed to find some niches in the political structure, . . . and it is likely, too, that even common soldiers among them were able to translate their professional status into minor official positions in those realms, or at least into places of economic advantage such as shopkeepers, artisans, or minor proprietors of the land. As the latter, they would have merged insensibly with the great majority of Muslim themselves who derived ultimately from the converts to Islam among the native populations of Visigothic Spain.

These *Muwallad*, or new Muslims, had from the beginning a somewhat lower status in the community, which derived from the fact that they were the conquered. Initially, they had been divided even among themselves socially and economically, depending upon whether they had submitted to the conquerors peacefully or had resisted and been subdued by force of arms. By the 11th Century that political distinction had long since been transmuted into one of simple economic status. . . . They had become simply those relatively humble Muslim who worked the land of the countryside as proprietors of small plots, practised a trade in one of the cities or villages, or ran small shops therein. . . .

Jews in Muslim Spain

A far more significant difference separated Muslim—any Muslim—and Jew. The Jew was *dhimmi*, of course, that is, one of the subject inhabitants of the dar-al-Islam who belonged to the special category of "people of the book." Like Christians, Jews were considered to possess an authentic, if imperfect and outdated, Revelation of the true God. As such, they were permitted to practice their own religion and live under the jurisdiction of their own law, insofar as that law did not conflict with the law derived from the *Koran*, which governed when conflicts at law occurred between Muslim and Jew. The authority of their rabbis over them was recognized by the Muslim rulers. . . .

Within this general framework, Spanish Jewry flourished in Muslim Spain during the 11th Century. In subsequent years it was to be regarded by its descendants as a sort of golden age. Medieval numbers are always hard to obtain, and are rightly objects of suspicion, but a serious estimate has at least been made that the Jewish population in Muslim territories at this time amounted to about 60,000, or one per cent of the total population. That population was higher in the cities, for the Jews were largely, if not exclusively, an urban group. In Sevilla they are held to have numbered 5,000 in the middle of the century. In the third quarter of the century they may have been 4,000 strong at Toledo. . . .

The Jews were without a doubt the most literate community of the peninsula. . . .

Indeed, the education and wealth of fair numbers of the Jewish population placed them among the governing elites. . . . Their abilities and their cosmopolitan character made them especially useful in the collection of taxes, not only among themselves but also from the population generally. Their often wide familiarity with the circles of international merchants made them useful business agents. . . .

In economic life, too, the Jew was often among the elite of the merchant class, sharing their life and journeys. Like the Muslim, the Jew found the Mediterranean of the 11th Century a community filled with fellows in almost every one of its ports and cities. The Jewish community seems to have shared in the economy of Spanish Islam at almost every level, from small agricultural proprietor, to artisan, to tradesman small or large. Also, at least the elite of Spanish Jewry entered into the intellectual life of the dar-al-Islam with zest and notable achievement, an aspect of their experience also best left to a general consideration of the context.

The Christian Community

As were the Jews, the Christians of Muslim Spain were also *dhimmi,* or people of the book. Their religion and law was tolerated, and they were allowed to live under the jurisdiction of their own bishops so long as they paid the special tax, which was the mark of their subjection to Islam, and generally did not disturb the good order of the dar-al-Islam. . . . They were far more numerous than the Jewish community, but also far more obscure in the surviving historical record. Their numbers, at least relative to the Muslim majority, were important, for they constituted for Muslim Spain a major weakness in its contest with the Christian kingdoms of the north. Even in the most passive aspect of that situation, that the Mozarabs [Arabic-speaking Christians] had maintained a Christian identity, which itself constituted them as an inferior group within Islam, meant that the Christian communities of the north continually acted as magnets. Almost from the original conquest of the 8th Century it is possible to trace the emigration of Christian groups from the areas controlled by Islam into those controlled by fellow Christians. In demographic terms, the constant tendency was toward a depopulation of the former and a corresponding population increase of the latter. . . .

The Mozarab population of Islamic Spain in the 11th Century was an uncomfortably large minority, perhaps something on the order of 30 per cent of the population. It had no appreciable political or even economic power of its own, to be sure. But . . . it could not be drawn upon for military purposes. In that sense, it was a handicap for Islam. But it could and would be exploited consciously by the kings of the north, who could draw upon its natural predispositions more easily to repopulate their own lands and to form an initial loyal nucleus of population in such lands as they might wrest from their weakened Muslim neighbors. More than ever, the Mozarabs of Muslim Spain weighed in the balance.

Life and Thought in Islamic Spain

For the vast majority of people, as always in an agricultural society, thought was practical and religious. It was bound up with the round of the seasons, the nurture of animals and plants, and the human cycle of birth, maturity, and death. As such, the contemporary human consciousness is not unfairly described as traditional, static, and preoccupied with its own limitations. . . .

Formal knowledge and education was an overwhelmingly urban affair and hence the preserve of a tiny minority. It was also predominantly a religious and a literary learning. As the former, learning was divided, ordinarily, into three provinces corresponding to the three sacred languages of the prevailing Revelations, Arabic, Hebrew, or Latin. . . .

The great secular learning of the period was poetry, for the most part lyric Arabic poetry whose major themes were nature, love, the hunt, and war. The conventions were those which had been set long before in the Levant. . . . The court of Sevilla became the center for this sort of literary exercise, and the rulers themselves, al-Mutadid (1012–69) and his son al-Mutamid (1069–1095), were avid practitioners. Even a famed theologian such as ibn Hazm (994–1064) could write perhaps the most famous single piece of this love poetry, *The Ring of the Dove*. This, too, was a genre in which a Jewish theologian, Solomon ben Judah ibn Gabirol of Zaragoza, could excel, writing in both Arabic and Hebrew.

There was also a certain development of prose as an instrument in literary studies, but it was subsidiary and largely limited to history, which, in the Arabic tradition, was what we should more properly call biography and genealogy. Prose was the instrument of the story also, but this latter was a popular rather than an erudite phenomenon.

If Arabic traditions and conventions dominated literary learning, philosophical and scientific learning derived from the classical world. Most of the Greek corpus of such writings that survive today had, in fact, been translated into the Arabic at Damascus in the 8th Century or Baghdad in the 9th, and had been more or less continuously commented upon in the dar-al-Islam ever since. Muslim Spain inherited this tradition and would absorb the products of it so far as they concerned the secular sciences. For example, the work of the scholars of the Near East, such as al-Battānī in astronomy and al-Khwārizmī in algebra, was received in Spain along with classical figures such as Ptolemy, Galen, and Euclid. The mathematics and the numerals of India which had been adopted in 9th-century Baghdad would also find their way west to Iberia. The caliphs of Córdoba had patronized learning of this sort, and al-Hakam is supposed to have collected a library of 400,000 books. . . .

Insofar as the inheritance was to deal with the philosophical corpus of the Greeks, however, the reception was rather more hesitant, not to say hostile. At the time, the great Muslim theologian and philosopher ibn Sīnna (980–1037), Avicenna to the later Christian West, was undertaking his daring attempt to rework the Greek philosophical vocabulary and conceptual apparatus in order to make it a vehicle and envelope for the religious thought of Islam. In the west ibn Hāzm of Córdoba (994–1064) wrote somewhat in this vein although much more tentatively. In this venture he was to find no immediate followers, and, in the long run of course, Islam generally would reject such an approach as blasphemous. His works on the *Koran* and the law of Islam would prove to be the products for which he was subsequently famous.

These same currents also permeated the world of Jewish scholarship. The work of the Cordoban Hasan ibn Mar Hasan on the Jewish liturgical calendar was frankly based upon the astronomical achievements of al-Battānī. So, too, Abū al-Waīd not only studied the medical works of Galen but was also drawn to the philosophical treatises of Aristotle. However, although he might accept the Aristotelian logic and some elements of the ethics, the metaphysics were finally to be rejected as too alien. Such conceptions as the eternity of matter were simply incompatible with Revelation as he understood it. On the other hand, ibn Gabirol (1020–1058), Avicebron to the later Latin West, although familiar with both the work of Aristotle and the commentaries upon it of the easterner al-Fārābī, chose rather to employ Neoplatonic thought in *The Fountain of Life*. But, although his book seems to have been widely read, the conservatism of the synagogue would ultimately reject both it and that approach to things divine generally. . . .

Formal learning among the contemporary Mozarab community must have been thinner and more closely confined to scriptural studies. What we know of it comes largely from the Mozarabic communities of the various Christian kingdoms, and there it is for the most part confined to the production of liturgical books, the recopying of collections of canon law, and the preservation of the secular legal collection of the *Liber Judiciorum* [the Visigothic legal code]. Such activities within the world of Islam would have been at least as restricted by the end of the 10th Century.

Battles Between the Spanish Christians and Muslims

Stanley G. Payne

A professor of history at the University of Wisconsin in Madison, Stanley G. Payne has written numerous books on Spain, including *Spanish Catholicism: An Historical Overview*. In the following excerpt from *A History of Spain and Portugal*, he explains that by the eleventh century much of Spain was governed by Muslim rulers, although Christian kings still controlled some regions. Throughout the 1000s, he writes, these rulers engaged in intermittent warfare as the Christians attempted to regain the lands under Islamic control and the Muslims beat back their advances. While the Muslim leaders were able to preserve most of their Spanish lands during this century, Payne states, the continual hostilities caused them to become increasingly distrustful of and intolerant toward their Christian subjects.

The collapse of the Cordoban caliphate in 1031 opened the way to a drastic change in the power balance of the Iberian peninsula. While Muslim leadership and strength splintered, the Christian principalities were expanding with vigor. . . . Key to the expansion were the recuperation of Leonese strength and unity and the reunification of Castile and León under the Castilian monarchy, accompanied by reinvigoration of the old Leonese program of imperial reconquest and Hispanic unity, first sketched out in the eighth century. A secondary factor of some importance was the development of mailed heavy cavalry, which had a distinct advantage over Muslim light cavalry and infantry, though it is not clear to how great an extent the Leonese-Castilian forces actually relied on heavy cavalry. Aragón and Catalonia also increased their military power, assisted by French adventurers and crusaders, but their forces remained much smaller than those of the large kingdom of León-Castile.

The Christian Resurgence

The reunification of León and Castile was accomplished by Fernando I (1037–1065), second son of Sancho el Mayor, who had inherited the county of Castile and raised it to the rank of kingdom in 1035. Meanwhile the young Leonese king, Vermudo III (1028–1037), had regained his capital after Sancho's death and begun to reassert the imperial sovereignty of the Leonese crown. In the process, he tried to reoccupy the territory in eastern León that had been seized earlier by Sancho for Castile, but was killed in battle by the Castilian forces of Fernando in 1037. Since Vermudo left no heir, he was succeeded by his rival, Fernando of Castile, who also happened to be Vermudo's brother-in-law, since Fernando was wed to a Leonese princess. Henceforth Fernando was ruler of "Castile-León," the younger and less-developed kingdom taking precedence in the royal title of the Sánchez dynasty because it was Fernando's inherited patrimony, whereas the larger and more important León was an acquired territory. In fact, the main role in the later reconquest by Fernando was played by the militant aristocrats and expansionist prelates of wealthier, more developed, and more imperial-minded León.

The united Castile-León of Fernando I fell heir to the historic Leonese imperial program, interrupted by a century of internal weakness and Muslim pressure. Nearly two decades were passed in recuperation, restoration of unity, and settlement of the border quarrel with Navarre, finally resolved in 1054 with the death of the Navarrese king, García. In the following year Fernando I launched the first of a series of assaults against the Muslim border taifas [regional kingdoms] that filled the last decade of his reign. The major territorial conquests were made in the southwest, where Viseu was seized in 1057 and Guarda and Coimbra in 1064. More important geopolitically and economically was the reduction to tributary status of the three leading taifa emirates along the frontier—Badajoz, Toledo, and Zaragoza. Large annual *parias* (tribute payments) swelled the resources of the Castilian-Leonese crown and encouraged the military mercenary, overlord, ethos that was developing more markedly in Castilian-Leonese society than in the Pyrenean counties.

Though Fernando I had adopted the imperial reconquest program of the traditional Leonese monarchy, he proved unable to resist the feudalizing inheritance policy that had been introduced by his father. He divided his domains among his three sons and awarded territorial grants to his two daughters, giving them the title of queen. This created intense conflict and rivalry after Fernando's death. At the end of seven years of internecine strife, the second son reunited the dual kingdom as Alfonso VI of Castile-León (1065–1109) and, in Leonese terminology, "Emperor of Hispania."

Leonese imperial policy could now be resumed. Within another decade most of Al-Andalus had been subjected to tributary status under the Leonese crown, and in 1082 Alfonso VI led an expedition to the southern tip of the peninsula, where he rode his horse out into the water in a symbolic gesture to show that all of Hispania was under Leonese suzerainty. The city of Toledo was a major prize, and key to the peninsula's fairly populous and productive central plateau. That entire region had been seized directly by 1085, moving the boundaries of Castile-León far southward from the Duero to the Tajo river valley and establishing Leonese dominion in the very center of Hispania. Reoccupation of the Visigothic capital gave further impetus to the imperial pretensions of the Leonese crown.

Territorial expansion and the large income from parias also opened a new era in the economic affairs of León and Castile. Urban life developed, as new towns were founded and the few already established grew. Commerce increased and began to acquire a significance it had never known before. This was stimulated by Alfonso VI's encouragement of the immigration of monks, merchants, and artisans, who helped form the nucleus of a middle class in the towns of northern Castile and León. It was also assisted by the growth in traffic along the road to Santiago de Compostela, whose shrine had become the destination of thousands of west European pilgrims. The new prosperity stimulated building, the endowment of churches, the development of the arts, and the general growth of Leonese culture. Population expanded, and by 1100 the greater kingdom of Castile-León numbered approximately two and a half million inhabitants. . . .

The Reconquest Checked

By the time of the incorporation of Toledo, Alfonso VI was collecting tribute not merely from Muslim frontier districts but from the taifas of Seville, Granada, and other important southern regions. He demanded that a lieutenant from among his officials be allowed to supervise the government of the emirate of Seville. Other military lieutenants occupied strategic fortresses in the south central, southern, and southeastern parts of the peninsula to ensure Castilian military dominance and continued tribute payments.

In 1085, there seemed nothing to hinder Castilian conquest of all the taifas of southern Hispania, though the economy and culture of the south continued to flourish. Silks, leather goods, cotton textiles, pottery, and farm products made the taifas the economic wonder of the peninsula, and their commerce remained extensive, but tribute payments were raised higher and higher, threatening to bleed away this prosperity. The only hope of respite from Castilian pressure was Muslim assistance from outside the peninsula.

Relief was available from the forces of a dynamic new Muslim power that had swept across Morocco from the western Sahara during the past generation. In 1039, a Maghrebi jurist and evangelist had been invited into the western Sahara to inculcate formal Islamic practice among the wild Touareg tribes of that region. This faqih [jurist], Ibn Yasin, preached a simple, ascetic, as well as militant interpretation of Islam and quickly collected a following calling themselves *al-murabitun* ("united for holy war"), westernized as *Almoravids*. In their fanatical fervor, the Almoravids preached the jihad [holy war] and spread across the western Sahara like the early followers of Mohammed. . . . The Almoravids' militant, puritanical doctrine—advocating strict, literal obedience to the Koran, daily ablutions, the shunning of money-making, the giving of alms and rejection of vice, and the fear of hell counterbalanced by hope of salvation, through militant implementation of the will of Allah—caught fire among the fierce, half-pagan tribesmen. Within twenty years the Almoravids carved out a loose, theocratic state that covered much of the western Sahara. Though in theory submissive to the sovereignty of the Fatimid caliphate at Cairo, the Almoravid state actually constituted an independent empire. It conquered the tribes of the upper Senegal, spilled over into western Algeria, and invaded sedentary and more cultured Morocco. The Almoravids brought a promise of lowered taxes and relief for the poor, and by 1080 nearly all Morocco had been conquered.

As early as 1077, the Almoravids had been approached for military assistance by taifa representatives. The conquest of northern Morocco was completed in 1084, one year before Toledo was incorporated into Castile. The need of the taifas was desperate, and in 1086 an explicit invitation to cross the straits was tendered by al-Mutamid of Seville, who at the same time sought to make sure that the taifas would not fall under Almoravid domination. The invitation to do battle in support of the emir of Seville against Castile was accepted by the Almoravid leaders as a logical extension of their jihad.

As usual, Alfonso VI seized the initiative, meeting the Almoravids on Muslim territory at Sagrajas (near Badajoz). The Almoravid forces relied chiefly upon compactly organized, trained infantry, armed with lances and javelins and protected by hippopotamus-hide shields. In addition, they included an elite corps of black African guards, light cavalry interspersed with small camel corps to frighten the enemy's horses, and units of archers and crossbowmen. At Sagrajas the forces from Seville bore the brunt of the formidable Castilian charge while a mobile portion of the Almoravids flanked the Castilian host and struck their camp from the rear. Defeated, the Castilians retreated in fairly good order, and the Almoravids retired to Africa without exploiting their victory.

The only real prospect for independence of what remained of Al-Andalus—still nearly two-thirds of the peninsula—seemed to lie in a permanent Almoravid military presence. This left the taifa rulers in a dilemma, for they were no more eager to be taken over by the fanatical, somewhat primitive Almoravids than by the equally rigorous Castilians. By 1090, however, an Almoravid party had formed among the people of some of the larger taifa cities. It was led by fanatical faqihs and supported by Muslim traditionalists increasingly conscious of their Muslim identity and fearful of Christian domination; also by the poor, hoping for relief. The Almoravid leader, Yusuf ibn Tashfin, had gauged the feebleness of the taifa emirs, weak in religiosity, many of them steeped in self-indulgence. He returned to the peninsula in 1090 and within two years had seized the main taifa capitals in the south. Soon nearly the entire southern half of the peninsula had been incorporated in the Almoravid empire. The frontier then for several decades was stabilized south of the Tajo, since the Almoravids were not strong enough to assault the new line of Castilian settlements in the very center of the peninsula.

There seems little doubt that Almoravid rule was at first fairly popular among Hispano-Muslims. Yet the Almoravid military elite was culturally inferior to its appanage, and the Almoravid period is sometimes painted as one of intolerant suppression of the "high culture" of the taifas by the puritanical and fanatic Africans. It is true that secular poetry and the use of musical instruments were discouraged, but the decorative arts, song, and popular poetry continued to flourish. The achievements of Hispano-Muslim culture in the second half of the twelfth century attest its survival under the Almoravids.

A Decrease in Islamic Toleration

With the eleventh-century shift in power and the subsequent establishment of the Almoravid empire in southern Hispania, the sense of ethno-religious identity among Hispanic Muslims and of intense hostility toward Christians was sharpened. The traditionalist Malikite rite, which had become less universal, was rigorously reimposed, and the *ulemas* (religious teachers) were employed as an instrument of policy. What remained of the traditional Hispano-Muslim "discriminatory toleration" ended with the Almoravids, who inaugurated a policy of direct persecution of the few remaining Christians in the south. Jews also suffered and for the first time were beginning to look to the Christian princes as saviors from Muslim persecution. This was a consequence of the Almoravid interpretation of the jihad, and something of the same degree of militance and intolerance was beginning to be shared by Hispanic Muslims as well. By the twelfth century the gap between Christian and Muslim Hispania was greater than ever before.

Terms of Surrender: El Cid at Valencia

Ibn 'Alqama

Rodrigo Díaz de Vivar, more commonly known as El Cid (from the Arabic *sayyidi*, which means "lord" or "master"), was one of the greatest Christian warriors of medieval Spain. Between 1088 and 1092, he steadily encroached on Muslim lands, carving out an autonomous domain in the eastern section of the Iberian Peninsula. When civil strife erupted between different Muslim factions in Valencia in 1092, El Cid took advantage of the internal rebellion to lay siege to the city. The siege lasted for twenty months, until the starving citizens finally capitulated. El Cid entered the city on June 15, 1094, and announced the terms of surrender that follow. Ibn 'Alqama, an Arabic chronicler who lived through the siege of Valencia, recorded El Cid's speech and the reaction of the Muslim audience.

Four days after [the Cid] took the city [of Valencia], he proclaimed throughout it that everybody should gather on the estate which he was occupying. People from the city and from the castles and settlements round about assembled. When they were all present, the Cid came out to meet them, seating himself in a spot which had been prepared with carpetings and drapes, and ordering that the principal men should sit near him. He began to speak by making them a few reproaches, and then continued:

> I am a man who never ruled, and none among my ancestors was a ruler either. From the day that I came to this city I was much pleased with it

and wanted it for myself, and prayed to our Lord God to give it to me: you can see how powerful God is from the fact that on the day I began to besiege Cebolla I possessed no more than a few crusts of bread, but now God has bounteously given me Valencia and I rule it. If I conduct myself justly here and put affairs in order, God will leave me in possession of the city; but if I do wrong here by injustice or out of pride, I know full well that He will take it from me. From today, let each one go to his estate and possess it as was his wont. If anyone finds his irrigated plot or his vineyard or his land empty, let him take possession of it at once. If he finds that his estate has been worked, let him compensate the occupier for whatever he has spent, and resume ownership of it as the law of the Moors [the Spanish Muslims] requires. Furthermore I order that those who collect the city's taxes should not take more than the proper tithe [tenth part], as your law stipulates. I have designated two days of the week, Monday and Thursday, for attending to your business; but if you have other matters which are urgent, come to me on whatever day it may be, for I will listen to you. It is not my habit to go off with women or to spend time singing and drinking, as your former masters did, making themselves unavailable to you. For my part, I wish to hear about all your affairs and to become a sort of companion to you, behaving towards you as friend to friend or relative to relative. I wish to be both judge and minister, and whatsoever dispute you have amongst yourselves, I shall try to resolve it.

After he had said this, he continued:

They told me that Ibn Yahhaf [the former chief magistrate of Valencia] wronged several of you, in taking from you possessions in order to present them to me, and that he took these from you because food was being sold at very high prices. I did not care to accept such presents from him, nor would I wish to take such goods or presents. If I should wish to take such things, I would do so, without asking him or anybody else; but may God not allow me to take such things improperly or unreasonably. Those of you who traded their own goods properly, may God give you a fair return from it. Those from whom Ibn Yahhaf took anything should approach him, for I shall order that he should return it all to you.

After this he said to them:

Did you see the property that I took from the messengers who were going to Murcia? It was mine by right, for I took it from them in war, and I took it from those who had broken the agreement they had made with me. But even though I took it from them by right, I intend to return it to them, down to the last farthing, so that they should not suffer the slightest loss. Now I want you to make me a solemn promise concerning matters I will explain to you. You are not to back out of it or get round it. You will obey my commands, and will not deceive me in any agreement that you make with me. Everything that I grant or do is to be respected, for I respect and love you well, and wish to give due attention to your needs and welfare, and I grieve at how much harm and suffering you endured from all the terrible starvation and great slaughter. If you had only done earlier what you are doing now, you would not have reached the state you did, and would not have had to pay a thousand *maravedís* for a measure of corn; but I will restore it to you at a single *maravedí*. Return to the possession of your lands, then, in safety, for I have forbidden my men to enter your city to trade or to buy and sell, ordering them to do all their trading in the Alcudia. I do this in order to avoid disturbance to you. I further order that nobody should bring any captive into the city, and if any should do so, take the captive and free him, and kill the man who brought him in without this counting as any crime.

He further said:

I do not propose to enter your city or dwell in it, but will build, close to the Alcántara bridge, a place in which I may take my ease at times and which I shall have ready, if needs be, for whatever may befall.

After he had said all this to them, he ordered them all to go about their business. The Moors left well content with the Cid, marvelling at the promises he had made to them and at the kindness he had shown them. They felt at ease in their hearts and lost the fear they had had, feeling that they had left behind all the evils they had suffered; and they felt sure the Cid would honour all the promises he had made to them.

The Muslim Dominion in India

S.M. Ikram

Despite some minor incursions by Muslims, until the eleventh century India was primarily a Hindu land. In the early 1000s, however, a Turkish leader known as Mahmud of Ghazni invaded deep into northern India and established Islamic rule over the region. In the following selection from his book *Muslim Civilization in India,* S.M. Ikram traces the chain of events that led to Mahmud's victories. He also examines the cultural legacy left by the Islamic rulers of India. A member of the Pakistan civil service for many years, Ikram was on several occasions a visiting professor of international affairs at Columbia University in New York City.

The Arab conquest of Sind and southwestern Punjab was completed by 714, and during the following three centuries there was no further extension of Muslim dominion in India. The second phase of Muslim expansion, beginning with the establishment of a Turkish Muslim dynasty in Ghazni, followed the traditional northwestern routes for the invasion of India.

In 642 the Arabs had defeated the Sassanid ruler Yezdegerd and become masters of Iran. After this, operating from Fars by way of Kirman, they set about conquering the eastern provinces of the Iranian empire. Under Qutaiba ibn Muslim they conquered Transoxiana as far as Khwarizm and Samarqand (711–712), and within a century of the death of the founder of Islam the Arabs were masters of

Khurasan, Balkh, and Mawara-un Nahr (Transoxiana). It was the Arab occupation of Transoxiana that paved the way for the Muslim conquest of India, for it established a link between the Turkish homeland and Islam. From this time the Turks were to play an important role in the Muslim world, and were the main force behind the conquest of the subcontinent.

Invasions from Ghazni

The first inroad into the heart of the area which is now Afghanistan was made by Yaqub ibn Lais, the Saffarid, who captured Kabul in 870 and founded Ghazni at about the same time. Kabul was, however, lost by his successor to Hindu rulers known as the Hindu Shahis, whose capital was at Waihind (Ohind), near modern Peshawar, and whose rule extended to Kabul in the west and the Bias River in the east.

In the meantime the Samanids (874–999) had established themselves at Bukhara and gradually brought the greater part of the territory to the east of Baghdad under their sway. Persian in origin, they favored the Persian language . . . and Persian replaced Arabic as the official language.

Under the Samanids Turkish slaves gained political and military importance. One of these, Alptigin, rebelled against his Samanid masters and established himself at Ghazni in 962. In 977, Subuktigin, a Turkish slave upon whom Alptigin had bestowed the hand of his daughter, ascended the throne of Ghazni and proceeded to expand his kingdom by annexing adjacent areas in Khurasan, Seistan, and Lamghan. Alarmed at the rising power of the new Turkish principality, Jaipal, Shahi raja of Waihind, took the offensive and advanced toward Subuktigin's capital. The two armies met between Lamghan (modern Jalalabad) and Ghazni. Jaipal was defeated, and was forced to agree to pay a large indemnity to the Turkish ruler. He defaulted and tried to avenge his loss, but he was again decisively defeated, and Subuktigin followed up his success by forcing Jaipal to cede the territory between Lamghan and Peshawar. . . .

Subuktigin paved the way for the more active efforts of his son Mahmud by occupying the key city of Peshawar and building roads leading to the Indian frontiers along which his son marched during his numerous expeditions.

Even more important was the development of Ghazni as a base of operations against India. It reached its zenith in the succeeding reign when it became a center of political power, organized administration, and literary culture, second in importance only to Baghdad in Muslim Asia. Even under Subuktigin it surpassed Bukhara in importance, and began to attract a large number of Turks who were to form the spearhead of the attack against the Indian subcontinent.

Mahmud of Ghazni

Subuktigin died in 997, and after a brief struggle his son, known to history as Mahmud of Ghazni, succeeded him. Brilliant and ambitious, Mahmud at once turned his attention to India. He had taken part in all of his father's campaigns against Jaipal, and knew the weakness of the Indian armies as well as the riches of the kings and temples. The series of invasions he launched against the subcontinent were to carry his armies farther than any previous Muslim ruler had penetrated. His first important battle was fought near Peshawar on November 28, 1001, and ended with the defeat and capture of his father's old opponent, Raja Jaipal. Jaipal obtained his release by paying ransom, but his repeated defeats had lost him the confidence of his people, and he named his son Anandpal as his successor. Following the Rajput custom, he immolated himself on the flames of a funeral pyre.

Three years later Mahmud made another expedition to India to punish the raja of Bhatiya (the modern Bhera), a principality that had been friendly to Subuktigin but had failed to provide help against Jaipal. The raja was defeated, but on his return Mahmud found himself in a difficult position. He lost most of his baggage in crossing the rivers of western Punjab, and was attacked by Abul Fath Daud, the Ismaili ruler of Multan. In 1005 Mahmud returned to punish Daud, but his passage was obstructed by Anandpal. Daud shut himself up in the fort at Multan and obtained pardon on payment of ransom and the promise to abjure Ismaili doctrines. Anandpal was defeated, and Mahmud appointed Sukhpal (a grandson of Jaipal who had accepted Islam and was now known as Nawasa Shah), as governor of Waihind and returned to Ghazni.

This first attempt to establish a center of Muslim authority east of the Indus through a scion of the old ruling family did not succeed. Nawasa Shah apostasized, started expelling Muslim officers, and proposed to rule either as an independent king or as the vassal of his uncle Anandpal. Mahmud returned to deal with the situation in 1008 and found Anandpal fully prepared. He had obtained help from the Hindu rajas of Ujjain, Gwalior, Kalinjar, Kanauj, Delhi, and Ajmer. It appears that by now Hindu India was alive to its peril. Not only did the rulers from northern and central India send their contingents, but, according to the historian Firishta, even the masses were highly enthusiastic, and the Hindu women sold their ornaments and sent their savings to help the army. The battle was fought at a place between Peshawar and Waihind. Mahmud took special precautions, for his army was breaking down under the charge of the warlike Khokhars when a fortunate accident decided the day in his favor. Anandpal's elephant took fright and fled with his royal rider. The Rajput army, believing the raja's flight to be intentional, broke up and dispersed, hotly pursued by the Muslims, thus converting what looked like a Hindu victory into a defeat.

The defeat of the great Hindu confederacy was a turning point in Mahmud's career. So far his campaigns had been confined to the neighborhood of the Indus. The breakup of the Hindu army emboldened him, and now he marched against the more distant Nagarkot (Kangra), where there was no resistance. Nagarkot contained an ancient temple which, like other Hindu temples of the period, was a great repository of wealth donated by rich votaries. Mahmud returned laden with booty, and for the rest of his life the ancient Hindu religious centers with their treasure hoards accumulated over centuries were to exercise a powerful fascination over him. His future expeditions went even farther afield. Tarain (1010), Thanesar (1014), the distant Kanauj (1018), and Kalinjar (1022) were scenes of Mahmud's exploits, in which he was uniformly successful. He did not try to establish his rule at any of these places, but he left a governor at Lahore in 1020, which now became incorporated into the Ghaznavid empire.

The most dramatic of Mahmud's campaigns was against Somnath, the wealthy religious center on the shores of the Indian Ocean. The dash to this distant goal, through an unknown and unfriendly area, across the deserts of Rajputana and marshes of Cutch, was a remarkable feat of courage, planning, resourcefulness, and tenacity of purpose. In spite of the hardships which Mahmud and his army had to suffer on the return journey, the expedition was completely successful in its object. Mahmud returned laden with riches of an extent until then unheard of in Ghazni.

Mahmud set out on the expedition to Somnath in October, 1024, and did not return to his capital until the spring of 1026. Except for a brief punitive expedition in the autumn of the same year against the Jats of Sind who had harassed him during his return from Somnath, Mahmud did not return to India. Henceforth affairs in Central Asia occupied him until his death in 1030.

Paving the Way

A brave and resourceful general during thirty years of ceaseless warfare, Mahmud never suffered defeat. He was a cultured monarch, and by his munificence attracted great poets and scholars to his court, making Ghazni the rival of Baghdad in the splendor of edifices and the number of men of culture and learning. He lacked the constructive genius of Muhmad Ghuri, and in spite of having overrun a great part of northern India, established Muslim dominion only up to Lahore, but he made the work of the later conquerors easier.

For our knowledge of India in this period we are indebted to one of the most remarkable of Islamic writers, Abu Raihan al-Biruni. His stay in what is now West Pakistan could not have been long, but his accounts of Indian customs and manners, as well as his observations on the Islamic conquest, are among the most penetrating that we have. He was born in about 973 in Khwarizm (modern Khiva) and soon distinguished himself in astronomy, mathematics, logic, and history. Some time before 1017 Mahmud was able to persuade him to come to Ghazni. . . . The work which is of special interest is his famous *Kitab-ul-Hind*, a masterly survey of the religion, sciences, and social customs of the Hindus, which was completed shortly after Mahmud's death. As a study of an alien civilization his book represents the peak of Muslim scholarship and remains unsurpassed as a masterpiece of erudite learning, penetrating observation, and unbiased appraisal of Hindu culture. . . .

The example set by Mahmud of Ghazni of raiding India and sacking its wealth, particularly that stored in the great temples, was repeated by his successors whenever the opportunity arose. The effect of this on the country can easily be imagined, and al-Biruni's description of the result of Mahmud's raids can scarcely be doubted. "Mahmud," he wrote,

> utterly ruined the prosperity of the country, and performed wonderful exploits by which the Hindus became like atoms of dust scattered in all directions, and like a tale of old in the mouth of the people. Their scattered remains cherish, of course, the most inveterate aversion towards all Muslims. This is the reason, too, why Hindu sciences have retired far away from those parts of the country conquered by us, and have fled to places which our hand cannot yet reach, to Kashmir, Benares, and other places.

The Cultural Legacy

. . . Of more lasting importance than the vicissitudes of the house of Mahmud is the cultural heritage of Ghazni, particularly in relation to that part of the Ghaznavid empire which now constitutes West Pakistan. The court chroniclers of Ghazni have not paid the subject much attention, but there are ample indications in contemporary literature that the Muslim government at Lahore was well organized and vigorous and that the city had become a great cultural center. . . .

Arab rule in the Sind had brought Islam to India, and had set a pattern for dealing with the conquered peoples as well as facilitating fruitful contact between Hindu and Islamic civilizations; the Ghaznavid occupation of Lahore had even more far-reaching cultural results. Persian, which was adopted as the court language and was the vehicle of literary and cultural expression during the Ghaznavid period, continued to hold this position throughout Muslim rule. The branch of Persian which remained current in Muslim India was the eastern branch in vogue in Afghanistan and Central Asia and not the pure Persian of Isfahan and Shiraz.

Partly because the linguistic affinity, and partly because the waves of the immigrants who established Muslim culture in India came through Ghazni and Bukhara, the entire cultural pattern of Muslim India was dominated by the Central Asian tradition. This continued until the days of the Mughals who, although themselves Turks from Central Asia, established closer contacts with Iran and Arabia. Even then, out of several strands which provided the warp and woof of Muslim civilization in India, the most dominant was the influence of Central Asia. After the establishment of Muslim Delhi, the administrative system was modeled on that of Ghazni. Muslim political institutions, military and administrative organization, ethics, and jurisprudence, in fact the entire pattern of Muslim life, bears the imprint of Ghazni and Bukhara.

The Golden Age of the Kingdom of Ghana

E. Jefferson Murphy

For several centuries, the kingdom of Ghana (located in present-day Mali) controlled the lucrative gold and salt trade between the Muslims of North Africa and the peoples of sub-Saharan Africa. In the 1000s, as E. Jefferson Murphy explains, Ghana was at the height of its power and prestige, ruling over an empire that stretched to the Atlantic Ocean. However, toward the end of the century, Islamic forces invaded Ghana and subjected the kingdom to two decades of war. Although the Muslims were only able to control Ghana for a few years, Murphy writes, the constant warfare sapped the empire of its strength and led to a slow decline. As an employee of the African-American Institute of New York City, Murphy lived for several years in various parts of sub-Saharan Africa. His books include *The Bantu Civilization of Southern Africa, Understanding Africa*, and *History of African Civilization*, from which the following is excerpted.

The western Sudan stretched from the Atlantic Ocean on the west, where modern Mauritania and Senegal are located, some thousand miles to the great bend of the Niger River in the east, in modern Mali. . . .

On the north the western Sudan stretches to the Sahara, and on the south, to the edges of the West African rain forest. Not an unusually vast region as African distances go, the western Sudan nevertheless includes more than one million square miles of sweeping grasslands. . . .

Sudanic civilization early reached its flowering, aided by trans-Saharan trade. . . . In the international, long-distance trading system that developed between the Sudan and North Africa, two items stood out: gold from sub-Saharan Africa and salt from North Africa. In the Sudan and the forests to its south there is virtually no natural salt. Coastal peoples made salt from sea water, but this supply was distant and expensive. Slabs of salt, however, could be mined from plentiful natural deposits in the Sahara and transported by camel southward to the markets of the Sudan. Several important gold-producing areas were located south of the Sudan. The most productive of these were in modern Ghana and Guinea. In these areas, the indigenous Negroid peoples learned to mine the gold, digging shafts as deep as fifty feet, and to wash out nuggets from the sands of streams. . . .

The Trans-Saharan Trade System

By about the eighth century, when the earliest written records appear, a thriving trans-Saharan trade system had been developed. It centered on the great market towns of the Mande of the western Sudan and the Berber of the southwestern Sahara. To Walata, Tichitt, Kumbi Saleh, Awdoghast and many other towns that have long since vanished streamed dozens of Berber camel caravans each year. The caravans, sometimes up to ten thousand camels strong, carried slabs of Saharan salt, finely wrought daggers, timepieces, silks, jewelry, and fine cloths of the Mediterranean world. Into these cities came traders and artisans of the Sudan. They brought gold, leather, cotton, kola nuts, pots of shea butter, baskets of millet and sorghum, bars of iron, and slaves. Mande kings developed strong states, to regulate the brisk and voluminous trade.

Thus the fabled empire of Ghana began. Within a few centuries after Christ, Soninke kings, inhabiting the grasslands in the far west of the Sudan, gradually accumulated the power and the wealth to regulate the rich trade in their great market towns.

In all the western Sahara, caravans could follow only two consistently reliable routes and still find occasional oases. One such route originated in the city of Marrakesh in Morocco and terminated in the city of Tekrur, on the Senegal River, roughly two hundred miles inland from the Atlantic. . . .

The route between Marrakesh and Tekrur ended in the land of the Tukulor peoples, who built a powerful state known to the ancient

Arabs as Tekrur. Arabic sources from the eighth and ninth centuries refer to Tekrur with considerable respect, and as frequently as they refer to Ghana. The kingdom probably began between about the third and sixth centuries of the Christian era, at about the same time as Ghana. By the tenth century, Tekrur had lost its independence to Ghana and the kings of Tekrur were required (probably very unwillingly, judging by later events) to pay tribute to the emperor of Ghana. In the eleventh century, when the Almoravid army invaded Ghana, the king and most nobles of Tekrur had already accepted Islam. They eagerly allied themselves with the Almoravids against their Ghanaian overlords, and the troops of Tekrur probably played a significant role in Ghana's defeat and destruction. . . .

Imperial Ghana

Although the Tukulor . . . had fashioned highly developed social, political, and economic systems, the Soninke people, who lived in the region where the most important trans-Saharan caravan route terminated, achieved a lustrous ascendancy through their great empire of Ghana. Even today Ghana inspires African intellectuals and political leaders as a crowning achievement of ancient Africa. The modern nation of Ghana, far distant from ancient Ghana's locale, chose its name to symbolize the resurgence of Black Africa to a new age of glory.

Actually, the Soninke kingdom that became Ghana was named Aoukar. Its kings were called ghana, meaning "war chief" in Soninke. Visiting Arabs, Berbers, and peoples from other parts of the Sudan used the king's title to refer to his kingdom, and by the ninth century, Ghana was recognized as the name of the great Black Kingdom below the Sahara.

Aoukar was situated on the grasslands north of the headwaters of the Senegal and Niger rivers. Its people inhabited the land as far north as the arid steppes of the Sahara's edge. There, no crops could prosper, and cattle, goats, and sheep of Berber pastoralists grazed each year after the rains had coaxed the sparse, wiry grasses into greenness. Farther south in Aoukar's territory, where rainfall was sufficient to support the cultivation of millet, sorghum, and other crops of the Sudanic complex, the Soninke developed their civilization.

Soninke country, not especially fertile compared to some more favored parts of the Sudan, supported a population that must have been at least several hundred thousand. It covered an area of some fifty to sixty thousand square miles in what is today the southeastern part of Mauritania, eastern Senegal, and western Mali. The Soninke, like most Mande peoples, lived in villages and towns rather than in dispersed homesteads. These settlements tended to cluster near the streams, lakes, and ponds that held water for some months after the annual rains. Because of the skill with which the Soninke preserved scant water supplies and raised good crops through the use of irrigation ditches, the kingdom was generally prosperous, if not bountifully favored. But strategic trade location added increments of wealth that early gave Ghana an advantage over other peoples of the western Sudan.

Salt, cloth, metalwork, silk, and other goods of North Africa flowed into Walata and Awdoghast, where teeming markets hummed with the bargaining of Berbers, Soninke, Dyula, Malinke, and other traders from both the Sahara and the Sudan. Into these two great markets, from smaller markets throughout Ghana, came smaller caravans of donkeys, each loaded with gold, pepper, kola nuts, elephant tusks, millet, sorghum, iron bars, and leather.

Astride the whole system of trade sat the king of Aoukar, the ghana, and his army of officials and tax collectors. Goods entering or leaving the kingdom were subject to carefully specified customs duties. In return for payment of duty, the palace troops and provincial conscripts protected the merchants against brigands and thieves. Cheating in the markets was forbidden, and royal edict required debtors to pay their creditors according to the terms of loan agreements.

Not all the products that passed through Ghana originated in the kingdom. Goods came from as far south as the forest region and from as far east as Songhai country, around Timbuktu and Jenne. Gold, Black Africa's most important product in those times, came from the land of Wangara, located in what is now the interior of Guinea. . . .

Arab Accounts

Although Ghana's rulers must have maintained accounts for the duties that flowed into the king's coffers, the empire never developed a system of writing. Thus, Ghana's history comes to us from carefully transmitted oral histories and from writings by early Arab historians and geographers, dating from the eighth century on.

The writings of the eighth-century Arab astronomer al-Fazari contain the earliest definite reference to Ghana. Al-Fazari called Ghana "the land of gold." The ninth-century Egyptian historian al-Hakan also mentioned the land of gold, and Ghana is found on the first important Islamic world map, which was produced in the ninth century by Mohammed Khwarizmi, a Persian geographer. Another Arab geographer, al-Ya'qubi, was the first to offer a description of Ghana. According to al-Ya'qubi's ninth-century account, "there is the kingdom of Ghana. Its king is mighty, and in his land are gold mines. Under his authority are various other kingdoms—and in all of this region there is gold."

References to Ghana appeared more frequently in books by Muslim scholars and travelers in the eleventh and twelfth centuries. The most helpful account that has been found is in al-Bakri's *Kitab al Masalik wa'l Mamalik*, written in Moorish Cordoba in 1067. Al-Bakri, regarded by modern researchers as an accurate reporter of his times, provides extremely useful information on Ghana's economy, its system of government and taxation, the magnificence of its court, and its trade and relationship with North Africa.

From al-Bakri's description and from linguistic and ethnological analysis, preliminary archaeological studies, oral histories, and information about trade in North Africa, historians have outlined Ghana's characteristics and history.

By the end of the tenth century, Ghana had conquered Tekrur, extending its territory all the way to the Atlantic Ocean. It had also incorporated a number of other states of the Mande-speaking peoples to the south and east of the Soninke state into the empire. In 990 Ghana captured the important Berber city of Awdoghast on the edge of the Sahara and thus established control of the caravan trade. During this period, when Ghana was at its peak of imperial expansion, it controlled a population of several million and a territory of roughly 250,000 square miles. It was a power no other African state was capable of challenging.

Although Ghana was in close contact with Muslim civilization, its culture remained purely Sudanic. Its capital, Kumbi Saleh, accommodated a large Muslim population concerned with the trans-Saharan trade, and Muslim ideas and skills were of great use to the kings of Ghana. But both the kings and the mass of people remained true to their own religion and way of life. The most vivid account of imperial Ghana at about the mid-eleventh century comes from al-Bakri:

> Ghana consists of two towns lying in a plain. One of these towns is inhabited by Muslims. It is large and possesses twelve mosques in one of which the people assemble for the Friday prayer. There are imams, muazzins and salaried reciters of the Koran as well as jurists and learned men. Around the town are wells of sweet water, from which they drink and near which they grow vegetables.

> The town in which the king lives is six miles from the Muslim one and bears the name Al Ghaba. The land between the two towns is covered with houses. The houses of the inhabitants are made of stone and acacia wood. The king has a palace and a number of dome-shaped dwellings, the whole surrounded by an enclosure like the defensive wall of a city. In the town where the king lives, and not far from the hall in which he holds his court of justice, is a mosque where pray the Muslims who come on visiting diplomatic missions. Around the king's town are domed buildings, woods, and copses where live the sorcerers of these people, the men in charge of the religious cult.

Al-Bakri also provides a classic portrayal of the pomp and majesty of the typical Sudanic kingship:

> The king adorns himself like a woman, wearing necklaces and bracelets, and when he sits before the people he puts on a high cap decorated with gold and wrapped in turbans of fine cotton. The court of appeal is held in a domed pavilion around which stand ten horses with gold embroidered trappings. Behind the king stand ten pages holding shields and swords decorated with gold, and on his right are the sons of the subordinate kings . . . all wearing splendid garments and with their hair mixed with gold. On the ground around him are seated his ministers, whilst the governor of the city sits before him. On guard at the door are dogs of fine pedigree, wearing collars of gold and silver adorned with knobs . . . the royal audience is announced by the beating of a drum which they call "deba" made out of a long piece of hollowed-out wood. When the people have gathered his co-religionists draw near upon their knees, sprinkling dust upon their heads as a sign of respect, whilst the Muslims clap hands as their form of greeting.

Al-Bakri also attests to the might of the king:

> . . . The king who governs them at present . . . is called Tenkaminen; he came to the throne in A.H. 455 [A.D. 1062] . . . Tenkaminen is the master of a large empire and a formidable power. . . . The king of Ghana can put 200,000 warriors in the field, more than 40,000 being armed with bow and arrow.

Al-Bakri's information on the size of the king's army is probably correct. But the king's forces were certainly not a standing army. More likely, the king had a thousand or so troops at his palace. These troops, drawn from slave ranks, were well armed, thoroughly trained and disciplined, and completely loyal to the king. They wore a kind of uniform that consisted of sandals, loose-fitting cotton breeches reaching to the knees, a sleeveless tunic, and a headdress of either cotton or leather, decorated with one or more feathers. Their weapons included iron-pointed spears, daggers and short swords, wooden battle clubs, and bows and arrows. By the ninth century, before al-Bakri's time, the king would also have had a small horse troop, armed with long lances.

These royal troops, whose only duty was to protect the king and lead his wars, trained rigorously and maintained themselves in peak physical condition. They were organized into companies and lived in special soldiers' compounds. Their commanders were close confidants of the king and often represented him on diplomatic missions to conquered and tributary rulers. In time of war, palace troops were augmented by the forces of lesser chiefs and vassal rulers and by slave and freemen conscripts from Soninke towns and villages; thus it was that the king could field the impressive army of which al-Bakri wrote.

Ghana's Collapse

The imperial might of Ghana was maintained for centuries on gold and other products of the empire, revenue from the trans-Saharan trade, and the considerable army the king had at his command. The kings of Ghana also probably controlled the empire's iron supply. There is no information available concerning the amount of difficulty the Soninke kings had in keeping restive subject kings quiet, but it is reasonable to suppose that occasional revolts and conspiracies took place. During the long centuries of Ghana's existence, there must also have been sporadic external threats, either from the Berbers to the north or from Sudanic states to the east. But until late in the eleventh century, no force was strong enough to threaten Ghana's power and territorial integrity.

Al-Bakri makes no mention of the war against Ghana that was commencing while he was writing his accounts. It was this war that sounded the death knell of the empire. In 1076, a powerful army of Almoravids, the desert Berbers who waged one of the greatest holy wars of the Muslim era, captured and sacked Kumbi Saleh, then the capital of Ghana.

Ghanaian seizure of Awdoghast in 990 and Ghana's subsequent control of the Saharan trade had resulted in a burning Berber hatred of Ghana. The Berbers, under Almoravid leadership, captured their city in 1054. Then, in alliance with the forces of rebellious Tekrur, they launched a determined campaign against the heartland of the great empire. It took twenty-two years to destroy the seat of empire, but Ghana was dealt a blow from which it never recovered.

The Almoravids spent their fervor in the conquest of Ghana, and were able to control the empire for only a few years. In 1087, their leader, Abu Bakr, was killed while attempting to suppress a revolt. The empire fell apart, never again to recover its former territory. For the next hundred and fifty years, the kings of various formerly subordinate states struggled against each other to pull the empire under their control. None succeeded.

Ghana, the first and most illustrious of the great Sudanic empires, lasted nearly a thousand years. It was eventually followed by Mali and Songhai, both even wealthier and larger in area, but these states never achieved the incredible longevity that was Ghana's greatest achievement. Today Ghana lives in the legends of the Sudan, but few great ruins mark its former glory.

Asia's Cultural Renaissance

PREFACE

In the eleventh century, the Chinese empire was the oldest in the world, having existed more than a thousand years. Although China had experienced periods of turmoil and division during its long history, the empire had never completely collapsed and had always eventually regained its unity and strength. The Chinese empire spent most of the tenth century mired in one of these tumultuous eras and was just starting to recover as the new millennium dawned.

China's problems had begun in the first decade of the tenth century, when the imperial T'ang dynasty came to an end. In North China, a series of ambitious military leaders usurped the throne in rapid succession. This period of political instability, which lasted approximately fifty years, is known as the Five Dynasties era because each new emperor made an unsuccessful attempt to found a lasting hereditary regime. Even though each of the five dynasties was short-lived, in many respects China remained stable; for instance, commerce and trade continued uninterrupted and even flourished. However, the emperors did face serious threats of invasion and disunity. Sensing the empire's weakness, semi-nomadic tribes such as the Tanguts and the Ch'i-tan increasingly harried the northern border regions. Meanwhile, the provincial governors and petty warlords of South China set themselves up as rulers of small independent kingdoms.

A sixth military coup in 960 succeeded in installing a strong ruler on the throne. Sung T'ai-tsu, the first emperor of the Sung dynasty, initially concentrated on restabilizing North China and then on subjugating the South China kingdoms and reincorporating them into the empire. His successors "usher[ed] in a period of unity, centralization, prosperity, and cultural flowering," as historian Charles O. Hucker writes. The Sung dynasty would be very different from the T'ang dynasty that preceded it. During the T'ang, members of the military aristocracy had governed China, but under the Sung, they were replaced in importance by the scholar-officials of the civil service. Young men now proved their worthiness to serve in the government not by commanding troops or winning battles but by studying hard and earning high scores on a series of difficult examinations. China already had a long tradition of revering scholarship, but the place of education in society became even more elevated as prestigious governmental positions began to be granted to distinguished scholars rather than to battle-hardened officers. This new emphasis on education led to a climate conducive to academic and cultural advancements.

The revitalization of China during the Sung dynasty also had roots in the surge of economic growth that occurred during the 1000s. Agricultural productivity increased rapidly, especially after the introduction of a strain of early ripening rice that allowed for as many as three harvests every year. The development of a new iron and steel industry also played an important role in the empire's economic expansion. Both internal and external commerce skyrocketed; trade relations with such partners as India and the Muslims added considerably to China's prosperity. According to historian Archibald R. Lewis, "This century saw China's economy grow spectacularly until, by the year 1100, it had developed what can only be regarded as the most advanced form of economic life to be found in all of Eurasia."

Clearly the Sung dynasty was a dynamic and energetic time for the Chinese empire. However, scholars have disagreed about its importance in Chinese history. In particular, many criticize the Sung dynasty's aversion to military campaigns and its readiness to repeatedly buy off hostile neighbors with gifts of silver and silk. They view the Sung dynasty's failure to dominate the geopolitical arena as a crucial weakness that negatively affected the ability of the Chinese to resist later invasions. These scholars tend to describe the Sung era as a pale imitation of the powerful and militaristic T'ang dynasty. On the other hand, as historians James T.C. Liu and Peter J. Golas explain, a growing number of experts "have come to see the Sung as one of the truly formative periods of Chinese history, a time of widespread social, economic, political and intellectual developments that shaped much of China down to the twentieth century."

At the same time that the first Sung emperor sparked China's resurgence, another Asian civilization was also at the threshold of a cultural awakening. Compared to the powerhouse of the Chinese empire, Japan in the year 1000 was insignificant, isolated by geography and barely participating in commercial growth and trade. Yet this little country burst forth in an unprecedented flowering of art and literature, including such innovations as the world's first novel. Considered in combination, eleventh-century China and Japan represent one of the greatest cultural renaissances of all time.

Life in China During the Early Sung Dynasty

Charles O. Hucker

Blessed with peaceful and prosperous times, eleventh-century China experienced a tremendous intellectual and cultural flowering. In the following excerpt from his book *China's Imperial Past: An Introduction to Chinese History and Culture*, Charles O. Hucker traces the beginnings of the Sung era, emphasizing those characteristics of the early dynasty that enabled China's cultural life to flourish. Hucker taught history for many years at the University of Michigan in Ann Arbor, where he also served as the chairman of the department of Far Eastern languages and literature. His books include *China to 1850: A Short History* and *The Ming Dynasty: Its Origins and Evolving Institutions.*

The fragmentation of China in the tenth century, after the long decline and final collapse of T'ang, was resolved after half a century by a new North China state called Sung, inaugurated in 960 by an army mutiny. Under the Sung dynasty, which lasted until 1279, scholar-officials finally replaced the old semifeudal aristocracy as the dominant class in Chinese society, and Chinese culture flourished as in the best of Han and T'ang times. But Sung China was hemmed in on the north and west by hostile nomadic empires and had to struggle constantly for survival. In 1126–27 the whole of North

China was lost to the alien state of Chin, ruled by proto-Manchu Jur-chen peoples.

The Southern Sung domain, limited to the Yangtze valley and the far south, enjoyed economic prosperity and cultural elegance for an-other century and a half, only to be overrun in the 1270's by the Mongols proper, who had already conquered all of inner Eurasia and probed into central Europe. . . .

Establishment of the Sung dynasty in 960 was not merely an event by which the two thousand years of China's imperial history may be conveniently divided at mid-point. It set the stage for the fulfillment of changes in the patterns of Chinese life that had been germinating since . . . the eighth century, . . . changes that gave life in the later im-perial age a notably different quality from that of either the Han or the T'ang dynasty. One major change has been suggested above: that as individual merit became the criterion for office, the old hereditary aris-tocracy disappeared, to leave civil servants the unchallenged elite in Chinese society and government. The style of governance became more autocratic, society more mobile and urbanized, the economy more commercialized. In thought, a revitalized Confucianism swept Buddhism and Taoism into the status of popular religions, only to turn increasingly introspective itself and lose much of its original empha-sis on social reform. In literature and art changes of equal significance came about, creating great new traditions in drama, fiction, and im-pressionistic painting. The rapid spread of printing and a consequent increase in literacy, along with various other technological develop-ments, were essential elements in many of these changes.

On a bolder level of generalization it can even be suggested that the Chinese spirit, having passed through a heroic, brash adolescence in the early imperial age, now experienced a chastened, sober, often grim and drab maturity. So, at least, it seemed to many thoughtful Chinese in the later empire, for whom the China of Han and T'ang times had powerful nostalgic appeal.

The Origin of the Sung Dynasty

The founder of the Sung dynasty was Chao K'uang-yin, known posthumously as Sung T'ai-tsu (r. 960–76). A capable young general in the service of the Later Chou dynasty, Chao was catapulted into prominence in 959 by his appointment as commander-in-chief of the palace army, the core of Later Chou military strength. Almost im-mediately a boy emperor succeeded to the throne, but at the begin-ning of 960 the army acclaimed Chao emperor instead; he took the throne at the age of thirty-two. It was not the first time in the Five Dynasties era that an army had engineered such a coup, and it seems likely that Chao was the instigator as well as the beneficiary of the mutiny. The times called for vigorous leadership.

The Sung dynasty inherited from its predecessors the dream of a restored T'ang empire, but it confronted serious external and internal problems. The increasingly powerful Ch'i-tan (Khitan) state of Liao loomed threateningly in the north and northeast. It had repeatedly interfered in North China politics since the end of T'ang, had taken control of 16 prefectures in traditional Chinese territory south of the Great Wall, and in 951 had helped establish a Chinese puppet regime, the Northern Han state, in Shansi province. In the northwest a federation of Tibetan tribes called Tanguts . . . had steadily expanded their territories during the tenth century and were soon to formalize their hostile independence by establishing an imperial state known as Hsi Hsia. South China remained fragmented among independent regional kingdoms. Though they did not threaten the north, they were obstacles to any northern ruler who hoped to consolidate manpower and other resources for a national effort to prevail over the nomadic raiders of the north and northwest. Moreover, in North China itself no government had yet consolidated power sufficiently to eliminate all separatist-minded warlords. The creation of Northern Han in 951 and the army mutiny that brought Sung T'ai-tsu to the throne in 960 were proof enough of North China's continuing instability.

Sung T'ai-tsu was a prudent and clever statesman who saw the folly of trying prematurely to regain territories lost to the Ch'i-tan and the Tanguts. His first priority was to centralize and stabilize North China. To this end, he persuaded his own chief military supporters to yield their commands in return for generous retirement pensions, thus forestalling the possibility of a successful mutiny against him. Gradually and tactfully, he also replaced militaristic regional governors with civil officials delegated from his court. Further, he transferred to the palace army, of which he retained personal command, the best units of the regional armies. In this way he created a military establishment in which the main fighting force was a large, mobile professional army garrisoned around the capital, while local forces consisted largely of substandard recruits.

T'ai-tsu also helped ensure his supremacy by expanding the examination-recruited civil service and entrusting the administration of government at all levels to its scholar-officials, who characteristically had no substantial power bases of their own but owed their status entirely to imperial favor, and by giving his central government the power to control the collection of all revenues and the appointment of all officials down to the county level. In these ways he created an institutional framework for an autocratic concentration of power in the throne beyond anything attained by earlier dynasties in a regular, institutionalized form; but T'ai-tsu did not abuse his powers. He honored civil servants, encouraged them to be imaginative and bold, and in general set an admirable precedent by seeking and heeding their advice. He built a modest palace at Kaifeng, which was located in the center of the productive North China plain and had been the capital of most of the Five Dynasties, and instituted practices that kept the whole Sung era freer of abuses by palace women and eunuchs than any other major era of Chinese history.

Conflict and Compromise

While establishing these fundamental dynastic policies, T'ai-tsu moved carefully and systematically to incorporate the South China kingdoms. In campaigns in 963, 964–65, 971, and 975 he subjugated one southern regime after another except the aboriginal state of Nan Chao in the far southwest, which retained its independence throughout the Sung dynasty, and the kingdom of Wu-Yüeh in Chekiang. T'ai-tsu died at the comparatively young age of forty-eight, his imperial ambitions only partially realized, but his younger brother, T'ai-tsung (r. 976–97), carried his plans forward; he accepted the peaceable surrender of Wu-Yüeh in 978 and then destroyed Northern Han, the Ch'i-tan protectorate in Shansi, in 979. Thus the traditional Chinese homeland was reunited except for the far northwest and the tier of 16 northern prefectures that Liao had seized.

The Tanguts in the northwest were sufficiently impressed by the new Sung dynasty to offer tribute and become nominal vassals. T'ai-tsung was satisfied with that because there was much greater popular resentment about the Ch'i-tan encroachment south of the Great Wall. In 979, immediately after subjugating Northern Han, T'ai-tsung personally led a campaign to recover the Peking area. Beaten off by the Ch'i-tan, he organized a second campaign only to be beaten off again, with heavy losses. T'ai-tsung then concentrated on building defenses, and defense was to be the Sung military posture through the remainder of the dynasty. The frontier situation stabilized in 1004, when a Liao probe in the direction of Kaifeng was checked. The opposing rulers then made a peace agreement that left the northern prefectures under Liao control and guaranteed "brotherly gifts" to Liao from the Sung court amounting to 100,000 taels (ounces) of silver and 200,000 bolts of silk each year. After several decades Liao demanded and got an increase of 100,000 units in each category; but the Ch'i-tan rulers kept the peace with China for more than a century. Meantime, the volatile Tangutan Hsi Hsia state provoked an inconclusive four-year war with Sung in the northwest in 1040–44. Hsi Hsia then promised to be peaceable in return for similar annual "gifts" of 200,000 taels of silver and 200,000 bolts of silk; but it continued to harass the Chinese, who launched ineffective punitive campaigns against the Tanguts in 1069 and again in 1081–1082.

Characteristics of the Sung Era

As always in times of prolonged domestic stability, China enjoyed great prosperity through the eleventh century. By mid-century the population regained its T'ang peak of sixty million, and by1100 it apparently approached one hundred million. The forces of change that were rooted in the breakdown of the old T'ang order in the ninth and tenth centuries now accelerated, and distinctively new patterns of Chinese life began to take shape. The socioeconomic realm was transformed partly by government initiatives and partly by private entrepreneurship of a more flamboyant type than China had seen since early Han times. New seeds and crops were introduced, there were successive advances in the organization and technology of both agriculture and industry, production boomed, and government revenues swelled in multiples of the T'ang totals. Kaifeng and other cities became large urban complexes, serving as the centers of regional and in some cases national marketing systems. Commerce flourished to an unprecedented degree, and for the first time in Chinese history a genuinely national urban class was emerging. New kinds of careers and life-styles developed in the commercial centers. Moreover, printing, which had developed rapidly in the Five Dynasties era, promoted literacy and education—to the point where, for the first time in Chinese history, common people had realistic hopes that their sons might achieve status in the elite official class.

The intellectual life of the eleventh century was probably more exciting than the Chinese had ever known. Scholarship, literature, and art all flourished in the hands of the greatly expanded, urban-oriented literate class. Most especially, foundations were laid for the Neo-Confucian philosophical system that would soon topple Buddhism from its long preeminence among Chinese intellectuals to become China's ideological orthodoxy into the twentieth century.

Eleventh-century China was the most populous, prosperous, and cultured nation on earth. It should also have been the most powerful, for the largest share of the increasing state income was spent on maintaining a huge standing army, well equipped with mass-produced iron and steel gear, and with various incendiary weapons supplementing the traditional bows and crossbows. Considering both the forces the dynasty had at its disposal, numbering some 1,250,000 at mid-century, and Chinese military successes against northerners in earlier periods of unity and prosperity, one might suppose Sung China should never have become the intimidated vassal of such neighbors as Liao and Hsi Hsia.

Among the many explanations that can be offered for Sung's failure to achieve military predominance over the northern nomads in the pattern of the Han and T'ang dynasties, the simplest is that the

Chinese were losing the will to fight. Sinicization was steadily weakening the warlike spirit of both the Ch'i-tan and the Tanguts, and the Chinese gradually realized that neither was going to engage in serious new aggressions against China. Keeping them appeased with silver and silk (the value of which never exceeded 2 per cent of Sung's state revenues) seemed a reasonable enough price to pay for peace, and Chinese of the eleventh century had more appealing and challenging things to do than struggle for the recovery of marginal territories. Such attitudes resulted in large part from the decay of the old military-minded aristocracy, a process that was hastened by the personnel policies of T'ai-tsu and T'ai-tsung. The military was subordinated to civil service control, careers in military service were disesteemed, the interests of scholar-officials became paramount in government, and the civilian values of the intellectual elite began permeating the whole society. The eleventh century produced no eminent military leaders, but it produced a galaxy of Chinese history's most distinguished and dedicated scholar-officials; and at no time in history were there more earnest efforts to achieve a golden age of benevolent government and popular welfare.

Economic Reform and Trade Development

Steven Warshaw, C. David Bromwell, and A.J. Tudisco

Steven Warshaw, C. David Bromwell, and A.J. Tudisco are the authors of several books on Asia, including *China Emerges: A Concise History of China from Its Origin to the Present*, from which the following selection is taken. The authors investigate the movement for economic reform that occurred in China during the 1000s. In particular, they discuss the reforms proposed by Wang An-shih, an adviser to the Sung imperial family. Wang An-shih's new policies greatly benefitted China, they maintain, contributing to a significant growth in trade and commerce that established Sung-dynasty China as an economic powerhouse.

During the Sung Dynasty Period, the movement for economic reform was led by Wang An-shih (1021–1086 A.D.). The son of a poor civil servant, Wang rose to become a minor official in the court bureaucracy. He was much noted for his bold ideas, as well as for his disdain for formal dress and etiquette. Wang An-shih suggested a change in the ancient practice by which learned Confucian scholars were given posts in government far too easily. Even under the Sungs, who worked steadily to improve the civil service, the office-seekers were often able to win government jobs simply by buying them or asking for them. The tasks of administration had become too complicated for such men to be effective, Wang argued. It seemed to him that a more efficient government would result from the appointment of some well-trained, well-paid specialists. When he advanced this program, however, he was bitterly condemned by a group of conservatives led by Ssu-ma Kuang (1018–1086 A.D.), a noted historian.

Tax Reform

The emperor Shen-tsung, the sixth ruler of the Sung Dynasty, agreed with Wang An-shih. In 1069 A.D., the year after he took power, he made Wang a special court adviser. Wang An-shih's greatest innovation was to build government granaries for the storage of grains collected as taxes. He used the granaries to control prices—distributing from them when there was a scarcity and collecting for them when there was a surplus. (These "ever-normal granaries" had been attempted by the earlier reformer Wang Mang, without success.) Wang also distributed surplus grain to the poor and made loans to the impoverished farmers. The state charged only twenty per cent interest on the loans, by contrast to the fifty per cent normally charged by landlords. To relieve farmers of forced labor, he put through legislation called the "Public Services Act," which required the government to pay for their services in construction projects. These projects were financed by a new taxation, with rich and poor paying their fair share of the burden.

Wang An-shih's tax program anticipated by more than eight centuries modern income taxes. To make taxation more effective, he brought the older register of lands up to date, surveying almost all estates of China. When the enormous task was completed, it was possible to gather taxes more efficiently and to plan the national budget more exactly. Large landowners could no longer escape the relentless government tax agents.

Many other sectors of Chinese life were affected by Wang An-shih's economic program. To improve the effectiveness of the army, he reduced the number of troops on the payroll from 1,600,000 to 600,000 and trained a militia of loyal farmers to ride and fight. Wang rewrote many Confucian texts for use in Chinese schools, which angered the literati. "If anyone has a poor harvest," wrote Wang An-shih, "I will give him all the grain I possess so that he has something to live on." But the Confucian historian Ssu-ma Kuang declared that to help the common people through loans and grain would only make them lazy. The conservative scholars pressured many officials into disobeying Wang's orders. When the emperor died, the conservatives wasted no time in stripping Wang's powers and repealing his reforms.

Wang An-shih's reforms might have wrought a permanent change in the character of China if they had been permitted to endure even a short time. His policy of encouraging merchants and industrialists by giving them tax benefits, his sponsorship of wider trading through the use of paper currency, and his willingness to help merchants to develop their trade associations, all encouraged the rise of a strong mercantile class. Such a class might have challenged the power of the gentry who traditionally ruled China through their ownership of land in an essentially agrarian economy. As in the Western nations and in Japan, this could have given rise to a more dynamic and modern society. But the merchants failed to win much political influence.

An Economic Powerhouse

Nevertheless, despite the triumph of conservatives over Wang An-shih, the Sung was a period of great commercial vitality and expansion. The forces of Islam were active to the west of China, and a lively new trade with the Muslims sprang up. Many new cities were founded and became prosperous, particularly on the southern coast, where a sea trade with India flourished. Merchants broke down the walls around their commercial centers and lined whole streets with shops. Their associations formed natural monopolies that further increased trade. Commerce also benefited from the spread of paper money issued by private Chinese bankers. In the larger cities, academies were founded which attracted outstanding scholars. These places became centers of new and more vigorous schools of Chinese thought.

The Importance of the Intellectual Class

Dun J. Li

Scholars and other intellectuals played an essential role in China during the early Sung dynasty. Those who passed the difficult civil service examinations were appointed to posts in the government bureaucracy, where they oversaw such functions as tax collection, education, and the justice system. As Dun J. Li notes in the following passage from his book *The Ageless Chinese: A History*, these civil servants kept the machinery of the Sung government running smoothly. Furthermore, Li writes, the examinations were open to men from almost every social class, which provided opportunities for students from poor backgrounds to advance their careers and social status. A professor of history for many years at William Paterson University in Wayne, New Jersey, Li has also taught at the National University of Political Science in Nanking, China.

If one happened to be intelligent and love book learning, one could not have been born to a better time than the Sung period, however humble one's background might be. With the exception of a small minority known as the "mean people," all Chinese were entitled to take part in the civil service examinations, and the examinations, being impartially administered, served as the greatest mechanism in keeping the political and intellectual elite in a continuous flux. Some may say that the increase of social mobility as generated by the examination system was more apparent than real since allegedly only the wealthy could afford to send their children to school. This assertion is valid only to a certain extent. To a family that had designated one of its sons (usually the brightest) to pursue an academic career, the major sacrifice was to lose him as a full-time worker on the farm. Since the farm was most likely small, his service on it might not have been needed in the first place. Tuition paid to a village teacher was nominal and could always be compounded into a few pints of rice. The length of formal schooling was also short because, once a student learned to read independently, he was practically on his own. If by then he had shown some promise as a scholar, there would be no dearth of eager, more affluent families that would try to help him out—to produce a distinguished scholar, as measured by the civil service examinations, was not only a matter of local pride, but it also had social and political implications that no farsighted person could ignore.

Countless examples of the Chinese version of from-rags-to-riches can be cited, but one of the best concerns Fan Chung-yen. Born to a poor family in Soochow, he was still an infant when his father died. Out of economic necessity his mother remarried, and he spent an unhappy childhood in his foster father's house. In 1011, at the age of twenty-one, he decided to make a name for himself. He left home for Honan where he studied with a private academy, later known as Ying-t'ien. For the next four years, we are told, he studied day and night, washing his face with cold water whenever he was too tired to continue and eating nothing more substantial than a daily fare of thin gruel. The endurance paid off in 1015 when he passed the metropolitan examination in his first attempt. He received appointment as magistrate of Kwangteh (located in modern Anhwei province), and among his first actions was to send for his mother, so she, too, could enjoy the glory and the material reward due to a holder of the *chin-shih* ("advanced scholarship") degree. From then on he rose steadily in the bureaucracy until he eventually became the prime minister. While in Kaifeng, he proposed reform for the enormous waste and inefficiency in the central government, but his proposal was rejected. During the Tangut war, he was called to head an army to defend the northwestern frontier after several Sung generals had failed. He stopped the Tanguts' advance and was in due course able to impose on them a peaceful settlement. During his long, distinguished career, he set aside part of his salaries to establish a relief fund to help the deserving poor. When in retirement, he was a good friend and fine neighbor, always kind and helpful to anyone who needed his counsel and advice.

The Intellectual Elite

People like Fan Chung-yen were the conscience of their time, and his maxim that "an educated man should suffer before anyone else suffers and should enjoy only after everyone else has enjoyed" may have been too lofty an ideal for all of his fellow intellectuals to reach. Nevertheless, there were enough intellectuals with a good conscience to make the Sung period a truly memorable one. They served as a buffer between an unbending bureaucracy bent on collecting as much tax as possible and the voiceless masses from whom most of them came. Often at the risk of their own careers, many of them spoke eloquently about social injustice and economic exploitation, sometimes with good results. When in retirement, they, as recognized leaders in their respective communities, supervised the maintenance of Confucian temples and the worship therein, the operation of communal granaries and relief work in time of famine, the establishment of schools and the proper education of the young, the continued operation of such welfare establishments as orphanages and houses for the aged, the administration of justice for crimes less serious than murder or armed robbery, and many other matters. Above all, they were the transmitters of Chinese heritage from one generation to another. They were supposed to set a moral example for others to follow and many of them did.

Wherever they lived or worked, these intellectuals formed part of a nationwide community. The community was not a society or association in its modern sense, with membership cards and paid dues; it was an informal comradeship of common interest, devotion, and pride. A successful candidate of the metropolitan examination would be an automatic member since his name would be immediately known to everyone in the community, and those who passed the examination in the same year had a special feeling for one another and called each other *t'ung-nien* ("same-year"), an affectionate term for "brother." For a person who had failed or, for personal reasons, had not tried to obtain a *chin-shih* degree, entry to this exclusive community was more difficult, since he had to do something special to attract nationwide attention. Maybe his essay on current affairs or on a specific point about Confucian philosophy was judged to have special merit; maybe some of his poems were so well phrased that they resembled the work of a genius. Even a *chin-shih* degree holder recognized that not everyone who had passed the examination was brighter than everyone who had failed it. Members of the community took their superiority for granted—so did practically everyone else. They protected one another's interests and formed a solid front as far as outsiders were concerned. If they failed as government officials, they could always return home as recognized leaders of their own communities. Even in total defeat, they were still regarded as better than anyone else.

Below the national community of intellectual elite were the second-echelon aspirants known only locally in their own communities. They were a mixed group, ranging from those who barely knew how to write a presentable letter to those who had passed the lower level of the civil service examination and had received the *hsiu-ts'ai* ("flowering talent") degree. The kind of influence they were able to exercise depended less upon their scholarship, which was difficult to measure, than upon their family background which was more tangible and familiar. A *hsiu-ts'ai* degree holder from a wealthy, established family might be a power in his own right, but his colleague from a poor background might have great difficulties in surviving since the government did not subsidize holders of lower degrees. To make a living, an impoverished *hsiu-ts'ai* might, for a fee, compose eulogies of the dead, write petitions for the illiterate or less well educated, or peddle calligraphy among the peasants who, following tradition, pasted calligraphic works on doors and walls when a special occasion such as the New Year had arrived. He might be able to secure a position in the magistrate's office as a secretary or clerk if he had good connections; more often than not, he became a schoolteacher. Despite his reputation as a scholar, his life was anything but enviable.

Importance in the Community

All the local scholars, rich or poor, held the *chin-shih* degree holders in awe as the kind of persons they themselves wanted, but failed, to become. A *chin-shih* living in his own community was an acknowledged leader whose opinion must be sought on all important matters. Even the local magistrate would not make an important decision without consulting him in advance. If, when a local issue developed, he was serving in the capital or some other part of China, and if, in the meantime, the issue had become too complicated to be settled to everyone's satisfaction, he might be requested to serve as an arbitrator; his decision, under normal circumstances, would be followed without fail. The general principle governing local disputes was to avoid litigation that would impose financial burden on all parties concerned. If two *chin-shih* degree holders stood on the opposite sides of a local issue, a *cause célèbre* ensued, no matter how insignificant the issue really was. Normally this would not happen since the intellectual elite preferred a united front vis-à-vis outsiders and would not wish to damage their own reputations and prestige in endless lawsuits.

While most intellectuals who became teachers did so out of economic necessity, there were others who purposely chose teaching as a lifelong profession. To them life as a bureaucrat, with its implied necessity of having to please one's superiors regardless of the issue involved, was simply too demeaning to entertain. Great masters emerged because, of all the things they could do in life, they preferred teaching. Ch'i T'ung-wen, a master teacher in the latter part of the tenth century, attracted students from all parts of China, and fifty-six of them later succeeded in passing the metropolitan examination. It was at the academy he founded, later known as Ying-t'ien, that Fan Chung-yen studied. Ying-t'ien, Pai-lu-tung (located in modern Kiangsi province), Shih-ku (located in modern Hunan province), and Yüeh-lu (also located in modern Hunan province) were then hailed as the Four Great Colleges of China. In Lower Yangtze there was a master teacher named Hu Yüan who, besides being a classicist, also specialized in acoustics. In the 1040's, after more than forty years of teaching in Huchow, he came to Kaifeng as a visiting professor in the Central University. So many students wished to enroll in his classes, or just be close enough to have a glimpse of him, that the regular dormitories were found to be inadequate and the university authorities, we are told, had to erect temporary buildings to accommodate the surplus. Sometimes a renowned scholar would travel hundreds of miles to engage in open debate with colleagues who held a different point of view, as the audience listened in awe of their erudition and eloquence. A scholar of this kind attracted followers from far and wide, and quickly he and his followers would found a new school of learning with a different philosophical emphasis.

Scholars and Politics

Scholars like Ch'i T'ung-wen and Hu Yüan were universally admired and respected because, among other things, they never allowed themselves to get deeply involved with political feuds and bickering. Being nonpolitical, however, was more an exception than a rule. While as individuals most Sung scholars could be characterized as good men, the Confucian obsession with "learning for the purpose of application" (*hsüeh yi chih yung*) could not but transform academic differences into practical politics, and scholars of different philosophical emphases soon found themselves political enemies as well. Various philosophical and political cliques emerged, and each of them made alliances and created enemies as the occasion arose. Before 1100 the political feuds were still conducted on a high level because, among other things, the participants were not only scholars but also gentlemen. Their differences were those of a policy or ideological orientation, and there was no personal vendetta of any kind. . . .

No intellectual was ever jailed or executed when his faction or clique lost power. The worst that could happen to him was the loss of his bureaucratic post and consequently his power base; he might even have to leave the capital and return home where he would remain a celebrity and an authoritative voice. In short, the political feuds of the Sung dynasty were the most gentlemanly ever recorded in Chinese history, never equalled before or since. Sung T'ai-tsu, a scholarly emperor, had made it a dynastic rule that no corporal punishment should ever be inflicted upon intellectuals, and his successors, for more than three hundred years, followed this rule without fail.

As the intellectuals formed the most powerful group in politics, traditional power blocks, such as the eunuchs and the emperor's maternal or spousal relatives, were completely overshadowed in terms of influence. One may argue, perhaps convincingly, that the Sung intellectuals, in power for more than three centuries, did not do any better for the Sung people than the groups they condemned did for their respective regimes. One may also argue, perhaps less convincingly, that their failings resulted less from personal faults than from the inherent imperfection of a chaotic world they had to face. Nevertheless, the very idea that the avenue to power was education, instead of birth, wealth, or any other consideration, was unique and refreshing. The examination system may not be the best way to measure a person's worth; still, no one in traditional China had been able to devise a better system. In any case, it kept alive the hope of a peasant's son who, with good intelligence, hard work, and much luck, might someday become one of the most powerful men in the nation. In view of the competition, the odds against his success were of course overwhelming; but few societies other than traditional China had ever even given him a chance.

Proposals for the Training and Selection of Government Officials

Wang An-shih

Wang An-shih, a scholar and government official, was the most important advocate of reform in eleventh-century China. In 1058, he sent the following memorial to the emperor of China, outlining the problems inherent in recruiting effective bureaucrats and suggesting corrective measures. The civil service examination is failing to produce able officials, Wang writes, because it places too much emphasis on literary style and rote memorization of the classics at the expense of practical knowledge. He suggests a return to the general principles of the ancient system of educating and selecting government officials, but he is also careful to specify that the content of the coursework should be updated for the current era.

Your servant observes that Your Majesty possesses the virtues of reverence and frugality and is endowed with wisdom and sagacity. Rising early in the morning and retiring late in the evening, Your Majesty does not relax for even a single day. Neither music, beautiful women, dogs, horses, sight-seeing, nor any of the other objects of pleasure distract or becloud your intelligence in the least. Your humanity toward men and love of all creatures pervade the land. Moreover, Your Majesty selects those whom the people of the empire would wish to have assisting Your Majesty, entrusts to them the affairs of state, and does not vacillate in the face of [opposition from] slanderous, wicked, traitorous, and cunning officials. Even the solicitude of the Two Emperors and Three Kings did not surpass this. We should expect, therefore, that the needs of every household and man would be filled and that the empire would enjoy a state of perfect order. And yet this result has not been attained. Within the empire the security of the state is a cause for some anxiety, and on our borders there is the constant threat of the barbarians. Day by day the resources of the nation become more depleted and exhausted, while the moral tone and habits of life among the people daily deteriorate. On all sides officials who have the interests of the state at heart are fearful that the peace of the empire may not last. What is the reason for this?

The Way of the Ancients

The cause of the distress is that we ignore the law. Now the government is strict in enforcing the law, and its statutes are complete to the last detail. Why then does your servant consider that there is an absence of law? It is because most of the present body of law does not accord with the government of the ancient kings. Mencius says, "Though he may have a humane heart and a reputation for humaneness, one from whom the people receive no benefits will not serve as a model for later generations because he does not practice the Way of the former kings." The application of what Mencius said to our own failure in the present is obvious.

Now our own age is far removed from that of the ancient kings, and the changes and circumstances with which we are confronted are not the same. Even the most ignorant can see that it would be difficult to put into practice every single item in the government of the ancient kings. But when your servant says that our present failures arise from the fact that we do not adopt the governmental system of the ancient kings, he is merely suggesting that we should follow their general intent. Now the Two Emperors were separated from the Three Kings by more than a thousand years. There were periods of order and disorder, and there were periods of prosperity and decay. Each of them likewise encountered different changes and faced different circumstances, and each differed also in the way he set up his government. Yet they never differed as to their underlying aims in the government of the empire, the state, and the family, nor in their sense of the relative importance and priority of things [as set forth in the ancient text, the *Great Learning*, chapter 1]. Therefore, your servant contends that we should follow only their general intent. If we follow their intent, then the changes and reforms introduced by us would not startle the ears and shock the eyes of the people, nor cause them to murmur. And yet our government would be in accord with that of the ancient kings.

The most urgent need of the present time is to secure capable men. Only when we can produce a large number of capable men in the empire will it be possible to select a sufficient number of persons qualified to serve in the government. And only when we get capable men in the government will there be no difficulty in assessing what may be done, in view of the time and circumstances, and in consideration of the human distress that may be occasioned, gradually to change the decadent laws of the empire in order to approach the ideas of the ancient kings. The empire today is the same as the empire of the ancient kings. There were numerous capable men in their times. Why is there a dearth of such men today? It is because, as has been said, we do not train and cultivate men in the proper way.

In ancient times, the Son of Heaven and feudal lords had schools ranging from the capital down to the districts and villages. Officers of instruction were widely appointed, but selected with the greatest care. The affairs of the court, rites and music, punishment and correction were all subjects that found a place in the schools. What the students observed and learned were the sayings, the virtuous acts, and the ideas underlying the government of the empire and the states. Men not qualified to govern the empire and the states would not be given an education, while those who could be so used in government never failed to receive an education. This is the way to conduct the training of men.

Selecting Officials

What is the way to select officials? The ancient kings selected men only from the local villages and through the local schools. The people were asked to recommend those they considered virtuous and able, sending up their nominations to the court, which investigated each one. Only if the men recommended proved truly virtuous and able would they be appointed to official posts commensurate with their individual virtue and ability. Investigation of them did not mean that a ruler relied only upon his own keenness of sight and hearing or that he took the word of one man alone. . . . Having inquired into his actions and utterances, they then tested him in government affairs. What was meant by "investigation" was just that—to test them in government affairs. . . . [But] it is not possible for the ruler to investigate each case personally, nor can he entrust this matter to any other individual, expecting that in a day or two he could inquire into and test their conduct and abilities and recommend their employment or dismissal. When we have investigated those whose conduct and ability are of the highest level, and have appointed them to high office, we should ask them in turn to select men of the same type, try them out for a time and test them, and then make recommendations to the ruler, whereupon ranks and salaries would be granted to them. This is the way to conduct the selection of officials.

[In ancient times] officials were selected with great care, appointed to posts that suited their qualifications, and kept in office for a reasonable length of time. And once employed, they were given sufficient authority for the discharge of their duties. They were not hampered and bound by one regulation or another but were allowed to carry out their own ideas. It was by this method that Yao and Shun regulated the hundred offices of government and inspired the various officials.

Today, although we have schools in each prefecture and district, they amount to no more than school buildings. There are no officers of instruction and guidance; nothing is done to train and develop human talent. Only in the Imperial Academy are officers of instruction and guidance to be found, and even they are not selected with care. The affairs of the court, rites and music, punishment and correction have no place in the schools, and the students pay no attention to them, considering that rites and music, punishment and correction are the business of officials, not something they ought to know about. What is taught to the students consists merely of textual exegesis [of the classics].

That, however, was not the way men were taught in ancient times. In recent years, teaching has been based on the essays required for the civil service examinations, but this kind of essay cannot be learned without resorting to extensive memorization and strenuous study, upon which students must spend their efforts the whole day long. Such proficiency as they attain is at best of no use in the government of the empire, and at most the empire can make no use of them. . . .

[Of old] those scholars who had learned the way of the ancient kings and whose behavior and character had won the approval of their village communities were the ones entrusted with the duty of guarding the frontiers and the palace in accordance with their respective abilities. . . . Today this most important responsibility in the empire . . . is given to those corrupt, ruthless, and unreliable men whose ability and behavior are not such that they can maintain themselves in their local villages. . . . But as long as military training is not given, and men of a higher type are not selected for military service, there is no wonder that scholars regard the carrying of weapons as a disgrace and that none of them is able to ride, or shoot, or has any familiarity with military maneuvers. This is because education is not conducted in the proper way.

In the present system for selecting officials, those who memorize assiduously, recite extensively, and have some knowledge of literary composition are called "splendid talents of extraordinary accomplishment" or "men of virtue, wise, square, and upright." These are the categories from which the ministers of state are chosen. Those whose memories are not so strongly developed and [who] cannot recite so extensively, yet have some knowledge of literary composition and have also studied poetry in the *shi* and *fu* forms, are called "advanced scholars." The highest of these are also selected as ministers of state. It can be seen without any question that the skills and knowledge acquired by men in these two categories do not fit them to serve as ministers. . . .

In addition, candidates are examined in such fields as the Nine Classics, the Five Classics, specialization [in one classic], and the study of law. The court has already become concerned over the uselessness of this type of knowledge and has stressed the need for an understanding of general principles [as set forth in the classics]. . . . When we consider the men selected through "understanding of the classics," however, it is still those who memorize, recite, and have some knowledge of literary composition who are able to pass the examination, while those who can apply them [the classics] to the government of the empire are not always brought in through this kind of selection.

Barriers to Effectiveness

It has already been made clear that officials are not selected with care, employed in accordance with their competence, and kept in office long enough. But, in addition, when entrusted with office, they are not given sufficient authority to fulfill their duties, but find their hands tied by this law or that regulation so that they are unable to carry out their own ideas. . . . Nevertheless, there has not been a single case in history . . . that shows that it is possible to obtain good government merely by relying on the effectiveness of law without regard to having the right man in power. On the other hand, there has not been a single case in history, from ancient times to the present, that shows that it is possible to obtain good government even with the right man in power if he is bound by one regulation or another in such a way that he cannot carry out his ideas.

Your servant also observes that in former times when the court thought of doing something and introducing some reforms, the advantages and disadvantages were considered carefully at the beginning. But whenever some vulgar opportunist took a dislike to the reform and opposed it, the court stopped short and dared not carry it out. . . . Since it was difficult to set up laws and institutions, and since the men seeking personal advantages were unwilling to accept these measures and comply with them, the ancients who intended to do something had to resort to punishment. Only then could their ideas be carried out.

Now the early kings, wishing to set up laws and institutions in order to change corrupt customs and obtain capable men, overcame their feeling of reluctance to mete out punishment, for they saw that there was no other way of carrying out their policy.

Printing's Contribution to Literacy and Education

Thomas H.C. Lee

The Chinese invented printing prior to the Sung dynasty, but it was not until the tenth century that the technology underwent vast improvements and became widespread. During the eleventh century, Thomas H.C. Lee explains, the new popularity of printing led to an unprecedented increase in the availability of books, which in turn created an explosion of literacy and scholarship. Lee is the author of *Education in Traditional China: A History* and *Government Education and Examinations in Sung China*, from which the following essay is excerpted. He is a professor of history and the director of the Asian Studies program at the City College of the City University of New York.

Contributing to the progress in the education of commoners was the mass utilization of printing skills in the century during which the Sung dynasty was founded. . . . The idea of duplicating written materials by seals or by engraving stones for later rubbing was by no means new in China. But the truly significant breakthrough in the history of "printing" in China came in the tenth century when

Excerpted from Thomas H.C. Lee, *Government Education and Examinations in Sung China.* Copyright © 1985 The Chinese University of Hong Kong. Reprinted with permission from The Chinese University Press.

wooden blocks started to be used. With them, it became economically feasible to distribute books by "printing" in large numbers. The Sung therefore benefited from the invention of block printing, a skill remarkably convenient and economical, which marked an important turning point in Chinese history.

Positive and Negative Effects

The widespread use of printing technology had both positive and negative effects on Chinese society. First of all, it definitely created an unprecedented opportunity for Chinese people to have access to books, resulting in an increase in the number of students who could take part in the civil service examinations. The rise in importance of the civil service examinations was as much a result of the general increase in the opportunities for education as a result of encouragement on the part of Sung rulers.

The second effect of the use of printing presses was the rise in literacy. The rate of literacy is a difficult social phenomenon to measure, but all indications suggest that there was an increase in literacy rate in the Sung. The effects of the increase were reflected in the following developments. First of all, Sung society saw the emergence of story-telling as a profession, which was responsible for the appearance of early novels. The rise of this profession, however, was doubtlessly a result of both a wealthy society which created a leisured class and an increasingly literate society which provided both story-tellers and an audience. Secondly, there was a rapid increase in all kinds of publications, including literary collections, encyclopedias, and most notably, the "moral books" (*shan-shu*). The last category of books was aimed at the populace at large. The rapid growth in book publication reflected an important social reality: the increased demand for books by a larger readership. Thirdly, though the increase in literacy was by no means sudden or extraordinarily spectacular, it did pose problems for ideological control. Many important ideological control measures were invented or revived in the Sung, chiefly because there was a need to reevaluate the significance and impact of widespread literacy. In a sense, then, increased literacy added a new dimension to the Chinese conception of education, and a rather complicated dimension at that.

Thirdly, the invention and the widespread use of printing technology most certainly led to a serious change in Chinese intellectual attitudes. More people were reading and becoming aware of the possible diversity of ideas. The result probably was the appearance of a number of people who, because of the chance to become literate, espoused extreme or even radical ideas. During the Sung, especially the Northern Sung, the emergence of such a new group of people advocating a wide range of reforming ideas must partially have been a result of easier access to printed materials. At least, it is probably fair to say that the unprecedented magnitude of Sung reform movements and their opposition owed a lot to the fact that an increased number of people were literate enough to become involved in the debates. The change in reading habits and the influx of ancient ideas, now popularized and inevitably modified by story-tellers in marketplaces, resulted in a different way of looking at nature and society. Chinese society was rapidly becoming secularized in the Sung, taxing the time and energy of the traditionalists who fought vigorously to forestall this trend.

Printing technology had an enormous influence on Chinese society. Although the speed and magnitude of the impact were not comparable to that of the Gutenberg Revolution, its importance should not be minimized. It not only created in Sung society various radicalized reforming groups, but also helped to shape the examination system and sustained it as a useful social institution. Its ultimate consequence was to broaden the reading public, a consequence that created new dimensions in China's social problems.

The Growth of a Native Culture in Japan

Edwin O. Reischauer

A leading expert on Japan, Edwin O. Reischauer was a professor of Far Eastern languages at Harvard University for almost forty years. He also served as the U.S. ambassador to Japan from 1961 to 1966. Among his numerous books are *East Asia: Tradition and Transformation*, *The Japanese Today: Change and Continuity*, and *Japan: The Story of a Nation*, from which the following selection is taken. According to Reischauer, for many centuries the Japanese modeled their civilization on that of China, but gradually they began to develop their own unique culture and art forms. By the early 1000s, he writes, this distinctive Japanese culture was rapidly blooming, especially in the area of literature.

The period of greatest learning [transmitted to Japan] from the [Chinese] lasted from the late sixth century until the middle of the ninth century, but then a subtle change began to take place in the Japanese attitude toward China. The prestige of all things Chinese remained great, but the Japanese were no longer so anxious to learn from China or so ready to admit the superiority of all facets of Chinese civilization over their own. The period from 710 to 794, when the capital was in the vicinity of Nara, was the time of the height of the political and cultural pattern borrowed from China. Even after the move of the capital in 794 to Heian, or Kyoto, the prestige of Chinese ways of doing things remained great, but by the early tenth century a profound shift in cultural emphasis had become apparent. As a consequence, the spirit of the Heian period, as the age from the ninth to the early twelfth century is called, came in time to be sharply different from that of the so-called Nara period. The emphasis was no longer on borrowing new elements of culture from China but on assimilating and transforming those that had already been borrowed to make them more congenial to Japanese tastes and better fitted to Japanese realities.

One reason for the lessened interest in learning from China was the political decay of T'ang, which became marked as the ninth century progressed. Perhaps even more fundamental was the intellectual growth of the Japanese themselves, for it resulted in a gradual reassertion of a spirit of cultural independence. Three centuries of assiduous learning from the Chinese had created, at least in the capital district, a cultured society with its own political and social institutions, patterned of course after Chinese models, but changed and adapted to fit Japanese needs by conscious experimentation and slow unconscious modification. The Japanese were no longer a primitive people, overawed by the vastly superior continental civilization and eager to imitate blindly anything Chinese. Japan was reaching a state of intellectual maturity and was ready to develop along her own lines.

One sign of the changing attitude was the ending of official contacts with China. The last of the great embassies left Japan for T'ang in 838 and returned the next year. Later embassies were proposed but were argued down by courtiers who felt their value no longer warranted the tremendous risks of the trip across the East China Sea. Some private traders and student monks continued to travel between the two lands, but for the most part Japan lapsed into her earlier state of virtual isolation from the continent. This isolation in turn made the Japanizing of the imported Chinese civilization all the more inevitable and rapid.

Developments in Writing and Literature

The cultural change is perhaps best illustrated by the development of an adequate means of writing the native tongue. This writing system was developed slowly during the ninth and tenth centuries by the process of using certain Chinese characters in greatly abbreviated form as simple phonetic symbols devoid of any specific meaning in themselves. Since the Chinese characters each represented one monosyllabic word, the phonetic symbols derived from them stood for a whole syllable, such as *ka, se,* or *mo.* The result was a syllabary rather than an alphabet. . . .

The Japanese syllabaries, called *kana,* formed more clumsy writing systems than alphabets, but they were, nevertheless, reasonably efficient for writing Japanese, and with their development appeared a growing literature in the native tongue. Even at the height of the Chinese period, poems had been composed in Japanese and laboriously written down by the use of unabbreviated Chinese characters to represent each syllable phonetically. . . . The simple phonetic systems of writing, however, made even the writing down of poems much easier than before. This fact may have contributed to what became a virtual craze among Japanese courtiers and their ladies to jot down poems on almost every conceivable occasion and exchange them profusely in their frequent love letters. . . .

Most of these poems, following a strict pattern of thirty-one syllables called the *tanka* ("short poem"), were quite brief. The *tanka* was too slight to do more than suggest a natural scene and, by some deft turn of phrase, evoke an emotion or some sudden insight, but within its narrow limits it could be both delicate and moving.

The *kana* syllabaries also made possible more extensive literary works in Japanese. In the tenth century, stories, travel diaries, and essays appeared, written in a Japanese which sometimes achieved considerable literary distinction. For the most part, educated men, much like their counterparts in medieval Europe, scorned the use of their own tongue for any serious literary purpose and continued to write histories, essays, and official documents in Chinese; but the women of the imperial court, who usually had insufficient education to write in Chinese, had no medium for literary expression other than their own language. As a result, while the men of the period were pompously writing bad Chinese, their ladies consoled themselves for their lack of education by writing good Japanese, and created, incidentally, Japan's first great prose literature.

The golden age of the first flowering of Japanese prose was the late tenth and early eleventh centuries. Most of the writers were court ladies living in ease and indolence, and their commonest form of literary expression was the diary, liberally sprinkled with "short poems" to commemorate moments of deep emotional feeling. Some of the diaries told of travels, but more often they concerned the luxuries, ceremonials, and constant flirtation and love-making which characterized court life at this time. The outstanding work of the period, however, was not a diary but an extremely lengthy novel, *The Tale of Genji,* written by Lady Murasaki early in the eleventh century. This is an account of the love adventures and psychological development of an imaginary Prince Genji. It is not only the earliest forerunner of a major genre of world literature, but both in itself and in Arthur Waley's magnificent English translation constitutes one of the great literary achievements of mankind. The diaries and novels by court ladies were clear evidence of the existence of a true native Japanese culture. They had no exact prototypes in Chinese literature: everything about them was distinctly Japanese. The transplanted Chinese civilization had flowered into a new culture, and the Japanese, a people but recently introduced to the art of writing, had produced a great literature of their own. . . .

Political Changes

Although the appearance by the tenth and eleventh centuries of a new and distinctive Japanese culture is perhaps best seen in the literature of the time, it is evident in other fields also. The arts of painting, sculpture, and architecture all showed definite and sometimes marked Japanese characteristics quite distinct from the original Chinese patterns, and political and social institutions changed so radically as to bear little resemblance to the Chinese prototypes.

The key figure of the Chinese political system was the bureaucrat, the scholar–civil servant who operated the complicated central government and went out to the provinces to collect taxes and maintain order. Thousands of these bureaucrats were required, and the recruiting of wise and capable men for the higher posts was a matter of crucial importance to the whole state. For this purpose, the Chinese had developed a system of civil service examinations. It centered around the great central university of Ch'ang-an, where periodic examinations were given on classical subjects. Candidates who succeeded best in the examinations went directly to high government posts. In this way, men of scholarly talents from all walks of life could reach positions of responsibility, and among the educated classes a vital tradition of public service was built up.

The Japanese borrowed only the outward forms of this system. With their strong traditions of family loyalty and hereditary rights, they could not bring themselves to accept its spirit. They created a central university where the Chinese classics were studied and examinations were held, but only in rare cases did scholars with little family backing attain positions of much responsibility. In the provinces, political authority remained in the hands of local aristocrats masquerading as civil servants appointed by the central administration, while at the capital courtiers of noble lineage held most posts of importance, leaving to the scholar-bureaucrats the humbler clerical jobs.

In China, the central government was constantly kept busy fighting the natural tendency for the tax-paying peasants and their lands to gravitate into the hands of powerful families with sufficient influence at court to protect their holdings from the encroachments of tax collectors. In Japan, this tendency was even stronger, for there was no powerful civil servant class to protect the interests of the state, and local aristocrats, in key positions as provincial officers, joined with court nobles in despoiling the public domain. The nationalized land system had probably never really been applied to more remote parts of the country, and during the late eighth and ninth centuries it decayed rapidly even in the capital district. Local men of influence built up tax-free estates, often by illegal means, and court aristocrats acquired in their own names large tracts of land as rewards for their services or through political manipulations of a less honorable nature.

On the one hand, the local gentry needed protection for their holdings from the tax collectors of the central government. On the other hand, powerful court families and great monasteries were acquiring large tax-free estates, and needed local men to represent their interests on these lands. From these reciprocal needs a pattern of landholding gradually developed in which provincial manors and estates were controlled and operated by local aristocrats, but were owned, at least in theory, by influential court families or powerful religious institutions in the capital district. The peasant, who came to have rights to the cultivation of his own little tract of land, gave to the local aristocrat, acting as estate manager, a generous portion of his produce; and the estate manager, in turn, passed on to the noble court family or great monastery a share of his income in payment for protection from the central government.

Tax-free manors grew and expanded during the eighth and ninth centuries, until by the tenth century, the national domain had virtually disappeared. With its disappearance, the income of the state from taxes, the economic basis for the Chinese form of centralized government, dwindled to almost nothing. As a result, provincial governmental agencies, which had never been strong, withered away almost completely, and left behind little except imposing administrative titles, such as governor or vice-governor. Even the central administration became largely an empty shell, a great paper organization with few working personnel, scanty funds, and pathetically reduced functions. The court nobles continued to sport high titles, and they were punctilious in maintaining the pomp and ceremony of court life. However, the complex system of actual rule through the eight ministries was for all practical purposes abandoned, and new and simplified organs of government were developed to handle what few political duties the central government still had.

The net result of all this was that centralized government ceased to exist for most parts of Japan. Each estate, freed from encroachment by tax collectors and other state agents, became a small autonomous domain, a semi-independent economic and political unit. The contacts it had with the outside world were not with any government agency, but with the great court family or religious institution to which it supplied a part of its produce and from which it received a loose sort of control. The noble court families and monasteries thus became multiple successors to the old centralized state. They had become, in a sense, states within the hollow framework of the old imperial government, each supported by the income from its own estates and, through family government or monastery administration, exercising many of the functions of government in its widely scattered manors throughout the land.

The Importance of the Fujiwara

The imperial family, though retaining great prestige because of its past political role and its continuing position as leader in the Shinto cults, became in fact simply one among these central economic and political units. It exercised a theoretical rule over a shadow government, but in reality it controlled only its own estates and lived on the income from them, not from government taxes. In time, even control over its own private affairs was lost, as one of the court families, the Fujiwara, gradually won mastery over the court and the imperial family by intrigue and skillful political manipulations.

The Fujiwara were a prolific family of many branches, descended from a courtier who had taken the lead in the pro-Chinese coup d'état of 645. The family had come to control many estates throughout the land and thus enjoyed an income probably greater than that of any other family, not excluding the imperial family itself. Its method of winning unchallenged dominance at the capital was to gain direct control over the imperial family through intermarriage. A daughter of the head of the family would be married to a young emperor, and the emperor, bored with the endless ceremonies required by his double role as secular and religious leader, would easily be persuaded to abdicate and retire to a simpler, freer life as soon as the son the Fujiwara girl had borne him was old enough to sit through these ceremonies in his place. This would leave a Fujiwara girl as empress dowager, and her father, the powerful head of a large and rich court family, as the grandfather of the new child emperor.

By such tactics the Fujiwara gained complete control over the imperial family during the middle decades of the ninth century. From that time on, it became customary for the head of the Fujiwara family, instead of an imperial prince, to act as regent for a child emperor or to occupy the new post of chancellor (*kampaku*) when an adult was on the throne. During the course of the ninth and tenth centuries, appointment to these two alternating posts, as well as to that of prime minister and to most of the other high offices in the central administration, became the hereditary right of members of the Fujiwara family. In fact, the family had become so dominant at court by the tenth century that the latter two-thirds of the Heian period is com-

monly called the Fujiwara period. The successive heads of the Fujiwara family completely overshadowed the emperors not only as the
real holders of the reins of government, but also as the openly recognized arbiters of taste and fashion at court. The greatest figure of
the whole Heian period was not an emperor or prince, but Fujiwara
Michinaga, who dominated the court between 995 and 1027, just at
the time when Lady Murasaki was writing *The Tale of Genji*.

In the late eleventh century, an energetic retired emperor tem-
porarily won back control over the court from the Fujiwara, and from
time to time other retired emperors repeated this feat. Of course, control over the empty shell of the Chinese-type government was in any
case becoming progressively less significant as power slipped away
from the imperial court. But the Fujiwara, despite occasional chal-
lenges by the imperial family, maintained their domination over the
court for exactly a millennium. Divided into a number of separate
lines, each with its own family name, they retained their virtual monopoly of all high court posts almost without interruption until the
great political transformation of the second half of the nineteenth
century.

In another country such a long and almost complete dominance
exercised by one family over the reigning family would probably
have resulted in a usurpation of the throne. Not so in Japan. Hereditary authority and the emperors' role in Shinto ritual were such
strong forces that outright usurpation was not to be contemplated.
Instead, the Fujiwara set a lasting Japanese pattern of control from
behind the scenes through a figurehead. For most of Japanese history, it has probably been the rule rather than the exception for the
man or group in nominal control to be in reality the pawn of some
other man or group. This fact has often helped to conceal the realities of Japanese life and confuse the casual observer.

Murasaki Shikibu's Literary Achievement

Ivan Morris

Written in the early 1000s by Japanese author Murasaki Shikibu, *The Tale of Genji* is widely considered to be the world's first novel—or at least the first "modern psychological" novel, in that it consists of a carefully structured narrative that delves into the psychological development of its protagonist. In the following selection, taken from his book *The World of the Shining Prince: Court Life in Ancient Japan*, Ivan Morris describes several qualities of *The Tale of Genji* that make it unique among the literary works of its time. He also argues that this thousand-year-old novel is still relevant today. A professor of Japanese history at Columbia University in New York City, Morris published translations of several Japanese works, including *As I Crossed a Bridge of Dreams: Recollections of a Woman in Eleventh-Century Japan.*

The first psychological novel in the literature of the world is also one of its longest. In its original form *The Tale of Genji* consisted of fifty-four books or chapters, which were separately bound and which often circulated independently. Arthur Waley's translation, which does not expand the original (and from which one of the books is missing), has some 630,000 words; this makes Murasaki's novel about twice as long as Miguel de Cervantes' *Don Quixote*, Leo

Excerpted from Ivan Morris, *The World of the Shining Prince: Court Life in Ancient Japan.* Copyright © 1964 Ivan Morris. Reprinted with permission from Alfred A. Knopf, a division of Random House, Inc.

Tolstoy's *War and Peace*, or Fyodor Dostoyevsky's *The Brothers Karamazov*, though only two-thirds the length of Marcel Proust's *A la recherche du temps perdu* [Remembrance of Things Past].

The action is spread over three-quarters of a century and involves four generations. There are about four hundred and thirty characters, not counting messengers, servants, and anonymous members of the working class. Most of these characters are related to each other, and early commentators devoted years to the sisyphean task of producing genealogical tables in which almost every character in the novel was included. The tradition has been maintained by modern scholars: Ikeda Kikan's recent *Encyclopaedia of the Tale of Genji* has over seventy closely printed pages of genealogy. Murasaki Shikibu belonged to a rigidly stratified society in which family connections were all-important, and while working on the novel she must have kept her own charts to show how her huge cast of characters were related. For never once is she inconsistent about the relationship of even the most obscure people in her book.

This methodical approach is even more striking in Murasaki's time scheme. There is hardly a passage in the entire novel that we cannot identify in terms of year and month and in which we cannot determine the exact age of each of the important characters. Occasionally Murasaki will depart from straight chronological order in telling her story. The events in one chapter, for example, may occur before those in the previous chapter, ('flashback'), or two chapters may overlap. But such deviations are deliberate and there is never any confusion. Commentators have subjected the time scheme of the novel to the minutest scrutiny. They are, one feels, almost hoping to find some inconsistency; until now they have been unsuccessful.

The Organization of the Novel

This precision is one aspect of Murasaki's talent for organizing her voluminous material in the most effective way. It immediately puts her work in a different category from *The Tale of the Hollow Tree*, the only extant precursor in the field of lengthy prose fiction. For one of the things that makes *The Tale of the Hollow Tree* so hard to read, and ultimately so unreal, is its disorganized construction and its chaotic time scheme.

The Tale of Genji does not ramble on amorphously as a haphazard sequence of loosely connected episodes. It is true that the books tend to be more independent than the chapters of most modern novels, especially since there is often a gap of several years between them; yet to view the work as a series of vaguely related short stories (as some critics have done) seems to me completely off the mark. Like the individual books of which it is composed, *The Tale of Genji* is an artistic unit whose shape has been carefully and deliberately designed. It is so constructed that the entire work can be resolved into certain general divisions, which represent its beginning (Books 1–12), its middle (Books 13–41), and its end (Books 42–54), and into a number of significant sub-divisions whose various chapters are closely bound together by the coherent development of character and event.

Above all, *The Tale of Genji* is constructed about a set of central ideas or themes, the historical theme of Fujiwara power, for example, and the human theme of impermanence, which combine to give it an artistic unity. This is one of the aspects (the use of realistic psychological detail is another) that allow us to describe Murasaki's work as a 'novel', a term that cannot be applied to any of its exact precursors.

One device that Murasaki uses with particular effect is anticipation or build-up. Frequently she will hint at the existence of some character long before that person enters the action of the novel, or she will adumbrate some sequence of events that is to take place many years in the future. There is a scene in one of the early books, for example, in which Prince Genji and his young friends stand on a hill and discuss the beauties of the countryside in the distance. 'If one were to live in such a place,' exclaims Genji, 'one could really ask for nothing more in this world!' Here Murasaki anticipates, not without irony, the events that are to happen eight years (and seven books) later. For the landscape at which Genji gazes so fondly is to be the place of his forlorn exile from the capital. His friend then tells him the story of the strange old lay priest of Akashi and his attractive little daughter. This arouses the young prince's curiosity, as well as the reader's, and paves the way for Genji's love affair with Lady Akashi and for all the complications that this entails in later years.

Sometimes Murasaki will speak about a character never mentioned before as though the reader already knew all about him. In the hands of a skilful writer this device can produce a curiously realistic effect and, as Arthur Waley has pointed out, it was used by Proust. Murasaki's more usual method of build-up, however, is to make different characters speak about someone from their respective points of view long before the person in question actually appears on the scene. For example, Kaoru hears various reports about Ukifune, the tragic heroine of the last five books, many years before he actually meets her. It is not until we have formed a fairly clear picture of the girl that she enters the action.

By far the best-known case of anticipation in *The Tale of Genji* occurs in Book 2 when Genji and his young friends meet on a rainy night to discuss the different types of women they have known and to compare their merits. This passage, with its detailed comments on various sorts of women that are to figure in the novel, has often been regarded as a key to the organization of the entire work, not unlike the first movement of a symphony in which the composer may suggest the themes that he intends to develop later. In fact the 'discussion on a rainy night' does not have nearly such a mechanical function as this might suggest. Of the many types of girls that the young gallants describe, only one can be identified with a specific character in the novel. This is Yūgao, the simple young woman whose love affair with Genji and whose weird death are described in the following two books. One of Genji's friends mentions that he has had an illegitimate child with Yūgao; mother and child have both disappeared and he has been unable to track them down. Here is another case of anticipation; for the child in question turns out to be Tamakazura, who enters the action of the novel seventeen years later.

Rhythms of Repetition

Another aspect of Murasaki's style that serves to tighten the structure of her narrative is the deliberate repetition of situations, settings, and relationships between characters. *The Tale of Genji* contains certain patterns of action that occur with variations at widely separated points of the narrative, not unlike the motifs in a musical composition. Here again we are reminded of *A la recherche du temps perdu* with its subtle use of internal 'rhythms'.

One of the best ways to understand the carefully balanced architecture of Murasaki's novel is to note how she places different characters, or sometimes the same character, in successive situations that 'correspond' with each other. Thus, when Genji finds out that his young wife, Princess Nyosan, has been seduced by Kashiwagi and that the little boy (Kaoru) whom everyone takes to be his own son and heir is in fact the result of this affair, he realizes that history has repeated itself to an uncanny degree. For some thirty years earlier Genji himself had seduced his father's new consort, Lady Fujitsubo, and she had given birth to a boy (Reizei), who was accepted as the Emperor's son and who as a result came to the throne illegitimately. As Genji holds the little child in his arms, it occurs to him that the old Emperor may secretly have known and suffered about Fujitsubo's unfaithfulness, in much the same way that he himself is now tormented by what Nyosan has done. The same pattern continues to unfold in later years. Just as Reizei was racked with doubts about his paternity, to the extent that he eventually resigned the throne, so when Kaoru grows up he is obsessed with the feeling that there was something strange about his birth, and this serves to intensify the neurotic aspect of his character.

There are many cases like this in which a pattern that has been developed in the early part of the novel, when Genji is the hero, is repeated with variations in the Kaoru books. For example, the relationship between Genji and Yūgao finds its echo, as it were, in the love affair between Kaoru and Ukifune some fifty years later. In each case the hero's interest is aroused by hearing about an attractive girl who belongs to a far lower social class than himself. It is only after careful anticipation that Murasaki puts her on the scene. The hero meets her by chance and is almost immediately captivated (Books 4 and 49). The love affair begins in the lady's humble town dwelling; and in the morning the hero lies listening to the unfamiliar street noises. He abruptly decides to move his mistress to some more isolated place and despite the protests of her attendants he takes her in his carriage to a gloomy country house. In both cases the relationships are marked by a sense of strangeness and end in tragedy. It is not surprising that such closely parallel situations should contain what Waley describes as 'balancing scenes', like those in Books 4 and 50 when Murasaki describes the sounds of the peasants and peddlers. The emphasis in the two scenes is on the unfamiliarity of the common surroundings in which the hero suddenly finds himself. Both men are fascinated by the street sounds, which in Genji's case are able years later to evoke the memory of his love. These are the scenes:

> (Book 4) . . . the dwelling, so different from those to which Genji was accustomed, seemed strange to him. It must have been nearly dawn. From the neighbouring houses he could hear the uncouth voices of workers who were just waking up: 'Oh, how cold it is!' 'We can't count on much business this year. It's a poor look-out for our hauling trade.' 'Hey, neighbour, wake up!' With such remarks they set out noisily, each to his own pitiful job.

> (Book 50) Soon it appeared to be dawn, but instead of the song of birds, Kaoru heard the raucous and unintelligible cries of pedlars calling out their wares from near the main street while they passed by in large groups. As he looked out at them staggering past in the dawn light with their loads, they appeared like phantoms. The experience of having passed the night in this simple dwelling seemed most strange to Kaoru.

Murasaki's deliberate repetitions are never as obvious as this may suggest. Nor are they exact. Psychological realism demanded that different types of people react differently in the same situation; however parallel the patterns may be, it is unthinkable that we should for example, find a resolute character like Genji handling a love affair with the diffidence and deviousness of a Kaoru.

The use of 'sustained imagery' (the repetition, that is, of a single central image in both the narrative passages and the poems) can also serve to connect different parts of the novel that are widely separated in time, or to tighten the structure of a particular series of books.

Throughout the novel, for instance, Murasaki rings the changes on the image of dreams and thereby evokes one of her central themes—the nebulous, unreal quality of the world about us, and the idea that our life here is a mere 'bridge of dreams' (the title of her final book), over which we cross from one state of existence to the next. . . .

Extensive Scholarship

Long as *The Tale of Genji* may be, it is the merest ant-hill in comparison with the mountains of commentaries and scholarly studies that have grown up about it. According to Professor Ikeda, more than ten thousand books have been written about *The Tale of Genji*, not to mention innumerable essays, monographs, dissertations, and the like; in addition there are several Genji dictionaries and concordances, and hundreds of weighty works in which Murasaki's novel has been used as material for the study of subjects like Heian court ceremony and music.

The basic textual commentary belongs to the early thirteenth century and consisted of fifty-four ponderous tomes, one for each of Murasaki's books; of these only a single volume is extant. Subsequent commentaries were rarely less than a thousand pages long; Ikeda's recent *Tale of Genji Encyclopaedia* has some 1,200 large, closely printed pages, of which about one hundred are devoted to listing earlier commentaries. No other novel in the world can have been subjected to such close scrutiny; no writer of any kind, except perhaps Shakespeare, can have had his work more voluminously discussed than Murasaki Shikibu. . . .

As the world of *The Tale of Genji* receded into the distant past, the language of the novel began to present even greater difficulties. The first Genji dictionary dates from the fourteenth century, and much of the work during the Muromachi period was devoted to linguistic interpretation. The study of manuscripts and the comparison of different versions also became important, as scholars tried to establish a definitive text of the work. . . .

Confronted with this formidable mass of scholarly material, the reader sometimes feels that, far from helping him to enter into the delicate spirit of *The Tale of Genji*, it imposes a block between him and the original novel. Indeed, as one wades through some of the more turgid commentaries, one wonders whether they are not trying to open a fragile persimmon with a hydraulic drill. Of course it would be the height of churlishness to question the value of the work by these generations of patient scholars; without it the novel would be as impenetrable as an Easter Island inscription. But it is important to remember that Murasaki was an artist, not a chronicler (still less a scholar), and that *The Tale of Genji* must be enjoyed above all as a work of literature, not as a source of information.

To what extent can we really understand what she was writing about? It has sometimes been suggested that the modern Western reader is so divorced from Murasaki in time and space, in patterns of thought and expression, in custom and in sensibility, that she might as well have belonged to a different planet, and that what we derive from the work of this court lady of tenth-century Japan can be only the palest approximation of what she intended to convey. According to this argument, even the modern Japanese reader, the child of Westernized industrial society, is hardly less cut off from the world of the shining prince than we in the Occident.

Murasaki's Enduring Relevance

I do not subscribe to this view. Indeed, it seems to me, one of the remarkable things about this novel of a millennium ago is how readily we can enter into the thoughts and feelings of its characters and respond to the total vision of life that its author communicated. The more we know about the times—social organization, religious ideas, marriage customs, literary conventions, and so forth—the greater our understanding will be. Yet, even with the most elementary knowledge of the Heian background, the sensitive reader can grasp the psychology of a character like Kaoru, for example, and appreciate the close connection between beauty and sorrow that is an underlying theme of the novel.

Many things that seemed important to Murasaki (calligraphic skill, for instance, or the court hierarchy) have little relevance in the present day; yet, when it comes to vivifying a character by psychological detail, or using imagery to evoke the feelings that death can inspire, she seems close to us and 'modern' in a way that no previous writer of prose fiction can approach.

The Art of Storytelling

Murasaki Shikibu

Murasaki Shikibu was born during the 970s into a minor branch of the powerful Fujiwara clan. She married a soldier of the imperial guard, but her husband died in 1001. Murasaki spent the next few years in seclusion, perhaps beginning *The Tale of Genji* during this time. Around 1004, her father arranged for her to enter the service of the young empress as a lady-in-waiting. Murasaki's chapters of *The Tale of Genji* circulated among the members of the royal court as fast as she could write them. Her name disappears from court records after 1025; it is thought that she either passed away at a relatively young age or retired from court life to become a Buddhist nun. In the following excerpt from Murasaki's novel, her protagonist Genji defends the art of storytelling in words that may well reflect her own opinions.

This year the rainy season lasted much longer than usual, and whereas the monotony of the downpour is usually relieved by an occasional day of sunshine, this time there was nothing but one continuous drizzle for weeks on end. The inhabitants of the New Palace found it very hard to get through the day and tried one amusement after another. In the end they mostly betook themselves to reading illustrated romances. The Lady of Akashi had, among her other accomplishments, a talent for copying out and finely decorating such books as these; and being told that everyone was clamouring for some occupation which would help them to get through the day, she now sent over a large supply to the Princess, her daughter. But the greatest enthusiast of all was Lady Tamakatsura, who would rise at daybreak and spend the whole day absorbed in reading or copying out romances. Many of her younger ladies-in-waiting had a vast stock of stories, some legendary, some about real people, which they told with considerable skill. But Tamakatsura could not help feeling that the history of her own life, should it ever come to be told, was really far more interesting than any of the tales with which her ladies sought to entertain her. True, the sufferings of the princess in the *Sumiyoshi Tale* had at certain points a resemblance to her own experiences. But she could see no reason why for generations past so many tears of indignation and pity should have been shed over the fate of this princess at the hands of her unscrupulous lover. Judged as an episode, thought Tamakatsura, her own escape from the violence of Tayu was quite as exciting.

The Lure of Books

One day Genji, going the round with a number of romances which he had promised to lend, came to Tamakatsura's room and found her, as usual, hardly able to lift her eyes from the book in front of her. 'Really, you are incurable,' he said, laughing.

> I sometimes think that young ladies exist for no other purpose than to provide purveyors of the absurd and improbable with a market for their wares. I am sure that the book you are now so intent upon is full of the wildest nonsense. Yet knowing this all the time, you are completely captivated by its extravagances and follow them with the utmost excitement: why, here you are on this hot day, so hard at work that, though I am sure you have not the least idea of it, your hair is in the most extraordinary tangle. . . . But there; I know quite well that these old tales are indispensable during such weather as this. How else would you all manage to get through the day? Now for a confession. I too have lately been studying these books and have, I must tell you, been amazed by the delight which they have given me. There is, it seems, an art of so fitting each part of the narrative into the next that, though all is mere invention, the reader is persuaded that such things might easily have happened and is as deeply moved as though they were actually going on around him. We may know with one part of our minds that every incident has been invented for the express purpose of impressing us; but (if the plot is constructed with the requisite skill) we may all the while in another part of our minds be burning with indignation at the wrongs endured by some wholly imaginary princess. Or again we may be persuaded by a writer's eloquence into accepting the crudest absurdities, our judgment being as it were dazzled by sheer splendour of language.

> I have lately sometimes stopped and listened to one of our young people reading out loud to her companions and have been amazed at the advances

which this art of fiction is now making. How do you suppose that our new writers come by this talent? It used to be thought that the authors of successful romances were merely particularly untruthful people whose imaginations had been stimulated by constantly inventing plausible lies. But that is clearly unfair. . . .

"Perhaps," she said, "only people who are themselves much occupied in practising deception have the habit of thus dipping below the surface. I can assure you that for my part, when I read a story, I always accept it as an account of something that has really and actually happened."

So saying she pushed away from her the book which she had been copying. Genji continued:

So you see as a matter of fact I think far better of this art than I have led you to suppose. Even its practical value is immense. Without it what should we know of how people lived in the past, from the Age of the Gods down to the present day? For history-books such as the Chronicles of Japan show us only one small corner of life; whereas these diaries and romances which I see piled around you contain, I am sure, the most minute information about all sorts of people's private affairs. . . .

He smiled, and went on:

But I have a theory of my own about what this art of the novel is, and how it came into being. To begin with, it does not simply consist in the author's telling a story about the adventures of some other person. On the contrary, it happens because the storyteller's own experience of men and things, whether for good or ill—not only what he has passed through himself, but even events which he has only witnessed or been told of— has moved him to an emotion so passionate that he can no longer keep it shut up in his heart. Again and again something in his own life or in that around him will seem to the writer so important that he cannot bear to let it pass into oblivion. There must never come a time, he feels, when men do not know about it. That is my view of how this art arose.

Clearly then, it is no part of the storyteller's craft to describe only what is good or beautiful. Sometimes, of course, virtue will be his theme and he may then make such play with it as he will. But he is just as likely to have been struck by numerous examples of vice and folly in the world around him, and about them he has exactly the same feelings as about the pre-eminently good deeds which he encounters: they are important and must all be garnered in. Thus anything whatsoever may become the subject of a novel, provided only that it happens in this mundane life and not in some fairyland beyond our human ken.

Comparing Scriptures and Fiction

The outward forms of this art will not of course be everywhere the same. At the Court of China and in other foreign lands both the genius of the writers and their actual methods of composition are necessarily very different from ours; and even here in Japan the art of storytelling has in course of time undergone great changes. There will, too, always be a distinction between the lighter and the more serious forms of fiction. . . . Well, I have said enough to show that when at the beginning of our conversation I spoke of romances as though they were mere frivolous fabrications, I was only teasing you. Some people have taken exception on moral grounds to an art in which the perfect and imperfect are set side by side. But even in the discourses which Buddha in his bounty allowed to be recorded, certain passages contain what the learned call Upaya or "Adapted Truth"—a fact that has led some superficial persons to doubt whether a doctrine so inconsistent with itself could possibly command our credence. . . . We may indeed go so far as to say that there is an actual mixture of Truth and Error. But the purpose of these holy writings, namely the compassing of our Salvation, remains always the same. So too, I think, may it be said that the art of fiction must not lose our allegiance because, in the pursuit of the main purpose to which I have alluded above, it sets virtue by the side of vice, or mingles wisdom with folly. Viewed in this light the novel is seen to be not, as is usually supposed, a mixture of useful truth with idle invention, but something which at every stage and in every part has a definite and serious purpose.

Thus did he vindicate the storyteller's profession as an art of real importance.

The Rise of New Civilizations in America

PREFACE

Of all the major societies of the world that existed in the 1000s, the least is known about the civilizations of the Americas. This is not due to a lack of accomplishments in the New World: Archaeologists have determined beyond a doubt that remarkable cities and cultures flourished in this region during the eleventh century. Instead, the gaps in our knowledge concerning the history of the Americas are directly related to the scarcity of written texts, for it is primarily through writing that information about ancient history is maintained and transmitted. Archaeologists can determine many facts about a civilization through careful examination of ruins and artifacts, but the historical and cultural information typically contained in written texts provides essential data that cannot otherwise be obtained.

Some of these ancient American societies were not yet literate: There is no evidence, for example, that either the Anasazi or the Mound Builders of Cahokia ever developed a system of writing. Those societies that were literate used elaborate and complicated forms of writing that for many years were almost entirely incomprehensible to researchers. Only in the 1960s did modern scholars discover the key to interpreting the Mayan hieroglyphs, and they still have not fully deciphered the glyphs nor translated all of the existing texts. Furthermore, the bulk of the writings of ancient Americans have been completely lost to posterity. As Mayan specialists Linda Schele and David Freidel explain, "The Maya wrote on paper, keeping thousands of books in which they recorded their history, genealogy, religion, and ritual; but their libraries and archives perished into dust or in the flames of their Spanish conquerors." Unfortunately, researchers may never be able to develop as full a picture of life in the Americas as they would like.

What researchers do know about the New World at the turn of the millennium is that it was a time of great and often sudden change. The heyday of the Maya was drawing to a close, and there is evidence that much of the Mayan homeland fell under the command of a militaristic elite based out of the city of Chich'en Itza. Researchers are not in complete agreement concerning what happened in the Mayan territory during this time period, but many conjecture that the rulers of Chich'en Itza were invaders, most likely Toltecs from Mexico. At the same time that the Mayan kingdoms were declining, the Toltecs were rising in power, building an empire that held sway over most of Mexico.

Important civilizations also sprang up in the area that is now the United States, most notably the Anasazi of the Southwest and the Cahokians in the Mississippi River valley. These societies engaged in extensive trade and maintained cities that in size and wealth rivaled many in eleventh-century Europe. Certain aspects of the culture of both the Anasazi and the Cahokians suggest that they were influenced by the Toltecs of Mexico. Whether or not they were in direct contact with the Toltecs is still a matter of conjecture; these cultural influences could well have been indirectly transmitted through an intermediary tribe that traded with both societies. However, some researchers believe that the Toltecs were aggressive conquerors who overran the Anasazi at the start of the 1000s, dominating them through violence and terrorization.

Recent archaeological research at Cahokia has suggested a similar pattern there. In 1993, archaeologist Timothy R. Pauketat demonstrated that Cahokia underwent a tremendous population explosion during the eleventh century, surging from a village of approximately one thousand people to a booming metropolis with a population well over ten thousand. He theorizes that around A.D. 1050, a powerful chieftain based in Cahokia subjugated the surrounding villages and consolidated control over a wide expanse of land. "The formerly independent chiefs of small neighboring communities seem to have been swept away [in the] summer [of 1050] and replaced by loyal and subordinate followers of Cahokia," Pauketat maintains. "Clan by clan and village by village, Cahokia absorbed the region. . . . Having gained total control of the area, the triumphant Cahokians used their rapidly burgeoning labor force to rebuild their large village into a grand regional capital that sprawled for more than two square miles." Whether the chieftain who led this devastating military campaign was a native Cahokian or an outsider is not known, but the intriguing possibility remains that he and his warriors were Toltec invaders.

As with the identity of the powerful Cahokian chief, much of the history of the Native Americans during this era is still a matter of speculation. Nevertheless, it is clear that the civilizations of the New World in the year 1000 were often as vibrant, sophisticated, and complex as those of the mighty empires across the ocean.

The Toltecs of Mexico

Michael D. Coe

Michael D. Coe is the author of numerous books on pre-Columbian America, including *In the Land of the Olmec*, *The Maya*, *The Art of the Maya Scribe*, and *The Jaguar's Children: Preclassic Central Mexico*. He is retired from Yale University where he served as both the Charles J. MacCurdy Professor of Anthropology and the curator of the Peabody Museum of Natural History. In the following excerpt from *Mexico: From the Olmecs to the Aztecs*, Coe traces the Toltecs' ascension to power in Mexico at the end of the tenth century. The Toltec civilization reached its height during the 1000s with an empire that dominated much of present-day Mexico and Guatemala, Coe explains.

There have been four unifying forces in the pre-Spanish history of Mexico: the first of these was Olmec, the second Classic Teotihuacan, the third Toltec, and the last Aztec. In their own annals, written down in Spanish letters after the Conquest, the Mexican nobility and intelligentsia looked back in wonder to an almost semi-mythical time when the Toltecs ruled, a people whose very name means 'the artificers.' Of them it was said that 'nothing was too difficult for them, no place with which they dealt was too distant.' From their capital, Tollan (Tula), they had dominated much of northern and central Mexico in ancient times, as well as parts of the Guatemalan highlands and most of the Yucatán Peninsula. After their downfall, no Mexican or Maya dynasty worth its salt failed to claim descent from these wonderful people.

The Origins of the Toltecs

Toltec society seems to have been composed of disparate tribal elements which had come together for obscure reasons. One of these, which would appear to have been dominant, was called the Tolteca-Chichimeca. The other group went under the name Nonoalca, and according to some scholars was made up of sculptors and artisans from the old civilized regions of Puebla and the Gulf Coast, brought in to construct the monuments of Tula. The Tolteca-Chichimeca, for their part, were probably the original Nahua-speakers who founded the Toltec state. They were once barbarians, perhaps semi-civilized Chichimeca originating on the fringes of Mesoamerica among the Uto-Aztecans of western Mexico. . . .

Led by their probably entirely legendary ruler Mixcoatl ('Cloud Serpent', i.e. Milky Way), who was deified as patron of hunting after his death, the Tolteca-Chichimeca by the beginning of the ninth century had entered civilized Mexico at the southern extension of the Sierra Madre Occidental, passing through what now comprises northern Jalisco and southern Zacatecas. It is no easy matter to reconstruct their history from the contradictory accounts which we have been left, but according to the widely accepted scheme of the Mexican ethnohistorian Wigberto Jiménez Moreno, Mixcoatl and his people first settled at a place in the Valley of Mexico called Colhuacan. His son and heir was the most famous figure in all Mexican history, a possibly real person named Topiltzin, born in the year I Reed (either A.D. 935 or 947), and later identified to the confusion of modern scholars with the Feathered Serpent, Quetzalcoatl. This king is described in the post-Conquest literature as being of fair skin, with long hair and a black beard.

The first event in the rule of I Reed Topiltzin Quetzalcoatl was the transfer of the Toltec capital from Colhuacan via Tulancingo to Tula, the ancient Tollan, a name signifying 'Place of the Reeds' but which to the ancients meant something like 'the city.' Some years after its founding, according to the annals, Tula was the scene of a terrible inner strife, for Topiltzin was supposedly a kind of priest-king dedicated to the peaceful cult of the Feathered Serpent, abhorring human sacrifice and performing all sorts of penances. His enemies were devotees of the fierce god Tezcatlipoca ('Smoking Mirror'), the giver and taker away of life, lord of sorcerers, and the patron of the warrior orders, the latter perhaps made discontented by the intellectual pacificism of their king.

As a result of this struggle for power, Topiltzin and his followers were forced to flee the city, perhaps in A.D. 987. Some of the most beautiful Nahuatl poetry records his unhappy downfall, a defeat laid at the door of Tezcatlipoca himself. Topiltzin and his Toltecs were said to have become slothful, the ruler having even transgressed the priestly rules of continence. Tezcatlipoca undermines the Toltecs by various evil stratagems: coming to Topiltzin in the guise of an old man and tricking him into drinking a magic and debilitating potion; then appearing without his loincloth in the marketplace disguised as a seller of green chile peppers, inflaming the ruler's daughter with such a desire for him that her father is forced to take him as son-in-law; next, as a warrior successfully leading a force of dwarfs and hunchbacks which had been given him in vain hope that he would be slain by the enemy; making a puppet dance for the Toltecs, causing them in their curiosity to rush forward and crush themselves to death. Even when they finally killed Tezcatlipoca by stoning, the Toltecs were unable to rid themselves of his now festering, rotted body.

At last, according to legend, Topiltzin Quetzalcoatl leaves his beloved city in exile after burning or burying all his treasures, preceded on his path by birds of precious feather. . . .

On his way trickster magicians cross his path again and again, trying to make him turn back. At last he reaches the stormy pass between the volcanoes Iztaccihuatl and Popocatepetl, where his jugglers, buffoons, and the pages of his palace freeze to death. He continues on, his gaze directed at the shroud of the snows and eventually arrives at the shore of the Gulf of Mexico. One poem relates that there he set himself afire, decked in his quetzal plumage and turquoise mask; as his ashes rose to the sky, every kind of marvelously colored bird wheeled overhead, and the dead king was apotheosized as the Morning Star. Another version of the tale . . . tells us that he did not perform an act of self-immolation, but rather set off with followers on a raft formed of serpents on a journey to the east, from which he was supposed to return some day.

It may be evidence of the historical core within this legend that Maya accounts speak of the arrival from the west, apparently in the year A.D. 987, of a Mexican conqueror named in their tongue Kukulcán ('Feathered Serpent'), who with his companions subjugated their country. There is also ample evidence in the archaeology of Yucatán for a seaborne Toltec invasion, probably assisted by the Putún Maya, successfully initiating in the late tenth century a Mexican period, with its capital at Chichén Itzá.

The Height of Tula's Power

With the sanguinary rule of the Tezcatlipoca party now dominant at Tula, the Toltec empire may have reached its greatest expansion, holding sway over most of central Mexico from coast to coast. At the height of its power, Tula is pictured in the poems as a sort of marvelous never-never land, where ears of maize were as big as *mano* stones, and red, yellow, green, blue and many other colors of cotton grew naturally. There were palaces of jade, of gold, a turquoise palace, and one made of blue-green quetzal feathers. The Toltecs were so prosperous that they heated their sweat baths with the small ears of maize. There was nothing that they could not make; wonderful potters, they 'taught the clay to lie.' Truly, they 'put their heart into their work.'

The end of Tula approached with the last ruler, Huemac ('Big Hand'). Triggered by a disastrous series of droughts, factional conflicts broke out once more, apparently between the Tolteca-Chichimeca and the Nonoalca. In 1156 or 1168 Huemac transferred his capital to Chapultepec, the hill-crowned park in what is now the western part of Mexico City, where he committed suicide. Some Tolteca-Chichimeca hung on at Tula for another fifteen years, finally themselves deserting the city and moving south to the Valley of Mexico and as far as Cholula, subjugating all who lay in their way. Tula was left in ruins, with only memories of its glories.

The Toltec Conquest of the Maya

J. Eric S. Thompson

The late archaeologist J. Eric S. Thompson was a leading authority on Mayan history and culture. He taught at Cambridge University in England and worked for many years at the Carnegie Institution of Washington, D.C. His books include *The Civilization of the Mayas*, *Maya History and Religion*, *Maya Hieroglyphs Without Tears*, and *The Rise and Fall of Maya Civilization*, from which the following passage is taken.

For several centuries prior to the 1000s, Thompson writes, the Mayan civilization flourished in Central America. On the eve of the eleventh century, however, the Toltecs of Mexico conquered a sizable portion of Mayan territory—including the great city of Chichén Itzá—which they ruled throughout the 1000s. According to Thompson, the impact of the Toltec conquest was a significant factor in the decline of the Mayan civilization.

The big invasion of foreigners and foreign ideas [into Maya territory] occurred in the century following the end of the Classic Period (*circa* A.D. 325–A.D. 925). They derive from Tula, the capital of the Toltec, in the state of Hidalgo, north of Mexico City, and are most apparent at Chichén Itzá. The shortest line by land between these two sites is no less than 800 miles, somewhat less than the distance between New York and Chicago. To us, living in the age of airplanes, . . . that is a matter of a few hours travel; to the peoples of Middle America in the tenth century the distance was immense, for the only form of transportation was shanks' mare or, for members of the aristocracy, a litter (part of the journey might have been accomplished in dugout canoes). Moreover, much of the intervening territory was hostile. Not only were the inhabitants unfriendly, but swamp, forest, and mountains were physical barriers. Yet there are the closest resemblances in the sculptural art, the architecture, the planning, the religious symbolism, and even the details of costume, ornaments, and weapons of the two cities. The extraordinary fact is that nowhere between central Mexico and Yucatán have buildings or sculptures in this distinctive style been found, although it is still possible they may turn up somewhere in southern Veracruz or coastal Tabasco.

Sixteenth-century Spanish accounts and the Maya books of Chilam Balam are at variance concerning who introduced Mexican culture and when. Here we will not list all the possibilities, but follow the interpretation I consider most reasonable, remembering that other interpretations have been proposed and yet others will be advanced before the problem is finally, if ever, solved.

The Invasion of the Itzá

Chichén Itzá, it should be recalled, was a Maya city of some importance during the Classic Period, as many buildings in the Maya tradition, sculptures in the Yucatecan classic style, and hieroglyphic texts bear witness. The dated monuments connected with these buildings cluster around the Maya equivalent of A.D. 889, which is approximately the end of the Classic Period in the Central area. . . . There is a transitional building in the inner temple of Kukulcan, which is in Maya style but with certain Mexican motifs, and then come the mass of Toltec buildings. As there are cases in which a Toltec house or wing has been built on to a Maya structure, but no example of the reverse process, it is clear that the Mexican style is later than the Maya. There are also cases of stones in Maya style being reused in Mexican buildings; for example, part of a Maya hieroglyphic stone lintel was recarved to serve as the tail of that typical Toltec feature, a feathered-serpent column, but the reverse is unknown. There is, accordingly, incontrovertible evidence that Mexican architecture is later at Chichén Itzá than the Maya style, and therefore its introduction dates sometime after A.D. 889 or perhaps 909, the latest dates associated with Maya architecture.

From various sources we learn that the Itzá, who were foreigners and spoke broken Maya, settled at Chichén Itzá in the twenty years between A.D. 967 and A.D. 987 (Katun 4 Ahau in the Maya calendar), and we also learn that Kukulcan, "the feathered [or quetzal] serpent," who was a Mexican leader, seized Chichén Itzá. Bishop Diego de Landa, our best Spanish source on Maya life, says, "The Indians are of the opinion that with the Itzá who settled Chichén Itzá there reigned a great lord called Cuculcan [Kukulcan] . . . and they say that he entered from the west, and they differ as to whether he entered before or after the Itzá, or with them." As, however, a Maya prophecy speaks of both Kukulcan and the Itzá coming again to Chichén Itzá in a katun 4 Ahau, and as in Maya opinion history always repeated itself, we can feel fairly sure that Kukulcan was the leader of the Itzá invasion which seized Chichén Itzá in the Maya katun 4 Ahau which ended in A.D. 987, and introduced Toltec religion, Toltec architecture, and Toltec art.

The problem remains who was Kukulcan and who were the Itzá. Kukulcan (*Kukul,* feather or quetzal; *can,* snake) is the Maya form of the Mexican Quetzalcoatl (*Quetzal,* the quetzal bird, the feathers of which were valued highly in ancient Middle America; *coatl,* snake). Quetzalcoatl was a ruler of Tula who was subsequently deified as god of the planet Venus and as a god of vegetation. Driven out of Tula by the machinations of his rival, the god Tezcatlipoca, he made his way to southern Veracruz or Tabasco, and embarking on a raft, was lost to view. According to another version, on reaching the sea, he made a pyre and cremated himself on it. Then, eight days later (the period of invisibility at inferior conjunction), he reappeared as the planet Venus at heliacal rising. Owing to the abbreviated method of dating used in central Mexico, the date of the expulsion of Quetzalcoatl is not certain, but Mexican archaeologists tend to favor A.D. 978 or a few years later.

That certainly rings the Maya bell (Katun 4 Ahau corresponding to A.D. 967–987), but before we become too sure, it is well to recollect that Quetzalcoatl was also the title of the Mexican high priest, and Quetzalcoatls seem to be as frequent in Mexican history as Roosevelts or Adamses in American public life. It seems almost too good to be true that the historical Quetzalcoatl and his Toltec followers, fleeing Tula, conquered Chichén Itzá. Moreover, other parts of the Maya area have traditions concerning the arrival of Quetzalcoatl.

Aside from the problem of the identity of Kukulcan, there is the mystery of who were the Itzá. Were they Toltec followers of Quetzalcoatl-Kukulcan, or were they some other group, perhaps even a Maya people from Tabasco, such as the Chontal, who had adopted the Quetzalcoatl cult and Toltec culture? At least, Itzá seems to be an old Maya name, for it is recorded for regions far from Yucatan. The terms "foreigners" and "those who speak our language brokenly" could well refer to a Chontal Maya group. On the other hand, they must have been thoroughly Toltecized if they were originally Maya, for we read in a Maya account (the Book of Chilam Balam of Chumayel) that the Itzá emblems were the bird, the flat precious stone, and the jaguar. The bird and the jaguar were the emblems of the warriors of Tula and of the warriors depicted on the walls and columns of buildings of the Mexican Period at Chichén Itzá.

This last is, I think, excellent evidence for identifying the Itzá as the rulers of Chichén Itzá during the Mexican Period; the innumerable symbols of the feathered serpent are equally good evidence for associating Quetzalcoatl-Kukulcan with their rule. As, however, there seem to be certain non-Toltec elements introduced from the Mexican area about that time, . . . it seems preferable to use the wider term "Mexican" to denote this period and culture rather than the more restricted "Toltec."

Difficulties with the Maya Calendar

The Itzá occupation of Chichén Itzá lasted for two centuries (i.e., from *circa* A.D. 987 to *circa* A.D. 1185) according to the Maya chronicles; it profoundly altered the Maya way of life. How much territory was ruled by Chichén Itzá at that time is not known; native sources speak of the whole country's being under the domination of Chichén Itzá, but Toltec art and architecture is not widespread outside the capital. We read of the Itzá conquest of cities such as Izamal and Mayapán. Maya sources speak also of a triple alliance between Chichén Itzá, Mayapán, and Uxmal, which lasted for the two hundred years (A.D. 987–1185) of Itzá rule at Chichén Itzá. Yet archaeology shows that Uxmal was deserted during the greater part of those two centuries and Mayapán was of little importance.

This is an interesting example of how archaeology can be used to check Maya accounts, which, as they have come down to us, are not too reliable. A good deal of Maya history was incorporated in prophecies because of the Maya belief that what happened in a certain twenty-year period (the katun) would repeat when that twenty years repeated. Each katun bore the name and number of the day on which it ended. On account of the construction of the Maya calendar, the katun had to end on the day Ahau, and as the attached numbers ran 1–13, a day such as 4 Ahau would repeat as the closing day and therefore the name of a katun after 260 Maya vague years (actually 256 ½ of our years because this type of Maya year—the tun—consisted of only 360 days). Again, because of the construction of the Maya calendar, the number attached to the day Ahau which ended each successive katun dropped by two, so that the katuns were named in this sequence. 11 Ahau, 9 Ahau, 7 Ahau, 5 Ahau, 3 Ahau, 1 Ahau, 12 Ahau (1 plus 13 minus 2 equals 12), 10 Ahau, 8 Ahau, 6 Ahau, 4 Ahau, 2 Ahau, 13 Ahau, and after that the count started again with 11 Ahau.

Eighteenth-century Maya antiquaries, trying to write the history of their people at a time when all the old knowledge was passing away, sought to disentangle these references to events which fell in certain katuns and to restore the events to their proper sequence. It is as though in the year A.D. 2500, with nearly all knowledge of European and American history lost, someone tried to reconstruct it from a couple of notebooks which contained abbreviated entries such as: Battle of Waterloo, '15; Surrender at Yorktown, '81; Defeat of the Armada, '88; Lincoln assassinated, '65; Fall of the Bastille, '89; Kaiser flees to Holland, '18; Battle of New Orleans, '14.

The historian might well decide that the surrender at Yorktown and the defeat of the Armada fell in the same century, the seventeenth, and, linking the Kaiser's flight to Holland with the Battle of Waterloo, place both events in the twentieth century, whereas the battle of New Orleans he might associate with the French and accordingly place it in the eighteenth century. The Maya antiquarians of the eighteenth century had the same problem, save that instead of having to figure out the century, they had to place events in cycles of 260 years. Their answers were not always right. The triple alliance, if such ever existed, probably fell not in the eleventh and twelfth centuries, where they placed it, but in the eighth and ninth, late in the Classic Period, when Uxmal flourished; or else the alliance did start when the Itzá conquered Chichén Itzá, but lasted but a few decades, not two centuries. Only those arrangements will meet the archaeological evidence that Uxmal was abandoned in the tenth century or very shortly thereafter.

New Religious Influences

The Mexican invaders introduced new religious cults, the most important of which was the worship of Quetzalcoatl-Kukulcan, the feathered-serpent god. Everywhere on these new buildings is displayed the feathered snake, its plumed body terminating at one extremity in exaggerated head with open jaws ready to strike, at the other end the warning rattles of the rattlesnake. Plumed serpents writhe on low-relief sculpture, the focus of lines of warriors who pay their god homage; they descend on balustrades which flank steep staircases; they rise behind warriors or priests performing human sacrifice; with head on ground and tail in air they serve as columns in triple doorways; in pairs they pugnaciously face one another with open jaws across cornices of altars, or in more friendly fashion intertwine their bodies to form guilloches reminiscent of Jacobean furniture. The repetition is excessive and monotonous; one is reminded of those Hitler youth rallies with their unending *heils* and swastikas, save that the Chichén artists were not so unimaginative. At Tula the feathered serpent is equally dominant. . . . Other

gods came to Chichén Itzá from Tula. Tezcatlipoca, the all-powerful deity who overthrew Quetzalcoatl, is there, but with a far less
formidable role; Tlalchitonatiuh, "sun at the horizon," god of the
warrior cult, had considerable prestige to judge by the number of
times he is represented; and Chicomecoatl, "seven snake," a corn
goddess, is represented, as in Veracruz, as a headless figure from
whose neck seven snakes radiate fanwise. There are, too, represen-
tations of the Mexican rain gods, the Tlalocs, but these foreign gods
were unable to displace their well-loved Maya counterparts, the
Chacs. A Mexican sun god peers earthward from countless solar
disks and an earth-monster of Tula origin displaces his less stereo-
typed Maya cousin.

With these manifestations of a new religion, aggressive militarism
is intimately associated. We [will] discuss . . . its impact on Maya
civilization, for which the best evidence is the art of Mexican
Chichén Itzá.

In sculpture and mural one finds line upon line of proud warriors,
who face toward an altar where sacrifice is made to the feathered
serpent or who receive the surrender of defeated Maya. The two
groups are recognizable by differences in their costume, and by such
details as spear-throwers, the identifying bird on the headdress and
the pectoral or helmet ornament, seemingly a conventionalized but-
terfly, which are worn only by the Mexicans and occur with equal
frequency in the art of Tula. From every side of countless square
temple columns a tall warrior with his weapons gazes vacantly to
left or right. Despite minor differences in costume, all look as though
they came from the same mold. . . .We are no longer dealing with a
theocracy, but with a society in which the soldier dominates the
priest who had called him into being.

That is not all. On friezes around pyramids and platforms jaguars,
pumas, and eagles, symbolizing the military orders, offer the hearts
of sacrificial victims to Tlalchitonatiuh, the rising sun, and walls,
carved with lines of human skulls impaled on poles grimly recall
that Mexican barbarity, the *tzompantli*, "the skull rack," on which
the heads of sacrificial victims were placed to the honor of blood-
thirsty gods and the glory of the warrior caste. It is, indeed, a sad
change from the Classic Period, when the current of life flowed
more gently.

Borrowed Words

That these ideas were foreign is demonstrated by the fact that Mexican terms for some of them were adopted by the Maya, presumably
because the Maya lacked words for such concepts foreign to their
culture. These borrowed words throw light on the new social organization introduced under inspiration from Tula.

With the shift from a theocracy to one in which lay influence, with a strongly militaristic cast, was dominant, we find the following words of Mexican derivation: *tepal* or *tepual*, "lord," and *macehual*, "common people"; *tecpan*, "large community structure" or "royal palace"; *tenamitl*, "fortified or wall town"; *tepeu*, "greatness," "glory."

Now it is obvious that the Maya had rulers long before the Mexican transformation, but, in view of the other terms introduced, we are justified in assuming that the change in rulership was sufficiently marked to necessitate a new word to describe it. The adoption of the term *tecpan*, which describes both a community structure and storehouse for weapons and also the residence of the ruler, as well as the newly adopted words for "fortified town" and "glory," similarly mark the shift from the old pacific and essentially introvert position of moderation to the militaristic and extrovert attitude of the belligerent Mexicans.

Even in words for weapons we can see some new introduction, for the Maya took over Mexican names for "shield" and "banner." They had, of course, shields before the Mexicans arrived and a Maya name for them, so it is probable that the Mexican term refers to some new type of shield introduced by the invaders. The term for "banner" almost certainly refers to the little flags the Mexican warrior wore on his back when he went into action, a custom unknown to the Maya of the Classic Period. The Maya also took over the Mexican name for a tight-fitting sleeveless jacket which was sometimes worn by fighters, and they borrowed Mexican armor, a thick-quilted garment of cotton, which was so efficient against native weapons that it was used later by the Spaniards.

Focusing on Defenses

In the highlands of Guatemala there was a marked shift after the close of the Classic Period from open ceremonial centers to easily defended sites, such as hilltops or tongues of land surrounded on two or three sides by deep ravines. The same thing happened in the Northern area. For instance, Mayapán, which was to become the capital of Yucatán after the decline of Chichén Itzá, is surrounded by a massive stone wall, now in a bad state of collapse, which has a circuit of over five miles and six main gateways.

Tulum, on the east coast of Yucatán and an important city after the Mexican invasions of Yucatán, has a wall on the land side, enclosing the city on three sides for a distance of nearly eight hundred yards, the fourth being protected by cliff. The walls are ten to fifteen feet high and as much as twenty feet thick, and are pierced by five narrow gateways. These are much better preserved than the ones at Mayapán, and some were clearly made with an eye to defense. In one case the doorway leading to the narrow passage is only four feet high, so that an attacker had to stoop to enter the passage and, coming from daylight into semidarkness, would clearly be at considerable disadvantage. Xelhá and Ichpaatún, also on the east coast, are similarly defended by stout walls, and both were of importance after the Mexican invasion. It is not certain when these walls were built around Yucatec cities; they may date from the time when Mayapán was dominant. The absence of a city wall at Chichén Itzá supports this view. The process of militarization, then, would have been lengthy, with walls of stone a late consequence of much earlier changes in the pattern of life. . . .

The picture we have, then, is of a complete reorientation of life. Alien gods and an alien ruling class impose a new way of life on the Maya of Yucatán and of the Guatemala highlands; the old agricultural life of the peasant continues as before, but now supports new masters who, from regarding warfare as a means to an end, have inevitably found that the means are far more important than the end; warriors organize to serve the gods, but the latter in turn become patrons of warfare.

Anasazi Culture at Its Height

J. J. Brody

The Anasazi settled in the canyons of what is now the southwestern United States, where they built elaborate cliff dwellings and ceremonial centers known as kivas. In the eleventh century, the Anasazi emerged as the predominant cultural power in the region, J. J. Brody writes in the following passage from his book The Anasazi: Ancient Indian People of the American Southwest. *According to Brody, by the end of the 1000s, the Anasazi had developed an extensive network of trade routes throughout the Southwest. They also constructed their greatest architectural monuments during this time period, he notes. Many details of Anasazi history are still unknown, the author concludes, but it is clear that their society at its apex was complex and highly advanced. Brody is a professor emeritus of anthropology and art history at the University of New Mexico in Albuquerque.*

The aptly named Classic Pueblo period began in about the eleventh century and continued into the fourteenth century. It was a time of cultural florescence. . . . Many of the most noteworthy Anasazi monuments—the great buildings of Chaco Canyon, the dramatic cliff houses of Mesa Verde, and the marvelous ruins of the Kayenta—date from this time. Those architectural achievements epitomize the era—they brought ancient Pueblo culture to the attention of nineteenth-century anthropologists, antiquarians, and historians, and their remarkable preservation continues to stimulate interest in the Anasazi.

Impressive Architecture

The first detailed published description of Anasazi culture was inspired by the Classic Pueblo "Great House" ruins at Chaco Canyon. These were examined in 1849 and reported upon a year later by Lt. James Simpson, a young military engineer attached to the American army. The Chaco sites were also among the first to be scientifically investigated, and studies there continue to the present. Appropriately enough, these are the earliest Classic Pueblo buildings. Many of the later but no less elaborate Classic ruins of the Mesa Verde and Kayenta also became well-known during the nineteenth century. The rock shelter towns, such as Cliff Palace at Mesa Verde and White House at Canyon de Chelly in the eastern Kayenta, are truly impressive, as are the curious, even bizarre towers of Hovenweep. But there are also larger if less spectacular sites on mesa tops and in valleys throughout the Anasazi country whose importance is only beginning to be appreciated.

South-facing rock shelters that could take advantage of solar energy during cold winters and supply shade in the very hot summers became favored building sites. . . . These are most commonly found in the Mesa Verde and Kayenta districts where there are many narrow sandstone canyons, cut by perennial streams which empty into the San Juan and Colorado Rivers. Many rock shelters are high, wide, and shallow; they encourage organization of multistoried, long, narrow, outward-facing communities. Storage buildings as well as houses at these sites are often located in dangerously high, well-protected crevices. . . .

As in earlier times, regional variations in architecture expressed aesthetic preferences while responding to differences in local environments, materials, community size, and building functions. But the similarities from place to place are very great. In all areas, the buildings are generally compact and blocky; many are multistoried and terraced, and their aesthetic character depends upon the play of light and shadow over plane surfaces. . . .

Many Classic period communities and virtually all of the Chaco style Great Houses, were initially planned or later renovated to be single, self-enclosed structures. Other towns, especially in the Mesa Verde district, were made up of a number of long buildings laid out in parallel rows. Even communities known to have grown slowly and by accretion follow these patterns. . . . If a village became old enough or grew large enough, the public space of its plaza or plazas was likely to become enclosed. Chaco plazas often held one or several Great Kivas (or ritual rooms) as well as smaller ones, [while] those in other districts generally contained only small kivas . . . .

As well as kivas, most Classic period villages included forty or fewer domestic rooms that were often organized into apartments of two or three connected rooms. These were usually entered by way of a doorway facing the plaza or street or, if on an upper level, by one facing a south terrace reached by ladders leaning against lower level walls. . . .

Population Growth

The community networks that prospered during the Classic era were, at least in part, responses to population growth. Following a pattern that began with the origins of Anasazi culture, this growth was supported by increasingly intense agricultural exploitation of the fragile, arid environment. The earliest manifestations of the Classic period are in the southeast, in the dry Chaco district. Later, the more verdant Mesa Verde area in the north became dominant, and locally important centers developed in the arid canyonlands of the western Kayenta region and in parts of the well-watered Rio Grande valley. But, throughout the period, it seems that the Four Corners Anasazi often expanded into areas that were dangerously marginal for successful agriculture.

There were many more Anasazi communities than ever before, and many were considerably larger than those of earlier times. Some may have had as many as 5,000 or 6,000 residents; but it is more likely that the upper limit was about 3,000 and, in any event, most housed 100 people or fewer. At present, there is no secure basis for accurately estimating populations for any of the Classic period districts. The problem is complicated by several factors, among them the difficulty of judging which rooms in a community were simultaneously occupied, of knowing when villages were abandoned after brief occupations, perhaps to be reoccupied a few years later, and of recognizing seasonal homes which would have multiplied the number of residences that a family might have. Nonetheless, it may be reasonable to surmise that the many Chaco Anasazi towns housed between 15,000 and 30,000 individuals among them, and that the later Mesa Verde communities may have had twice that many people. It is likely that population densities were lower in the other Anasazi regions during the Classic period, so that the total number of people was probably on the order of 50,000 to 100,000.

Many villages were located near to each other and some, especially in the Chaco and Mesa Verde districts (but also at places such as Cedar Mesa and Black Mesa in the Kayenta area and in some valleys of the upper Rio Grande), were close enough to be considered neighborhoods of a disjunctive town rather than independent settlements. Hispanic descriptions of sixteenth-century Anasazi towns, as well as some modern-day Pueblo settlement patterns, support that interpretation, but even so it is unlikely that many such conglomerate villages housed more than a few thousand individuals. It seems

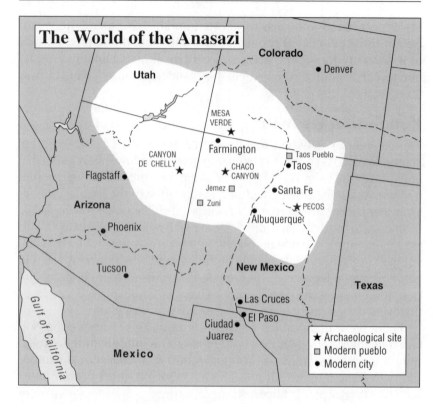

The World of the Anasazi

that the monumental architecture of the period and the economic, social, and ritual activities that it supported would have required participation of most people living within a relatively large area, as well as commitment of a large proportion of available regional resources.

Stronger leadership and greater social stratification than were characteristic of earlier Anasazi times apparently marked the Classic period. Yet material prosperity seems to have been evenly distributed, and there is little evidence that people who lived in smaller, less impressive communities were any less well-off than those living in large and architecturally more elaborate ones. Anasazi society may have been more highly organized than in earlier days, and there were certainly more people living in a larger area, but it seems to have remained essentially egalitarian. Thus, important questions remain open regarding the motivation for building such monuments as the Chaco Great Houses and Great Kivas or the towers of Hovenweep and the other Mesa Verde communities.

Despite the material evidence for greatly increased complexity of religious, political, economic, and social systems, there are surprisingly few entirely original innovations. Water management systems were more sophisticated, but for the most part elaborated on earlier Anasazi methods, and, while pottery and many other arts and manufactures burgeoned, these were mainly refinements and variations upon older themes and technologies. Similarly, the elaborate calendrical and ritual concerns evidenced by solstice markers and Great Kivas had much older prototypes. Virtually all the technological and intellectual aspects of Classic Pueblo culture appear to have had their origins in earlier Anasazi practices. . . .

Elsewhere in the Southwest, Anasazi styles in building, village organization, economics, ritual, and many other aspects of material and intellectual life became widespread. By the end of the period, the Anasazi had spread well beyond the upper Colorado River and Rio Grande watersheds, especially to the south where they encroached deeply into territories formerly identified with the Mogollon. Even the more distant Hohokam now showed influence of Anasazi ideas. Relationships between the Southwest and Mesoamerica may also have intensified, though the evidence for that is at best equivocal. In any event, Anasazi culture became a dominant force within the Southwest during the Classic period, and each of its major regional variants exerted great influence upon neighboring peoples.

The Chaco District

Chaco Canyon is a valley located in about the middle of the 20,460 square-mile San Juan Basin, which comprises the eastern portion of the Colorado Plateau. It is in one of the more arid parts of the Southwest, about 6,000 feet above sea level, in a region of special beauty that can be searingly hot in the summer and bitterly cold in the winter. The Chaco River (or Chaco Wash) which drains it is merely an intermittent stream that feeds into the San Juan River. . . .

Because of its extreme aridity, it seems an unlikely place to have become the hub of a widespread cultural system that depended upon agriculture. Nonetheless, by the end of the eleventh century, hundreds of miles of roads terminated there, linking it to at least 100 related communities which we call "Chaco outliers." These outliers are found throughout the San Juan Basin, some as far as 100 miles from Chaco Canyon, and are recognized primarily by their use of the unique Chaco architectural style. . . . This widespread system of related communities is sometimes referred to as the "Chaco Phenomenon," but not all scholars agree on what is meant by that phrase.

It is generally agreed that Chaco Canyon was the center of a trade network, and it may also have been a ritual center. The outliers and the roads that linked them brought a wide variety of regional goods and resources to Chaco Canyon including food, timber, turquoise, and other rare and desirable minerals. They seem also to have directed raw materials and manufactured goods from as far away as the Pacific Coast and central Mexico. Some of these materials may have been processed at Chaco for redistribution throughout the Southwest. The Chaco Phenomenon may even be thought of as an economic and political system that was integrated and perhaps directed by religious activities centered upon the nine Great Houses and eighteen Great Kivas located within about eight miles of each other at Chaco Canyon. Some scholars have even suggested that the Chaco roads were used primarily as thruways for ritual processions and that many rooms of the Chaco Great Houses were dormitories for participants at ritual gatherings. . . .

The Great Houses and small villages at Chaco Canyon could conceivably have been home to as many as 6,000 people. Chaco farmers used efficient agricultural methods, and their water control systems, which included terraces, dams, reservoirs, and irrigation canals, were designed to utilize all available water resources. Even so, they could not have raised enough food for so large a group. Either the normal population was considerably smaller than the capacity, or great quantities of food were regularly imported from other places. The potential number of people living in Chaco outliers was probably many times larger but, since we have no present way of knowing if—or when—Chaco people moved from place to place within their network, we cannot know how many of them there were.

The Functioning of the Chaco Network

Recent excavations suggest that the normal population at Chaco was considerably fewer than 5,000 people. At Pueblo Alto and several other Great Houses, comparatively few rooms were used as regular living quarters. Instead, many were storerooms adjacent to the roads, and others, of unknown utility, lacked fire pits and other domestic features. Rather than serving the Great House communities, the storerooms might have had warehouselike functions, holding food or other goods imported from one part of the Chaco network for transshipment to another. Considering the aridity of the land and constant threat of locally devastating droughts and other natural disasters, it may be postulated that the San Juan Anasazi chose centrally located Chaco Canyon to be a food storage and redistribution center. Adding other economic functions and ritual and political roles would have followed logically upon the original purpose.

Neither the Chaco people nor any of the other Anasazi had draft animals or wheeled vehicles, therefore the Chaco roads were built for foot traffic. Nonetheless, they are a consistent thirty feet wide for great distances, smoothly finished, curbed, and built to go directly from point to point, across valleys, mesas, and up or down cliffs on staircases cut from the sandstone. Communication between towns also utilized line-of-sight signalling stations, some of which also served as observatories and as religious shrines. Other shrines saw use as stellar or solar observatories, and it is clear that ritualists kept track of solar, lunar, and stellar cycles. Like the modern Pueblos, it appears that Chacoan priests maintained complex calendars in which the ritual and mundane spheres were fused, and practical activities such as planting were sanctioned by and invested with religious authority. That fusion of religious and secular spheres went well beyond agriculture: religion permeated the economic, political and social ends served by the roads, the signalling stations, indeed all of the material manifestations of the Chaco Phenomenon. . . .

It is architecture, roads, and the social, political, economic, and ritual implications of these grand material accomplishments which set Chaco apart most emphatically from the rest of the Anasazi until the twelfth century. The elaboration of Anasazi architecture, which began late in the tenth century, spread during the eleventh century, and reached its climax before A.D. 1130. For reasons that are not yet clear, the Chaco system ended by about A.D. 1150.

Were the Anasazi Cannibals?

John Elvin

In the following article, John Elvin examines the controversial discovery of apparent evidence of cannibalism among the Anasazi. As Elvin reports, several archaeologists believe that physical evidence found at Anasazi sites—such as butchered human bones and burned skull fragments—proves that cannibalism began to occur in Anasazi settlements around the beginning of the eleventh century. Some experts maintain that Toltec invaders were the culprits, using cannibalism as a way to intimidate and control the Anasazi population. However, others theorize that the desert-dwelling Anasazi turned to cannibalism in times of drought and crop failures, the author relates. Elvin is the national correspondent for the weekly news magazine *Insight*.

One of history's most perplexing riddles involves the disappearance of the cliff-dwelling Anasazi Indians, known popularly as a remarkably advanced, mystical, peaceful and agrarian culture that once inhabited the parched, desolate, vast Four Corners region of present Colorado, Utah, Arizona and New Mexico in the late pre-Columbian era. The stark and stunning sandstone pueblos they abandoned around the 14th century are among America's great wonders, attracting hordes of tourists to Mesa Verde, Chaco Canyon and numerous other sites of mythical fame.

Evidence of Cannibalism?

What happened? Why did the Anasazi clear out as though vaporized, leaving a treasure trove of worldly goods behind? Christy G. Turner II, bioarchaeologist at Arizona State University and author of the controversial book *Man Corn*, has been on the case for more than 30 years. After looking at some 15,000 sets of butchered, broken and burned bones, his verdict: cannibalism.

Turner theorizes that the American Southwest in the centuries around the turn of the first millennium was the stomping ground of a band of Charles Manson-type cannibals: Toltec thugs from Mexico who ate their way through the local population. This sensational scenario has brought him enormous publicity; his claims have been examined by *National Geographic*, *Discover*, the *New Yorker* and the *Los Angeles Times*, to name a few popular forums. In his book Turner states point-blank that "cannibalism was practiced intensively for almost four centuries" in the region inhabited by the Anasazi. The public, shall we say, seems to be eating it up.

But in an area more remote from the eyes of the general public—in the scientific journals and at the specialist conferences—Turner is taking a beating. In public comments and in a growing stack of professional papers, many scientists who have worked the same territory as Turner are criticizing his conclusions for what may be political reasons.

Alternate Theories

Prominent among the critics is Debra L. Martin, professor of biological anthropology at Hampshire College in Amherst, Mass. Martin, who heads the college's U.S. Southwest and Mexico Program in the School of Natural Science, is reviewing Turner's book for a scholarly journal and working with a Hopi archaeologist on a rebuttal of his findings. She has worked on many of the sites and collections studied by Turner.

The bone damage Turner insists is evidence of cannibalism also could be "found in a number of other kinds of contexts such as ritual dismemberment, secondary burial, ceremonial reduction and presentation of bones as in ancestor veneration, witchcraft execution, and disturbed burials," Martin states.

> It might have been torturing and killing enemies, but it might have been veneration, honoring the dead by keeping their remains around, or ritual eating—it's very complex. What if some of it was the opposite of violence, curating bones a particular way to keep the power of the grandparents available?

While each of these possibilities might take a few hours in the classroom to explain in full, the point is that any number of "variables" could account for the damage but "they are not taken into consideration by Turner," she says. In addition to her problems with the cannibalism theory in general, Martin also disputes Turner's "Toltec-thug" scenario as a "flawed, simplistic model" that ignores many alternative explanations.

Turner, in published statements, has said he believes that colleagues are challenging him because he has shattered the politically correct stereotype of the spiritual, pastoral American Indian. Martin, for instance, rips into him on his very use of the word "cannibal." One of her concerns is that the general reader will view the term in keeping with modern notions that focus on nutritional desperation or psychopathic depravity.

The term itself, Martin notes, was concocted by Christopher Columbus when he thought he had encountered people subject 'to the Khan, or "canibes." Martin, who takes a rather political view of the matter, says Columbus promoted the idea that the indigenous people were "flesh-eaters" in support of a campaign of conquest, Christianization and slavery. "Turns out they were not [human] flesh-eaters, but [his] term became equated with all flesh-eating."

Martin says that the word covers a range of behaviors that were quite acceptable to the groups practicing them, such as the symbolic gesture of eating a bit of an ancestor or fearsome enemy to obtain power. She mentions exocannibalism, eating those not of your ethnic group, and endocannibalism, only eating those within your group, adding: "The point is Turner uses the word quite loosely and then smoke-screens the whole thing in pseudoscience with the bone data. Those of us who do skeletal analysis think it's pretty shoddy science."

At the same time, Turner has influential allies. David Wilcox, curator of the Museum of Northern Arizona, told the *Los Angeles Times*, "We are in a period where everything Native American is [seen as] spiritual, sensitive and wonderful. We would like to believe that all of the nasty stuff was introduced by the Europeans, and before that it was all truth, beauty and love. Sorry, that's just not so." David Roberts, an archaeologist and author of the book *In Search of the Old Ones: Exploring the Anasazi World of the Southwest*, says he reviewed the evidence with Turner and is "absolutely convinced" of Anasazi cannibalism.

Paleoanthropologist Tim D. White of the University of California at Berkeley added considerable credibility to Turner's findings with his book *Prehistoric Cannibalism at Mancos*, his study of an Anasazi site where he developed the concept of "pot polish"—marks left on bone tips as a result of being stirred in cooking pots. At that site, White found what he terms evidence of the cooking of 17 adults and 12 children. He described the process as he envisions it for an interviewer with *Science* magazine: "They skinned them, roasted them, cut their muscles off, severed their joints, broke their long bones on anvils with hammer-stones, crushed their spongy bones, and put the pieces into pots."

Archaeologist Brian Billman, a professor at the University of North Carolina, is the former project director at an Anasazi site excavated on land now belonging to the Mountain Utes. He and his staff found extensive evidence of humans processed much in the manner of elk or deer, including cutting tools with residue of human blood. He submitted a human coprolite, or fossilized excrement sample, from the site for examination by a pathologist at the University of Colorado Health Sciences Center. It came back positive for myoglobin, a protein that only should be present if human skeletal muscles or hearts were eaten. Billman's only disagreement with Turner is with regard to an invasion by Toltecs. He believes cannibalism was a terror tactic used among fairly local and desperate competitors for scarce resources.

A Challenge to the "Noble-Savage" Image

Few of Turner's colleagues dispute his "politically incorrect" evidence of grotesque violence having been the order of the day in the Four Corners region at the time the Anasazi disappeared. But the idea does meet resistance among those with a stake in the image of the cliff-dwellers as a peaceful, spiritual and rather advanced people. . . .

Younger Indians, brought up in an age when Robert Redford and his ilk have taken the earlier romanticized "noble-savage" image and stripped it of the savage element altogether, choose to neglect that part of their history steeped in war, torture and routine raiding of rival camps. They believe it was the invading cultures from overseas that were brutal, genocidal and treacherous, a viewpoint that certainly has substance—but does not cleanse them of the thoroughly documented cruelties of their own past.

Kurt Dongoske, a tribal archaeologist at the Hopi Reservation in Kykotsmovi, Ariz., is among those who bristle at Turner's cannibalism assertion. He insists that the damaged bones result from some other activity. Dongoske was on extended leave as this article was being written, but in comments published elsewhere he has termed Turner's conclusions "a real stretch." He told the Raleigh, N.C., *News & Observer* that no one has "conclusively demonstrated that people were eating people. What they've proven is that, for whatever reason, the remains of those people were treated violently. That doesn't mean flesh was consumed." Peter Bullock, an archaeologist with the Museum of New Mexico in Santa Fe, joins Dongoske, telling an interviewer that he finds Turner's conclusions "somewhat preposterous" and "constructed to prove a point."

Many of Turner's critical colleagues point out that his findings also might be explained as a way of combating witchcraft. Even into modern times, Indians of that region have been obsessed with the extermination of witches. Common tactics of old summed up recently by anthropologist J. Andrew Darling, an expert on mortuary practices, included dismemberment, defleshing, burning, pounding and scattering of body parts.

In an interview with *Science* magazine, Turner responded, "There's no known mortuary practice in the Southwest where the body is dismembered, the head is roasted and dumped into a pit unceremoniously, and other pieces get left all over the floor." One of his oft quoted blasts at his politically correct critics: "Let's open our eyes and look at the darker side of ourselves."

Not everyone is ready to join that activity. "There is tremendous social pressure not to study certain things, even among scientists," Robert Pickering, curator of anthropology for the Denver Museum of Natural History, told the *Los Angeles Times*. "Cannibalism is one of those things. There are taboos." That observation has not escaped scientists who not only are researchers but educators as well. Professor Glenn Stone, an anthropologist with Washington University in St. Louis, is part of a team of experts in various fields who have led students into various Southwestern sites as a part of a multidisciplinary program funded by Hewlett-Packard.

Stone's students looked at the Anasazi disappearance from various angles, focusing on how the Indians may have brought about their own demise by "wrecking their environment." They looked at possibilities such as drought, overuse of trees and soil depletion, "and then the cannibalism thing broke and we used that to explore the concept that you have to have a way of living with your neighbors that is sustainable." Cannibalism, he says with a wry chuckle, "is not a sustainable adaptation."

Stone says Park Service officials during his most recent visit to the sites responded to his inquiries and those of his students by asserting that reports of cannibalism are "unscientific." He then pointed out that the reports had appeared in "the scientific literature" and his students asked if there was a "government line" on the subject. They were told that individual interpreters can shape their own talks.

Stone and his students visited a site with one such interpreter, "a Navajo who asserted descendency from the Anasazi, which is simply inaccurate," Stone says. "He was talking about the great spirituality of these people and the spirituality of their descendants and made no reference to violence or cannibalism." Stone says he asked the guide innocently about the meaning of the word "Anasazi" and the guide bristled, saying it was the name of a people, such as French or German. "Etymologically, it is Navajo for 'ancient enemies' and most Navajo will tell you that," Stone notes. Increasingly, though, this is toned down to "the ancient ones." Stone observes, "The Park Service has tended to stress the peaceful view of these people, and archaeological literature is starting to question their approach as 'whitewashing.'"

Despite Turner's efforts to homogenize the unpleasant data into a single, catchy explanation, Stone says that the answers probably will be a long time coming and probably will be varied. "I'll put any amount of money on that it's not some bunch of Charles Manson-crazy-Toltecs who wandered up here a thousand miles to run around eating people to show them who's boss," he concludes.

The Mound Builders of Cahokia

Lewis Lord

In the year 1000, the Native American inhabitants of the region near present-day St. Louis, Missouri, were developing a city known as Cahokia that rivaled the major centers of Europe in size. Lewis Lord, a senior writer for *U.S. News & World Report*, explains that Cahokia appears to have been influenced by Mesoamerican culture: For instance, the Cahokians built large earthen mounds that closely resemble the pyramid temples of the Maya and the Toltecs. The Cahokians also maintained a far-reaching trade network and developed an effective astronomical system, Lord states. On the other hand, he notes, by the close of the eleventh century, Cahokia was beginning to suffer from the overpopulation and depletion of resources that would eventually lead to the city's demise.

A merica was different then. Eagles soared over the oak and poplar forests of Manhattan, where the fragrance of wild roses filled the air and deer, turkeys, and great horned owls inhabited what would become Fifth Avenue. Boston teemed with beavers. Herds of buffalo trod Chicago. And in the heart of the Midwest in that year—A.D. 1000—the first city in what is now the United States was on the verge of becoming an Indian metropolis.

Reprinted from Lewis Lord, "The Americas," *U.S. News & World Report,* August 16–23, 1999. Copyright © August 23, 1999, *U.S. News & World Report.* For additional information visit www. usnews.com. Reprinted with permission.

Archaeologists know it as Cahokia, the busiest spot north of the Rio Grande when the new millennium began. At a time when few settlements had even 400 or 500 residents, this 6-square-mile community on the Illinois side of the Mississippi River boasted several thousand. In its 12th-century heyday, Cahokia may have had 20,000 or 25,000 residents, roughly the number in contemporary London. Not until 1800, when Philadelphia counted 30,000, would any U.S. city have more.

Cahokia enjoyed the same advantages that strengthened urban centers of the 19th and 20th centuries: a specialized labor force, an organized government, public construction projects, and a trade network that extended the length of the Mississippi River and reached east to the Atlantic and west to Oklahoma and Nebraska. But it also was bedeviled by problems not unlike those that plague modern cities, especially the havoc created by too much growth. Five or six centuries after its birth, America's first city, unable to cope with change, was a ghost town.

Yet, while the people vanished, their monuments remained, as can be seen in a visit to Cahokia Mounds State Historical Site, a 2,200-acre tract of open fields and Indian mounds 8 miles east of downtown St. Louis maintained by the state of Illinois. Among the scores of mounds still intact in the rich river bottomland is Monks Mound, towering as high as a 10-story building and covering more ground than the biggest of Egypt's pyramids. From atop this grassy structure—the largest prehistoric earthen mound in the western hemisphere—visitors see in the distance St. Louis's Gateway Arch. Much closer, they hear the whine below of 18-wheelers on an interstate highway built in the 1960s across the ancient city's site.

An Emerging Civilization

One millennium ago, Cahokia was emerging from centuries in which people in the region foraged for nuts and berries. Cahokia's rise very likely began with a breakthrough, the introduction around A.D. 800 of a variety of corn suited as much for the Midwest as for Mexico, the land where corn began. New technology also helped: Someone fastened a stone blade to a pole, and farmers in the heartland began cultivating soil with a hoe instead of scratching it with a digging stick. All around Cahokia, corn-fed villages sprang up on the plain made fertile by floods of the Mississippi and Illinois rivers.

Indians for centuries had built mounds in many shapes—octagons, circles, even the zigzag of a snake. Around A.D. 900, Cahokia developed another form: the four-sided pyramid with a flat top. To this day, no one has shown that a single Mexican ever visited Cahokia. But someone, somehow, had Mexican ideas: Cahokia's earthen mounds were very similar to the stone pyramids built by

Mexico's then fading Mayans. And atop Cahokia's mounds stood thatched-roof temples and houses for the privileged, like structures crowning the Mayan platforms.

To build Monks Mound (so named after a local 19th-century Trappist monastery), Cahokians hauled 55-pound basket loads of dirt on their backs from nearby borrow pits. After they did this 14.7 million times over three centuries, constructing one rectangular platform atop another, the 22-million-cubic-foot mound was complete.

Cahokian Society and Culture

The French explorers who ventured into the Mississippi Valley in the 1600s found nothing around Cahokia but vine-covered mounds, which they probably mistook for natural hills. But further south along the Mississippi, they came across Indian tribes with lifestyles that scholars believe were remarkably like Cahokia's. The Cahokians are considered perhaps the earliest of a people known to anthropologists as "Mississippians"—Indians of the Mississippi Valley and the Southeast who formed villages beside rivers, raised corn, built temple mounds, and worshiped the sun. In the early 1700s, in what is now Mississippi, French colonists settled among perhaps the last Mississippian tribe—the Natchez—and, before annihilating them 30 years later, kept detailed accounts of their habits.

Along with archaeological findings at Cahokia, the Natchez records give scholars plenty of clues about Cahokian life. Evidence suggests, for instance, that each morning at Cahokia a millennium ago likely found a cluster of old men in a house atop Monks Mound raising their arms and emitting frightful howls as a man covered in tattoos arose from his bed. Not once did the Great Sun, as Mississippian chiefs were known, bother to look at them. Instead, he stepped outside and howled a greeting to his perceived brother, the real sun, as it emerged over the wooded flatlands. Then he lifted a hand above his head and drew a line across the sky, from east to west. That showed the sun which way to go.

Cahokia's great suns apparently expected an eternity of female companionship. Excavation of a small mound a half mile south of Monks Mound revealed the skeleton of an early leader, a man about 40 years old, resting on a bird-shaped platform of nearly 20,000 marine-shell beads. Nearby lay the remains of more than 100 women between 15 and 25 years old, plus four male skeletons—apparently the chief's attendants—with no heads or hands. When a Natchez son died, many of his subjects volunteered to be strangled so they could join him in his afterlife. A mass sacrifice, scholars believe, was also precipitated by the death of Cahokia's great son.

A re-creation of the Cahokia chief's burial, complete with the 20,000 beads, is part of a life-size diorama at the historical site's museum near Collinsville, Ill. Among other scenes: a young woman grinding corn, children playing with a doll made of cattails, a man with tattoos on his face and shoulders (indicating high status) trading salt for a knife, and a boy heating rocks for a sweat lodge, where townspeople expected steam to cleanse their bodies and spirits.

Cahokians could neither read nor write, but they had a knack for astronomy. West of Monks Mound stands a reconstructed circle of 48 wooden posts that scholars dubbed "Woodhenge" because of its functional similarity to England's Stonehenge. Nearly 10 centuries ago, such a circle apparently served as the Cahokians'calendar: A pole at the center, when aligned with the circle's easternmost post and the front of Monks Mound, marked the equinoxes of spring and fall.

The Seeds of the City's Demise

The original Woodhenge went up when the city was on the rise, and its replica symbolizes Cahokian achievement. Just east of Monks Mound stands another re-creation—a portion of a 20-foot-high wall—that represents the community's decline. "More and more people were settling in Cahokia, and a lot of problems developed," explains archaeologist William Iseminger, the museum curator. "They likely had smog from all the fires that burned every day. You could probably smell Cahokia before you saw it."

Most of the trees from the nearby forests, Iseminger suspects, were cut for construction and firewood. This damaged the habitat of animals that provided meat for diets not only in Cahokia but also in surrounding communities. Reduction of the forests also probably led to silt buildups in streams, resulting in floods that wrecked croplands. "Cahokia was competing with other people for resources," Iseminger says, "and warfare may have resulted."

What ensued was a defense program that apparently helped spell Cahokia's demise. Around A.D. 1100, the Cahokians enclosed their inner city within a 2-mile-long stockade built from the foot-thick trunks of 20,000 oak and hickory trees. Problems endured, but the wall didn't. Thrice in the next 200 years, the Cahokians rebuilt their wooden perimeter, each time at a cost of 20,000 trees and 130,000 work-hours. Cahokia's forests were being exhausted and so, too, were its people.

By 1200, a gradual exodus from the inner city and its suburbs was under way. The wall still shielded Cahokia from rival chiefdoms, but inside the city, shortages of fuel and food grew steadily worse. No one is sure whether other problems emerged, such as inept leadership, the rise of a more charismatic chief somewhere else, a ruinous change in climate, or diseases brought on by diminished diets and faulty sanitation.

Nor does anyone know where the Cahokians were going. Conceivably they canoed down the Mississippi to Memphis or Natchez, or up the Ohio and the Tennessee to Alabama or Georgia. In all those places, Mississippian communities with platform mounds and a culture akin to Cahokia's would emerge and endure into the 16th century, only to vanish in the wake of Hernando De Soto's epidemic-spreading 1540 trek across the South. Whether Cahokia's refugees inhabited any of the towns is anyone's guess. But the archaeological findings that focus on Cahokia itself are clear: By 1400, it was abandoned.

After a half-millennium run, the country's first city had become its first victim of urban stress.

990s
Approximate date of the invasion of the Yucatan by the Toltecs.

1000
Mahmud of Ghazni begins his raids into northern India. The Icelanders adopt Christianity as the country's official religion. Approximate date of the Viking discovery of North America and the Toltec incursion into the Anasazi territories.

1001
Approximate date of the beginning of the composition of *The Tale of Genji*.

1002
In the St. Brice's Day Massacre, the Danes living in southern England are slaughtered at the instigation of the king, Ethelred the Unready.

1003
Sweyn Forkbeard, the Danish king, attacks England in retaliation for the St. Brice's Day Massacre.

1008
Mahmud defeats a large confederation of Hindi rulers. The Muslim caliphate in Cordoba enters a troubled period of contested successions and political assassinations.

1009
Al-Hakim, the caliph of Egypt, orders the destruction of the Church of the Holy Sepulchre in Jerusalem. Muslim settlers move into northwest India.

1013
Sweyn invades England; Ethelred flees to Normandy.

1014
Sweyn dies; Ethelred returns to England and is restored to power. Irish forces led by Brian Boru, the high king of Ireland, defeat the Vikings at Clontarf.

1015

Sweyn's son Canute invades England.

1016

Ethelred dies in April and is succeeded by his son, Edmund Ironside, who signs a treaty dividing England between Canute and himself. Edmund dies in November, and Canute is accepted as the sole king of all England.

1020

Mahmud conquers Lahore and incorporates it into the Ghaznavid Empire.

1021

Al-Hakim disappears, presumably murdered.

1024

The world's first paper currency is printed in China.

1025

Mahmud destroys the temple of Shiva in the city of Somnath, an important center of Hinduism in the region of Gujarat.

1030

Mahmud of Ghazni dies in April and is succeeded by his son Mas'ud.

1031

The Cordoban caliphate collapses and is divided into small independent kingdoms (taifas).

1039

The Almoravid sect of Islam begins to form.

1040

At the Battle of Dandankan, Mas'ud and the Ghaznavid army are defeated by the Seljuk Turks, marking the foundation of the Seljuk Empire. The Chinese go to war against the Hsi Hsia.

1041

Approximate date for the Chinese invention of movable type, which greatly simplifies the process of printing.

1042

Edward the Confessor, son of Ethelred the Unready, becomes the king of England.

1044
·The war between China and the Hsi Hsia ends inconclusively; the Sung emperor agrees to pay tribute to the Hsi Hsia in exchange for peace.

1045
The Seljuk Turks begin their incursions into the Byzantine Empire.

1054
The Almoravid armies march on Ghana, capturing Awdoghast. The pope and the patriarch of Constantinople excommunicate each other, beginning the schism between the Roman Catholic Church and the Greek Orthodox Church.

1055
Fernando, the king of Castile-Leon, launches an attack against the Spanish Muslims.

1059
In the Treaty of Melfi, Pope Nicholas II formally recognizes the authority of Robert Guiscard over southern Italy. The Lateran Council approves a decree regulating papal elections.

1060
Robert Guiscard starts the Norman invasion of the Muslim-held island of Sicily. The Seljuk Turks seize Baghdad and consolidate their control over Persia and Iraq.

1062
Tenkaminen begins his reign as king of Ghana.

1064
Harold Godwinson travels to Normandy; William the Conqueror later claims that Harold came to confirm William's status as the official successor of Edward the Confessor.

1065
Sancho Ramirez, king of Aragon, receives assistance from other Christian kingdoms of western Europe in his battles against the Spanish Muslims. A famine begins in Egypt that lasts until 1072.

1066
Edward the Confessor dies on January 5; the next day, Harold Godwinson takes the throne. Harold Hardrada, the king of Norway, is defeated by Harold Godwinson at the Battle of Stamford Bridge

on September 25. William the Conqueror arrives in England on September 28 and defeats Harold Godwinson in the Battle of Hastings on October 14. William is crowned king of England on December 25.

1069
Wang An-shih is appointed as special advisor to the emperor of China and begins to institute his ambitious program of reform.

1071
Robert Guiscard captures Bari, the primary Italian port of the Byzantine Empire, in April. The Seljuk Turks decimate the Byzantine army at the Battle of Menzikert in August and subsequently take over much of Asia Minor. The Seljuks also wrest control of Jerusalem from the Egyptian Muslims.

1072
Robert Guiscard and his brother Roger seize the Muslim-controlled city of Palermo in Italy.

1075
Pope Gregory VII bans the investiture of clergy by secular rulers. The Seljuks capture the Byzantine city of Nicaea and make it their capital in Anatolia.

1076
Henry IV, the Holy Roman Emperor, protests Gregory's lay investiture decree and convenes a council during which the German bishops renounce their allegiance to Gregory. The pope responds by excommunicating Henry. The Almoravids sack Kumbi Saleh, the capital of Ghana. Wang An-shih is dismissed from his post due to opposition to his reforms.

1077
In January, Henry humbles himself before Gregory at Canossa and is absolved from excommunication.

1080
On March 7, Gregory excommunicates Henry for the second time. Henry convinces the German bishops to elect an anti-pope on June 25. Along with his son Bohemund, Robert Guiscard launches an invasion of the Byzantine Empire.

1084
Henry drives Gregory out of Rome and installs his anti-pope in

March. Answering Gregory's request for aid, Robert Guiscard arrives in Italy in May and expels the Germans from Rome—but then his Norman troops plunder the city.

1085

Gregory dies in exile on May 25. Alfonso VI of Castile takes Toledo from the Muslims and proclaims himself emperor of all Spain. The Seljuks seize the Byzantine city of Antioch. On December 25, William the Conqueror orders a massive survey of England that is subsequently recorded in *The Domesday Book.*

1086

The Almoravids land in Spain to aid the beleaguered Muslim rulers. On October 23, they defeat Alfonso at Sagrajas.

1087

Following the death of the Almoravids' leader, the Ghana Empire collapses.

1088

El Cid begins his campaigns against the Muslim rulers of Spanish territory.

1091

The Almoravids capture Seville. The Normans complete their conquest of Sicily. The Seljuk Empire starts to disintegrate.

1094

Valencia surrenders to El Cid after a twenty-month siege. In the Middle East, several important Muslim leaders die or are murdered in short succession. The Egyptian caliphate falls into a rapid decline.

1095

Pope Urban II declares the First Crusade at the Council of Clermont on November 27.

1096

The crusaders arrive in waves at Constantinople. The Seljuks destroy the main contingent of the Peasants' Crusade near Nicaea in October.

1097

The combined forces of the crusaders and the Byzantine army capture Nicaea in June. On July 1, the crusaders defeat the Seljuk Turks in the Battle of Dorylaeum. They lay siege to Antioch in October.

1098

Antioch falls to the crusaders in June. The Egyptians recover Jerusalem from the Seljuks.

1099

The crusaders conquer Jerusalem on July 15 and establish the Latin Kingdom of Jerusalem. On August 12, they solidify their victory by routing an invading Egyptian army at Askelon.

Western Europe

Frank Barlow, *Edward the Confessor*. Berkeley: University of California Press, 1970.

Richard F. Cassady, *The Norman Achievement*. London: Sidgwick and Jackson, 1986.

H.E.J. Cowdrey, *Pope Gregory VII, 1073–1085*. Oxford, UK: Clarendon Press, 1998.

Richard Erdoes, *A.D. 1000: Living on the Brink of Apocalypse*. New York: Harper & Row, 1988.

Archibald R. Lewis, *Nomads and Crusaders, A.D. 1000–1368*. Bloomington: Indiana University Press, 1988.

Bryce D. Lyon, ed., *The High Middle Ages, 1000–1300*. New York: The Free Press of Glencoe, 1964.

John Man, *Atlas of the Year 1000*. Cambridge, MA: Harvard University Press, 1999.

Colin Morris, *The Papal Monarchy: The Western Church from 1050 to 1250*. Oxford, UK: Clarendon Press, 1989.

Karl Frederick Morrison, ed., *The Investiture Controversy: Issues, Ideas, and Results*. New York: Holt, Rinehart, and Winston, 1971.

John Julius Norwich, *The Normans in the South, 1016–1130*. London: Longman, 1967.

James Reston Jr., *The Last Apocalypse: Europe at the Year 1000 A.D.* New York: Doubleday, 1998.

H. Daniel-Rops, *Cathedral and Crusade: Studies of the Medieval Church, 1050–1350*, trans. John Warrington. New York: E.P. Dutton, 1957.

Pauline Stafford, *Queen Emma and Queen Edith: Queenship and Women's Power in Eleventh-Century England*. Oxford: Blackwell, 1997.

Schafer Williams, ed., *The Gregorian Epoch: Reformation, Revolution, Reaction?* Boston: D.C. Heath, 1964.

The Norman Conquest

R.J. Adam, *A Conquest of England: The Coming of the Normans*. London: Hodder and Stoughton, 1965.

R. Allen Brown, *The Norman Conquest*. London: Edward Arnold, 1984.

David C. Douglas, *William the Conqueror: The Norman Impact Upon England*. Berkeley: University of California Press, 1964.

Brian Golding, *Conquest and Colonisation: The Normans in Britain, 1066–1100*. New York: St. Martin's Press, 1994.

David Howarth, *1066: The Year of the Conquest*. London: Collins, 1977.

Edwin Tetlow, *The Enigma of Hastings*. New York: St. Martin's Press, 1974.

Terence Wise, *1066: Year of Destiny*. London: Osprey, 1979.

The Vikings

Peter Brent, *The Viking Saga*. New York: Putnam, 1975.

Johannes Brøndsted, *The Vikings*, trans. Kalle Skov. Baltimore, MD: Penguin Books, 1965.

James Robert Enterline, *Viking America: The Norse Crossings and Their Legacy*. Garden City, NY: Doubleday, 1972.

Gwyn Jones, *A History of the Vikings*. Oxford, UK: Oxford University Press, 1984.

Michael Hasloch Kirkby, *The Vikings*. New York: E.P. Dutton, 1977.

Ole Klindt-Jensen, *The World of the Vikings*, trans. Christopher

Gibbs and George Unwin. Washington, DC: Robert B. Luce, 1970.

H.R. Loyn, *The Vikings in Britain*. New York: St. Martin's Press, 1977.

Magnus Magnusson, *Viking Expansion Westwards*. London: Bodley Head, 1973.

Peter Sawyer, ed., *The Oxford Illustrated History of the Vikings*. Oxford, UK: Oxford University Press, 1997.

The First Crusade

Robert Chazan, *European Jewry and the First Crusade*. Berkeley: University of California Press, 1987.

Michael Foss, *People of the First Crusade*. New York: Arcade, 1997.

John France, *Victory in the East: A Military History of the First Crusade*. Cambridge, UK: Cambridge University Press, 1994.

Jonathan Riley-Smith, *The First Crusade and the Idea of Crusading*. London: The Athlone Press, 1986.

————, *The First Crusaders, 1095–1131*. Cambridge, UK: Cambridge University Press, 1997.

The Islamic World

Titus Burckhardt, *Moorish Culture in Spain*, trans. Alisa Jaffa. New York: McGraw-Hill, 1972.

Thomas F. Glick, *Islamic and Christian Spain in the Early Middle Ages*. Princeton, NJ: Princeton University Press, 1979.

Hugh Kennedy, *Muslim Spain and Portugal: A Political History of al-Andalus*. London: Longman, 1996.

K.S. Lal, *Early Muslims in India*. New Delhi, India: Books and Books, 1984.

Ira M. Lapidus, *A History of Islamic Societies*. Cambridge, UK: Cambridge University Press, 1988.

Maurice Lombard, *The Golden Age of Islam*, trans. Joan Spencer. Oxford, UK: North-Holland, 1975.

F.E. Peters, *Allah's Commonwealth: A History of Islam in the Near East, 600–1100 A.D.* New York: Simon and Schuster, 1973.

Jan Read, *The Moors in Spain and Portugal*. Totowa, NJ: Rowman and Littlefield, 1975.

Francis Robinson, ed., *The Cambridge Illustrated History of the Islamic World*. Cambridge, UK: Cambridge University Press, 1996.

Edward C. Sachau, trans., *Alberuni's India*. New York: Norton, 1971.

Margaret Shinnie, *Ancient African Kingdoms*. New York: St. Martin's Press, 1965.

Desmond Stewart, *Early Islam*. New York: Time-Life Books, 1967.

China and Japan

Rose Hempel, *The Golden Age of Japan, 794–1192*, trans. Katherine Watson. New York: Rizzoli, 1983.

James T.C. Liu, *Reform in Sung China: Wang An-shih (1021–1086) and His New Policies*. Cambridge, MA: Harvard University Press, 1959.

James T.C. Liu and Peter J. Golas, eds., *Change in Sung China: Innovation or Renovation?* Lexington, MA: D.C. Heath, 1969.

Winston Wan Lo, *An Introduction to the Civil Service of Sung China*. Honolulu: University of Hawaii Press, 1987.

Ivan Morris, trans., *As I Crossed a Bridge of Dreams: Recollections of a Woman in Eleventh-Century Japan*. Harmondsworth, UK: Penguin, 1975.

Alfreda Murck, *Poetry and Painting in Song China: The Subtle Art of Dissent*. Cambridge, MA: Harvard University Press, 2000.

George Sansom, *A History of Japan to 1334*. Stanford, CA: Stanford University Press, 1958.

Donald H. Shively and William H. McCullough, eds., *The Cambridge History of Japan*, vol. 2, *Heian Japan*. Cambridge, UK: Cambridge University Press, 1999.

Amitendranath Tagore, *Moments of Rising Myth: A Collection of Sung Landscape Poetry*. New York: Grossman, 1973.

Burton Watson, *Su Tung-P'o: Selections from a Sung Dynasty Poet*. New York: Columbia University Press, 1965.

The Americas

Richard E.W. Adams, *Ancient Civilizations of the New World*. Boulder, CO: Westview Press, 1997.

J. Richard Ambler, *The Anasazi: Prehistoric People of the Four Corners Region*. Flagstaff: Museum of Northern Arizona, 1989.

Elizabeth P. Benson, *The Maya World*. New York: Thomas Y. Crowell, 1977.

Michael D. Coe, *The Maya*. New York: Thames and Hudson, 1999.

Nigel Davies, *The Toltecs, Until the Fall of Tula*. Norman: University of Oklahoma Press, 1977.

Richard A. Diehl, *Tula: The Toltec Capital of Ancient Mexico*. London: Thames and Hudson, 1983.

Donald G. Pike, *Anasazi: Ancient People of the Rock*. New York: Harmony Books, 1986.

Linda Schele and David Freidel, *A Forest of Kings: The Untold Story of the Ancient Maya*. New York: William Morrow, 1990.

Biloine Whiting Young and Melvin L. Fowler, *Cahokia: The Great Native American Metropolis*. Urbana: University of Illinois Press, 2000.

INDEX